British Rule & Islam in Palestine

Taylah Kable

Abstract

This examines the British approach to institutional Islam in mandatory Palestine from 1917 to 1929. By looking at the establishment of Islamic institutions such as the Supreme Muslim Council (SMC), I clarify the process by which the Christian power transferred oversight over Islamic affairs to the local Muslim community. The period studied covers the beginning of British rule in Palestine, the elevation of the mufti of Jerusalem to the position of Grand Mufti, the riots at the Nabi Musa festival of 1920, the establishment of the SMC under the presidency of the mufti Hajj Amin al-Husayni, and the subsequent struggle between the Council and Zionists over the Western Wall from 1928-29. My work challenges the idea that the British decision to create autonomous Muslim-run institutions was an abdication of Britain's duty as a colonial power or was an act of appeasement towards the Arab population. Through a study of British archival material, memoirs from colonial officials and leading Arab observers, British and Zionist intelligence reports, newspaper reports, and select records from the SMC, I identify how British policy towards religion was driven by a vision of Palestinian society as divided along communal lines and how the creation of a separate Muslim-run institution was an attempt to recreate the supposed communal structure of the Ottoman millet system. I also reinvestigate the controversy over the SMC's participation in nationalist politics, arguing that its emergence as a political actor was produced in large part by the same communalist approach that led to its creation.

Table of Contents

Introduction
The Place of Palestine in Empire

I – Introduction

In early October 1920, the Criminal Investigation Department of the Palestine government reported that the Pan-Islamic movement was planning "a significant move…in furtherance of the agitation." What followed was a report on the decision by local Muslim prayer leaders (*khatib*s) to dedicate their Friday sermons (*khutba*s) to the Ottoman Caliph for the first time since the British occupation of Jerusalem in December 1917.[1] This intelligence would prove accurate, for prayers were offered to Sultan Mehmed VI Wahid al-Din at al-Aqsa mosque in Jerusalem on October 30, 1920. This small change in the khutba generated many questions for officials in the Palestine government. Was this a political act or an innocent change? Was the introduction of the Sultan's name simply a sign of respect or was it designed to turn the population against the British? Would the change lead to unrest? Most importantly, what should be done?[2]

Looking at British correspondence from the period, we can find a colonial administration that was deeply confused and divided about the meaning of this change.

---

[1] Quigley to Civil Secretary, October 4, 1920. ISA 2/5/163/78/CID/S. Quigley viewed the leading figures in this movement as 'Arif al-'Arif (who had been a central figure in the Nabi Musa riot) and Shaykh Abdul Qadir al-Muzafar (a member of the *Nadi al-Arabi* political society and later a member of the Arab Executive).

[2] This incident and the politics surrounding this incident are discussed in greater detail on pages 267-271.

Some officials viewed this development as part of a wider Pan-Islamic movement, some argued that it was part of a French plot to undermine British rule, while others saw it as clear evidence that the Arab population was turning towards the Turks. Their solution was simple—the Palestine government had to intervene to end the practice. In contrast, a number of other officials argued that the change in the khutba was not a political development at all and suggested that the government do nothing. In the end British anxiety proved to be unwarranted; the introduction of the sultan's name was found to be neither a harbinger of unrest nor a foreign plot to undermine British rule. In fact, what appeared to be an innovation to the British was simply a return to the practice found in Palestinian mosques during the Ottoman period. After seeing little response from the local population and having received reassurances from Muslim leaders, the Palestine government realized that their fears were unfounded and decided not to intervene. In the end this "khutba scare" faded as quickly as it had began.

Although this incident is little more than a footnote in the history of British Palestine, it is a good illustration of the fear that Islam and, more specifically, Islamic politics could generate among British officials. That a small alteration in the prayer dedication could induce such concern, tells us a great deal about the uncertainty of British officials towards the Muslim community that they ruled over. While the police warnings about a Pan-Islamic threat were eventually recognized as gross exaggerations, such suspicions about Muslim intentions resonated with a basic British view that Middle Easterners were more prone to fanaticism than Westerners, that Arabs were more easily led than Europeans, and that Muslims were more apt to combine church and state than Christians.[3] And it wasn't just stereotypes that played into this fear of political Islam, for British memories of the Mahdist revolt in Sudan made colonial officials wary of the power of Islam to move people. While British officials tended to see the Arab population as having little aptitude for politics, they worried that Islam could be used to incite the people to rebellion.[4] The khutba incident was not the first, nor would it be the last time that British officials worried about Islam's impact on Arab politics. The rioting at the Nabi Musa festival of 1920, the violent conflict at the Western Wall in 1929, and the Palestine Arab revolt of 1936-39 were moments in which Islam was accused of driving the population to violence. As a result, keeping Islam under control was seen by British officials to be a necessary part of keeping order in Palestine.

Concerns about the place of Islam in Palestinian politics should be familiar to anyone who studies the contemporary Arab-Israeli conflict. The Israeli government's war with Hamas in the Occupied Territories is well known, but a better parallel to the British situation is the government's dealings with Muslim institutions within Israel

---

[3] These stereotypes about Arabs were most famously articulated in Lord Cromer's assessment of the Egyptian population in his highly influential 1908 work, *Modern Egypt*:

> Want of accuracy, which easily degenerates into untruthfulness, is, in fact, the main characteristic of the Oriental mind. The European is a close reasoner; his statements of fact are devoid of any ambiguity; he is a natural logician, albeit he may not have studied logic; he is by nature very sceptical and requires proof before he can accept any proposition; his trained intelligence works like a piece of mechanism. The mind of the oriental on the other hand, like his picturesque streets, is eminently wanting in symmetry. His reasoning is of the most slipshod description. Although the ancient Arabs acquired in a somewhat higher degree the science of dialectics, their descendants are singularly deficient in logical faculty.

Lord Cromer, *Modern Egypt*, vol. 2 (New York: MacMillan, 1908), 146.

[4] The Report of the Commission of Inquiry into the Jaffa Riots for example argued that Arabs are usually obedient to authority, except when they are aroused for religious or racial reasons. PRO CO733/5/43345.

proper. Israeli concerns with these institutions go back to the earliest years of the

state, when the government worried about the potential for Arabs to rally around a

religious body. Like the British before them, Israeli officials saw Islam as a prime

motivation for Arab politics. Such a view was based on an official assessment, as

quoted in Alisha Peled's book *Debating Islam in the Jewish State*, that "the political

claims of the Arab minority are frequently linked with their pleas in the religious

realm, and very often deliberately confused with them."[5] Peled's book details how

Israeli officials developed an "Islamic policy" towards Muslim communal institutions,

as a way to deal with the threat that they saw in Islamic politics. Hers is a timely

investigation, for recent years have seen increasing tension between the Israeli state

and Islamic groups within the Israeli Arab community, such as the Islamic Movement

and the Waqf Administration in Jerusalem, particularly over the status of Muslim

religious sites in Jerusalem.

Peled makes clear in her work that Israeli policy was built out of and in some

cases was a reaction to British policy towards the Muslim community. This should

not be surprising, for the nascent Jewish state faced much the same question of how to

administer Islam in 1948 as the British administration had faced some thirty years

earlier. A comparison of British and Israeli policy towards Muslims would thus be

highly useful for studying the continuities and differences between the two colonial

projects. It would also be helpful for understanding how contemporary Islamic

institutions in Palestine have been shaped by policies towards Islam that were

---

[5] Alisha Peled, *Debating Islam in the Jewish State* (Albany: SUNY Press, 2001), 6.

originally developed in the mandatory period. But unfortunately, such a comparison is difficult to make for there is no equivalent of Peled's book for the British period. While much has been written about the political and economic issues of the mandatory period, religious issues have received much less coverage. And those studies that look at Islamic institutions in detail have tended to say rather little about how British policy shaped the establishment and development of local institutions.

This study aims to correct this lacuna by looking at British policy towards Islam in Palestine from 1917-1929. I will investigate the way in which the British authorities created, worked with, and reacted to institutions for running Islamic affairs and how those institutions developed over the course of the first decade of British rule. In doing so, I consider the logic behind Britain's approach to the administration of Islam, an approach that was criticized at the time and remains controversial among scholars today for granting Muslim institutions in Palestine almost unchecked autonomy.

II - The Nature of British Rule

Before we begin, it is important to understand the political constraints that limited Britain's approach to the local population in terms of political and social development, for such constraints also had a role to play in its approach to Islam.

One of the most important factors to understand was the fact that Palestine was part of the mandate system but was a mandate like no other. It was formally recognized in 1922 as one of five new mandates carved out of the Arab territories of

the Ottoman Empire but had first emerged as a separate country at the end of the First

World War with Britain's conquest of the Ottoman districts of Jerusalem, Acre, and

Nablus. During that war various plans and commitments to divide the Middle East

had been developed, with Palestine and its holy places "promised" to a future Arab

state in the Hussein-McMahon correspondence of 1915, envisioned as an international

zone in the Sykes-Picot agreement of 1916, and pledged as the future site of a Jewish

National Home in the Balfour Declaration of 1917. It was the latter commitment to

Zionism that became part of the terms of the Mandate for Palestine of 1922, and

although this commitment was challenged during the mandate, it remained the guiding

principle of British rule in Palestine.

This commitment to Zionism made Palestine unique among the Middle Eastern

mandates. Class A mandates, such as Palestine, had been recognized in Article 4 of

the League of Nation's Covenant (1919) as "independent states" that needed tutelage

by outside (i.e. Western) powers in order to prepare them for survival in the modern

world. This meant that the eventual national independence of the population was built

into the concept of the mandate system from the beginning. To be sure, this was

mostly a fig leaf to cover up the naked imperialism of Britain and France. For Britain,

mandatory rule was never about helping the Palestinian Arab community to develop,

but was about ensuring the security of the Suez Canal and by extension the route to

India. But it is also true that in other mandates, the Arab population was given some

form of representative government and Iraq in 1932, Lebanon and Syria in 1943, and

Transjordan in 1946 would emerge as partially or fully independent Arab nations.

Palestine, as Rashid Khalidi has argued, represented "a striking anomaly among the

Class A League of Nations mandates."[6] British commitments to the creation of the

Jewish National Home precluded any real possibility of the Arab population being

granted independence and led officials to consistently resist Palestinian Arab calls for

autonomy or representative government.[7]

Palestine was instead placed under direct British rule for the entirety of the

mandate. For the first two years of its existence, British Palestine was controlled by a

military administration (the Occupied Enemy Territory Administration South or

simply, OETA) under the leadership of a chief administrator. Then from June 1920,

the country was placed under civilian government (referred throughout this study as

the Palestine Government) headed by a high commissioner. Assisting him in

Jerusalem was a civil secretary (from 1922 known as the chief secretary), an attorney

general, two assistant civil secretaries, and the heads of such departments as the

education department, the public works department, and the Palestine police

department. These positions were all held by Britons throughout the mandate period.

---

[6] Rashid Khalidi, *Iron Cage: The Story of the Palestinian Struggle for Statehood* (Boston: Beacon Press, 2006), 37.

[7] A promise to offer the Arab population the opportunity for independence after ten years was made in 1939 in the build-up to World War II but was forgotten after the war—at no other time did British officials discuss the possibility of Arab national independence. The only attempt to build a representative government in Palestine—the proposal to create a legislative assembly in 1923—did not offer Arabs proportional representation and never came into existence anyway. In drawing this distinction between Palestine and the other mandates, I do not want to suggest that the other mandatory regimes adhered to the spirit of benevolent tutelage at the core of the mandate system of rule. The failure of the French to allow Arabs real participation in government in Syria and Lebanon is well known and argues against the notion that mandatory rule ably prepared those populations for independent rule. However, it is clear that the promise of Arab independence had a much greater resonance in these mandates, while it remained a dream permanently deferred in Palestine.

District governors (called district commissioners from the late 1920s onwards) were also British, as were the senior members of their staffs. The local population found employment in the Palestine government but only in lower ranking jobs, such as teachers in government schools, civil servants in the colonial bureaucracy, or as drivers and laborers.[8]

There were occasional proposals to give the Arab community more political representation, such as the attempt in 1923 to create a legislative council in which local Muslims, Christians, and Jews would serve alongside British officials. In the same year there was also a plan establish an Arab Agency that was intended to have been an equivalent to the Jewish Agency. But such proposals were always crafted in a way that protected Britain's commitment to the Jewish National Home by ensuring that Arab representatives could always be outvoted, as will be discussed in Chapter Five. As Charles Smith has aptly put it, Arab inclusion in the Palestine government "was designed to 'emasculate Arab nationalist opposition to the mandatory system' while excluding them from position in which they might be able to exert influence against the system."[9] Palestinian Arabs were keenly aware of British intentions and complained that British proposals neither addressed their desire for political representation nor fulfilled the mandatory power's obligation towards the local population. As Jamal al-Husayni, the secretary of the Arab Executive, made clear in

---

[8] The government's reluctance to share power was shown in the famous mistreatment of the Cambridge educated George Antonius, who was repeatedly passed over for promotion by junior and inferior British colleagues in the Education department despite his strong qualifications. See Susan Boyle, *Betrayal of Palestine: The Story of George Antonius* (Westview: Boulder, CO: 2001).

[9] Charles D. Smith, *Palestine and the Arab-Israeli Conflict* (Boston: Bedford, St. Martins: 2007), 125.

an article in 1932, Palestinians were also aware of how they were treated differently

than other Arabs under mandatory rule:

> The term "mandate" and the provisions of Article 22 of the Covenant
> of the League of Nations which defines it, particularly with regard to
> the territories that have been released from Turkey, both import the
> existence in a mandate of two distinct governments—the foreign
> mandatory and the local government under his mandate—the one as
> master to teach and the other as pupil to learn. The legal meaning
> involves two persons, a guardian and a minor.
>
> There is scarcely any relation between this actual conception of
> a mandate and the mandate that the Palestinian Constitution recognizes.
> For here the Mandatory is His Majesty's Government, and the
> government under its mandate is His Majesty's Government, which
> actually directs, and its British nominees who actually execute the
> Mandate. In this combination the people of Palestine have no political
> existence other than that of a very low-grade colony. They are not the
> pupils to learn until "such time as they are able to stand alone," because
> they have no responsibility and they are not the minors to gain
> experience, because according to this Constitution they are offered no
> real opportunities to do so.
>
> Conditions in Iraq and Transjordan, both "A" mandated
> territories and both under the Mandate of Great Britain, present a very
> different aspect in this question. Both have local responsible
> governments assisted technically by British advisors nominated by the
> Mandatory. The duration of the Mandate in these territories seems to
> be limited in the case of Trans-Jordan, and in the case of Iraq its life
> seems be only a question of days.[10]

It is not surprising then that Arab leaders ended up rejecting British proposals for

political reform.

Britain's strong grip on the reins of political power was less detrimental to the

Jewish community. British support for the Jewish National Home meant that the

Jewish community in Palestine, the *yishuv*, was granted a degree of autonomy denied

to the Arab community. According to Khalidi, "this autonomy included full-fledged

---

[10] Jamaal Bey Husseini, "The Proposed Palestine Constitution," *Annals of the American Academy of Political and Social Science,* Vol. 164, Palestine, A Decade of Development (Nov., 1932), 25.

representative institutions, internationally recognized diplomatic representation abroad via the Jewish Agency, and control of most of the other apparatuses of internal self-government, amounting to a para-state within, dependent upon, but separate from, the mandatory state."[11] In addition, as the economic historian Barbara Smith has pointed out, the British not only permitted but encouraged the creation of a separate and superior Jewish economy.[12] This approach was determined by the assumption that Jewish industry would drive the economic development of the country, when in fact it ended up benefiting only the Jewish community.

The denial of meaningful political representation, the economic inequality of the mandatory period, the lower level of education and technical training of Arabs compared to Jews, and the fractiousness of the Arab political elite, frustrated Palestinian Arab attempts to gain independence or even political representation. And as is well known, this frustration would lead to violent conflict, as seen at the Nabi Musa festival in Jerusalem in 1920, at the May riots in Jaffa in 1921, and the conflict at the Western Wall in August 1929, as well as during the most disruptive period of the mandate, the Palestine Arab Revolt of 1936-39.

The fact that British rule was never completely accepted by the predominantly Arab population of Palestine, and at times was actively opposed by it, led to British policymaking being dominated by security concerns. From the beginning, British

---

[11] Khalidi, *Iron Cage*, 37.

[12] Barbara Smith, *The Roots of Separatism in Palestine: British Economic Policy 1920-29* (Syracuse: Syracuse University Press, 1993). The divided economy of Palestine is the subject of two other strong accounts, Gershon Shafir, *Land, Labor, and the Origins of the Israeli-Palestinian Conflict: 1882-1914* (Berkeley: University of California Press, 1996) and Jacob Metzer, *The Divided Economy of Palestine* (Cambridge: Cambridge University Press, 2002).

plans for development were tempered by concerns about how educational reform or economic modernization, for instance, might upset the local political situation, an approach that encouraged conservative rule. Such security concerns would be even more important when it came to Islam, for religion was understood by British officials to be a primary motivator for the actions of the Arab population.

III – Research Questions

The British arrival in Palestine in December 1917 ended four hundred years of Ottoman rule and brought to a close centuries of Muslim control of the holy city of Jerusalem. For the first time since the twelfth century, Jerusalem was under Christian rule. The city's political status also changed, as it became the capital of the newly formed country of Palestine. Another major change, perhaps the most significant of all, was the commitment of the new occupier to support the establishment of a Jewish National Home.

The transition from Ottoman to British control, from Muslim to Christian rule naturally raised all sorts of questions. What would happen to the administration of holy sites? Would religious communities retain their rights or would the British alter the religious balance of power that had favored the Muslim majority? Would the Christian churches, in particular Protestantism (a relative newcomer to Jerusalem), be favored over other faiths? Would Judaism be favored? The greatest uncertainty lay with the future of Islamic institutions. Under the Ottomans, Islam was the religion of empire and the state effectively controlled Muslim religious affairs. The empire's Islamic court system and system of pious endowments (*awqaf*) were supervised by religious bureaucracies in Istanbul, while the appointment and dismissals of qadis (Islamic judges) and muftis (jurisconsults) was overseen by Ottoman governors. Institutional Islam was for all intents and purposes a branch of the state. In contrast, the Jewish and Christian communities enjoyed almost complete autonomy under the so-called *millet* (literally "nation" but best translated as "religious community") system. This granted recognized religious minorities control over their religious affairs, gave them the right to self-taxation, and enabled them to provide their own social, religious, and educational services. For those communities the change in leadership did not necessitate a new approach, but for Islamic institutions, cut off from their parent bodies in Istanbul, a new type of religious administration had to be devised. It is the development of the British policy to Islam and the consequences of that policy that is the subject of this dissertation.

What was Britain's Islamic policy? Who did they identify and promote as leaders of the Muslim community? How did the colonial government administer the country's Islamic court system, its Islamic pious endowments, its Muslim holy places, and its Islamic schools? What was the logic behind colonial decision-making? What was the outcome of British policies? And how did the local population respond to British policies? These are some of the questions that I consider in an investigation of how British officials worked to organize and control Islam.

In the pages that follow, I shall show how British Islamic policy was developed out of British officials' selective reading of Ottoman precedent and their limited understanding of Palestine and Palestinians. I will also demonstrate how this policy was influenced by Britain's geopolitical interests and most significantly by events on the ground. The policy that emerged was developed across a range of political departments, owing to the fact that there was never a single department of religious affairs in the Palestine government. Nevertheless, I argue that British policy ended up being built around a single basic principle: the extension of the Ottoman concept of the millet to the Muslim community of Palestine. By applying this concept to the Muslim community, the British chose an approach that ensured that the Palestine government stayed out of religion, a strategy that fit the conservative and parsimonious character of colonial governance in Palestine. But this choice had another objective: by dividing the population into three religious communities, the government would be able to treat the Arab population as two separate religious communities rather than as a unified nation.

In practical terms, British policy led to the creation of an entirely new religious institution, the Supreme Muslim Council (SMC), which was created in 1922 to give the Muslim community control over its own religious affairs. It also led to the elevation of the mufti of Jerusalem to the position of Grand Mufti and to his election as the president of the SMC. These changes made the mufti of Jerusalem the de facto head of the Muslim community. Such measures created a more concrete and hierarchical religious structure for Palestinian Islam, useful attributes for a government that wanted to work with only one agency for Muslim affairs. This concentration of power into the hands of one institution—the Supreme Muslim Council—and ultimately into the hands of one individual—the mufti of Jerusalem—would become highly controversial for giving control of Palestinian Islam to a single family, the al-Husayni family, who proved to be unreliable allies of the Palestine government. As we shall see, for better or worse, the success or failure of Britain's Islamic policy would come to hinge on the actions of Muhammad Amin al-Husayni, the mufti of Jerusalem from 1921 until 1937. When he cooperated with the British, as he did for much of the 1920s, British policy towards Islam was hailed as a success, but when he seemed to work against the Palestine government that policy was assailed for being too tolerant and trusting of the Muslim community.

Although I touch on some of the history of Palestine in the 1930s in my conclusion, the decision to concentrate on events from 1917-1929 is predicated on the idea that those years comprise a distinct period in the history of Palestine. The end of 1917 was an obvious time of transformation, but 1929 was a watershed as well. The end of that year saw rioting between Arabs and Jews at the Western Wall in Jerusalem and subsequent Arab attacks against Jewish communities in Hebron and Safad. These violent actions opened up British eyes to the obvious fact that the Arab population had in no way accepted the terms of British rule. In the aftermath of the Western Wall conflict British officials confronted a truth that they had tried to deny, namely that Palestine was home to two irreconcilable nationalisms. As Bernard Wasserstein has argued,

The absolute nature of the Arab-Jewish conflict, the increasing stature
of the Arab and Jewish quasi-governments, the gulf between British
official perceptions of the conflict in London and Jerusalem, and the
hollowness of the concept of a political community in mandatory
Palestine, were all suddenly illuminated by the riots of 1929. The riots
were symptoms of these deeper ills. In seeking to palliate these, the
mandatory government more often merely accentuated the fundamental
division between the two national groups in the country. To a large
extent it thereby nurtured the seeds of its own decay. British officials
were right when they insisted that their task was almost an impossible
one. The British mandate in Palestine was doomed from the outset.[13]

By the end of 1929, British hopes for a functional one-state Palestine were doomed

and within a decade British officials would propose a plan for partitioning the country.

But in the period from 1917 until 1929 the hope for a productive and peaceful

Palestine was still very much alive. This is why the early years of the mandate were

marked by colonial efforts to develop the country for Jews and Arabs, although such

efforts would be fatally limited by the British commitment to the Balfour Declaration.

An investigation of the way in which the British put together their policy

towards Islam can reveal much about the tenor of those times. How did the mandatory

power's mission to develop the country influence its treatment of Islam? How did the

security concerns of the occupation affect Britain's relationship with the Muslim

community? Did Britain's postwar geopolitical interests have any bearing on its

Islamic policy? Questions like this can help to uncover the logic behind the colonial

project in Palestine, which is often reduced in scholarship to a simplistic analysis of

whether Britain was pro-Zionist or pro-Palestinian.

---

[13] Bernard Wasserstein, *The British in Palestine: The Mandatory Government and the Arab-Jewish Conflict 1917-1929* (Blackwell: Oxford, 1991), 243.

A second research question that is addressed in this study is how the mandatory regime borrowed from and used the Ottoman past. Although British and French officials presented their occupations as opening up a new era for the Arab Middle East, they in fact kept intact many of the political, legal, and religious institutions of the Ottoman period. Using Ottoman concepts to justify their policies, colonial administrators presented their rule as fitting in with Middle Eastern traditions, particularly when it came to religion. However, in invoking the past, these officials distorted and stretched Ottoman traditions to fit their own agendas, as will be explored below. This practice of recycling "traditional" practices and institutions within colonial administration was, of course, far from unique—one only has to look at the British use of the *zamindar* system in India—but the use of Ottoman practices by the succeeding British and French administrations has not been studied in great depth. Scholars of the interwar period have recently begun to track the continuities and disjunctions between the late-Ottoman period and the period of European colonialism that followed, and the present study is intended to be a contribution to this field.[14]

A third issue that I consider is the way in which Britain's policy towards Muslim affairs shaped Palestinian Islam, notable politics, and the Palestinain nationalist movement. Why did certain religious actors and institutions rise to power in the Muslim community and not others? Why was a single Supreme Muslim

---

[14] An important recent work in this field has been Eugene Rogan, *Frontiers of the State in the Late Ottoman Empire* (Cambridge: Cambridge University Press, Second Edition, 2004). In terms of Palestine/Israel this transition has been explored in Ruth Dockser Marcus, *Jerusalem 1913: The Origins of the Arab-Israeli Conflict* (New York: Penguin, 2008) and in a recent dissertation: Abigail Jacobson, "From Empire to Empire: Jerusalem in the Transition between Ottoman and British Rule, 1912-1920," Ph.D Thesis, Chicago: University of Chicago, 2006.

Council founded and not a series of religious institutions? What was the logic behind the decision to empower Hajj Amin al-Husayni and his Jerusalem notable family, at the expense of others? Answering these questions allows us to see how British officials shaped a new system of patronage in Palestine, an important step for understanding what Albert Hourani has described as the "politics of notables".[15]

Finally, by studying the political activities of Islamic leaders and institutions we can begin to understand the impact of religion on Palestinian nationalism. Were appeals to Islam an important part of the nationalist message? Did religious officials and institutions—most notably the Supreme Muslim Council—become involved in nationalist politics? What was the relationship between Palestinian political societies and religious institutions? Such questions can help us understand the place of religion in nationalism, a subject that will be missed by scholars who adopt Benedict Anderson's model of nationalism as a secular enterprise.[16]

IV - Literature of the Field

This study is above all intended to be a contribution to the historiography of mandatory Palestine, a field in which Islam's relationship with the colonial state has not been a major topic of analysis. Part of the reason for this is the influence of the Arab-Israeli conflict on the types of historical questions that interest scholars. Seeing

---

[15] The concept of the "politics of notables" refers to the situation in the Arab provinces of the Ottoman empire, especially in provincial capitals like Damascus, in which leaders of the local notability acted as intermediaries between the Ottoman state and the local population. This relationship was based on a *quid pro quo*. The Ottoman government granted these notables political and religious offices in return for their help in making sure that there was order in their provinces. Albert Hourani, "Ottoman Reform and the Politics of Notables," *The Modern Middle East: A Reader*, eds. Albert Hourani, Philip Khoury, Mary Wilson (Berkeley : University of California Press, 1993), 83-109.

[16] For an expansion of this point, see page 19.

the mandatory past as a prelude to today's conflict, the lion's share of attention has

been paid to Palestinian and Zionist political groups, nationalist organizations, and

paramilitaries. This does not mean that historians have ignored Islamic affairs, but

such matters have tended to be pushed into the background, only becoming part of the

narrative when there is controversy and conflict involving Muslims.

This tendency is well illustrated in Charles D. Smith's *Palestine and the Arab-Israeli Conflict: A History with Documents*, probably the most popular general history

of Israel/Palestine.[17] Smith devotes two chapters (chapters 4 and 5) of his book to the

British mandate and uses those chapters to discuss the development of Zionism and

Palestinian nationalism. Long passages describe the development of Labor and

Revisionist Zionism in Palestine and abroad, the intricacies of Arab politics in

Palestine, and above all the competition between Jews and Arabs over land,

immigration, and labor. Religious matters receive less attention, only coming into

view when Smith discusses Arab and Jewish competition over religious space, such as

at the Western Wall riots of 1929. The mufti Hajj Amin al Husayni and the Supreme

Muslim Council are mentioned but not discussed at length, despite the fact that these

were the two most important institutions in Palestinian Islam and would end up

playing a central role in Palestinian politics, as will be detailed in Chapter 6.[18] The

Palestine government's policy towards Islam gets only a cursory glance.

---

[17] Charles D. Smith, *Palestine and the Arab-Israeli Conflict: A History with Documents*, sixth edition (New York: Bedford St. Martins, 2007).

[18] Interestingly, the index to the book includes no separate entry for the Supreme Muslim Council but does include references to Arab political clubs such as the *Nadi al-Arabi* (Arab Club), the *Muntada al-Adabi* (Literary Society), and the Muslim-Christian Association.

A similar story is found in other general histories of the period, such as James Gelvin's *The Israel-Palestine Conflict: One Hundred Years of War*, another well-written and diligently researched study of the conflict.[19] Like Smith, Gelvin concentrates on the evolution of political organizations in order to track the strength of Palestinian nationalism and Zionism and spends less time talking about religion in Palestine. While his account is stronger in its coverage of the internal politics of the Palestine Arab community, and does a good job of concentrating on the role of the non-elite, his focus, like Smith, is on the community's political and social organizations not its religious groups.

The choice to concentrate on the political rather than the religious almost certainly comes from a widely held but largely unexamined view among scholars that religion has less impact on the life of modern individuals than politics or economics. This is clearly shown in Rashid Khalidi's *Palestine Identity*, a seminal work on the development of Palestinian national consciousness. Khalidi explicitly links the rise of Palestinian nationalism to a decline of religion in public life.[20] This idea is fleshed out in Chapter 7, "The Formation of Palestinian Identity: The Critical Years, 1917-1923," where he explains how the Arab inhabitants of Palestine began, in his words, to "imagine" themselves as part of a single national community. This was made possible because of the loss or weakening of other forms of identification. For Khalidi, the secularism of the Young Turk period and the destruction of the Ottoman Empire in the

---

[19] James Gelvin, *The Israel-Palestine Conflict: 100 Years of War* (Cambridge: Cambridge University Press, 2005).

[20] Rashid Khalidi, *Palestinian Identity: The Construction of Modern National Consciousness* (New York: Columbia University Press, 1997), 19.

First World War led to a situation in which "two of the central pillars of identity before 1914, Ottomanism and religion, were seriously diminished in importance by the end of World War I. This left the field open for nationalism, the ideological rival of both, which had been growing rapidly in influence in the late Ottoman period."[21]

I bring up Khalidi's view about the origins of Palestinian nationalism here not so much to question its validity but to discuss how it shapes his coverage of Palestinian politics. His account of nationalism during the earliest years of the British mandate centers on the activities of the notable elite because this was the only strata of the Arab community that was affected by Arab nationalism and secular education during the Ottoman period. More specifically, he concentrates on individuals involved in secular activities. His protagonists are the editors of Palestinian nationalist newspapers and Arab politicians who founded political and cultural organizations under British rule. In contrast, he writes very little about those members of the notability who were involved in religious institutions, such as the al-Husayni family, despite the fact that those institutions came to be seen by many Arabs as also representing their communal interests.

Khalidi's use of the word "imagine" suggests a reason why he insists on a secular reading of Palestinian nationalism.[22] That term evokes Benedict Anderson's conception of nationalism as developed in *Imagined Communities: Reflections on the*

---

[21] Khalidi, *Palestinian Identity*, 158.

[22] Khalid seems to acknowledge the weak ground he is on when he makes this statement by also pointing out that "for many sectors of the population, and perhaps for most people in the successor states of the Ottoman Empire, religion has remained the most important single source of identification and community feeling. This has been true not only of the lower classes and the rural populace, but also of many members of the upper classes and among city dwellers, particularly the older ones." Ibid.

Origin and Spread of Nationalism.[23] For Anderson, the rise of nationalism was tied to and ultimately dependent upon two developments in European history—the rise of print capitalism and the emergence of a secular civil society. The first development could be seen in the rise of newspapers and books in vernacular languages, hence Khalidi's concentration in *Palestinian Identity* on Arab newspapers. This transformation enabled individuals to see themselves as part of a common "imagined" ethno-linguistic community, an important step towards nationalism. The second was tied to the loss of power of the Catholic Church, through the Reformation and the Enlightenment, leading to the rise of secular states and the consignment of the supranational concept of "Christendom" to the dustbin of history. This model of nationalism, which most properly describes the history of nation-state building in Western Europe, has been extended to non-European contexts by Anderson himself and by many scholars who have followed. But such a model reflects a Eurocentric and teleological view of national development that is problematic, especially when applied outside Europe, as Partha Chatterjee most famously argued in *The Nation and Its Fragments: Colonial and Post Colonial Histories.*[24]

To his credit, Khalidi offers a fuller account of the Muslim authorities in his most recent work, *The Iron Cage: The Story of the Palestinian Struggle for Statehood* (2006). Here the Supreme Muslim Council plays a much larger role, with its president,

---

[23] Benedict Anderson's *Imagined Communities: Reflections on the Origin and Spread of Nationalism* (London: Verso, 1991.

[24] Partha Chatterjee, *The Nation and Its Fragments: Colonial and Post Colonial Histories* (Princeton, NJ: Princeton University Press, 1993).

the mufti Hajj Amin al-Husayni, identified as a prominent nationalist leader. But it is

also clear that Hajj Amin does not fit Khalidi's ideal of a nationalist leader:

> Hajj Amin al-Husayni was far from the archetype of the Arab
> nationalist leader of the interwar period…Among all the other leaders
> of national movements in Arab countries during the interwar period
> (with the sole exception of Libya), and among Palestinian leaders as
> well, the mufti was alone in being a religious dignitary, whose base of
> power was a "traditional" religious institution, albeit a newly invented
> one, created and endowed with resources by the colonial power. In this
> unique institution, created by Britain in the singular circumstances of
> this specific mandate, we find one of the crucial differences between
> Palestine and Arab countries like Egypt, Syria, Lebanon, and Iraq.
> There, largely secular political parties and other movements, however
> weak or poorly organized they may have been, were the primary
> vehicles for nationalist leaders, until control over the state and its
> resources could be achieved. The Wafd in Egypt, the National Bloc in
> Syria, and various grouping and movements in Lebanon and Iraq
> played this function. There was no true analogue to them in Palestine,
> although political parties began to be founded in the late 1920s and
> early 1930s.[25]

It is not surprising then that rather than being a nationalist hero, Hajj Amin al-Husayni

turns out to be a collaborator. Instead of being an authentic nationalist, he chooses to

work with the government because of the religious office that it gave to him. As a

result, al-Husayni's religious nationalism is a dead end, a movement that diverted the

Palestinian Arab community from building a proper secular nationalism.

This presentation of the mufti and the SMC is not entirely wrong. As will be

shown in Chapters 4 and 6, the Muslim authorities were allied to the Palestine

government for much of the period under discussion in this dissertation. For this

reason, it is entirely appropriate to see the SMC as a moderate force in Palestinian

---

[25] Rashid Khalidi, *The Iron Cage: The Story of the Palestinian Struggle for Statehood* (New York: Beacon Press, 2006), 60-61.

politics from 1917-1929. But as we shall also see, the mufti and the SMC were also able to exploit their position of independence, particularly at the end of the 1920s, to engage in nationalist agitation against the Jewish community and the colonial government. In other words, the fact that the SMC was not a particularly militant group should not lead us to conclude that it was apolitical.

It would be a mistake however to go to the opposite extreme and regard the mufti as a central political player during this period. Such a position has often been taken in Zionist and Israeli historiography, especially in popular histories, where the mufti often appears as an evil mastermind who incited Arabs to rise up against their Jewish neighbors. In this narrative, the mufti is held responsible for the violence of the mandatory period, from the first riots at Nabi Musa in 1920 until the Palestinian Arab Revolt, during which the mufti fled the country. The failure of Arabs and Jews to get along during the mandate period can thus be pinned on the uncompromising mufti, rather than seeing it as a product of the conflict between two legitimate nationalisms.

Khalidi argues in *The Iron Cage* that there is an "amnesiac element in the vilification of the mufti in much Zionist and Israeli historiography."[26] This is true in the sense that these accounts often overlook obvious historical details, but in another way these portraits of the mufti are very much tied to the past, for they repeat and amplify accusations about the mufti that were made by Palestine Zionist Executive during the mandate period. Even more importantly, such views are influenced by the

---

[26] Khalidi, *The Iron Cage*, 61.

mufti's brief history of cooperation with the Nazi regime during the Second World War. It is for this reason that the Muslim leader's connection to Nazism and not his experiences as a religious leader in Palestine that have grabbed the attention of Zionist authors.[27]

This notion that the mufti was the central player in Palestinian politics has also played a part in Palestinian historiography, with partisans of the mufti presenting his actions as being dedicated to the Palestinian nation. Hajj Amin's own book about the mandate period and Zuhayr al-Mardini's hagiographic biography, *Alf Yawm ma'a al-Hajj Amin* [One Thousand Days with Hajj Amin] (1977), are two of the most obvious examples of revisionist works that repackage the mufti as a nationalist hero for leading his people's struggle against Zionism and colonial rule. Similarly, 'Izzat Darwaza (an

---

[27] Early books of this type were Simon Wiesenthal's, *Grosse Mufti: Grosse Agent der Achse* [Grand Mufti: The Great Agent of the Axis] (1947), Moshe Pearlman's, *The Mufti of Jerusalem: The Story of Haj Amin el-Husseini* (1947), and Joseph Schechtman's influential *The Mufti and the Fuerher: The Rise and Fall of Haj Amin el-Husseini* (1965). More recently, neoconservative authors in the United States have discovered this topic, as seen in the publication of two books by right-wing talk radio hosts: Chuck Morse's, *The Nazi Connection to Islamic Terrorism: Adolf Hitler and Haj Amin al-Husseini* (2003) and David G. Dalin's and John F. Rothmann's, *Icon of Evil: Hitler's Mufti and the Rise of Radical Islam* (2008).

The political agenda of these recent works is made clear in a statement from the publisher that Dalin's and Rothman's work "links the fascism of the last century with the terrorism of our own." See Random House, "Icon of Evil: Hitler's Mufti and the Rise of Radical Islam," Random House, http://www.randomhouse.com/catalog/display.pperl?isbn=9781400066537 (accessed June 1, 2009).

The failure of their attempt is best summed up in the concluding paragraphs of a scathing review of the book published in *The New York Times* by the eminent Israeli journalist and historian Tom Segev:

> Throughout the book, Dalin and Rothmann tend to blur the terms radical Islam, anti-Semitism and Nazism, and numerous Arab and Muslim leaders are grouped together as disciples of the mufti. Anwar Sadat and Yasir Arafat are among the villains, though one is left to guess in what way the mufti's spell led them to strike historic deals with Israel.
>
> In spite of all this, the book is worth noticing, as it belongs to a genre of popular Arab-bashing that is often believed to be "good for Israel." It is not. The suggestion that Israel's enemies are -Nazis, or the Nazis' heirs, is apt to discourage any fair compromise with the Palestinians, and that is bad for Israel.

Tom Segev, "Courting Hitler," *New York Times*, September 28, 2008, Arts Section.

associate of the mufti) has written accounts of the mandate that exaggerate the mufti's role in fomenting opposition to Jewish immigration.[28]

Philip Mattar has rightly criticized these Zionist and Palestinian accounts for being "so partisan and polemical that the historical al-Husayni and the movement he led were scarcely discernible."[29] If we are to understand the SMC and its leader we need to move away from such black and white portraits of the mufti and the institution that he led. In this regard, Mattar's *The Mufti of Jerusalem: Al-Hajj Amin al-Husayni and the Palestinian National Movement* (1988) and Taysir Jbara's *Palestinian Leader Hajj Amin al-Husayni* (1985) are useful in presenting the ambiguous political position of the mufti, who was stuck between the Palestine government to whom he owed his position and his Muslim constituency who chafed under the weight of colonial rule. But as one might expect, the focus of these biographies does not move very far from the person of Hajj Amin or the Israeli-Palestinian conflict. Yet again, the British side of the story remains hidden.

There are a number of interesting works on the personalities and institutions of the Palestine government that can be used to understand British policymaking. Bernard Wasserstein's, *The British in Palestine: The Mandatory Government and the Arab-Jewish Conflict 1917-1929* is the standard text for understanding the inner workings of the colonial governance during the first decade of British rule. A. J.

---

[28] In his biography of the mufti, Zvi Elpeleg argues that Darwaza rewrote the history of the 1929 Western Wall riots by later arguing that Hajj Amin al-Husayni had planned the riots in advance, an argument that was designed to burnish the mufti's nationalist credentials. See Elpeleg, Zvi Elpeleg, *The Grand Mufti: Haj Amin al-Hussaini, Founder of the Palestinian National Movement,* Trans. David Harvey (London: Frank Cass, 1993).

[29] Philip Mattar, *The Mufti of Jerusalem: Al-Hajj Amin al-Husayni and the Palestinian National Movement* (New York: Columbia University Press, 1988), xiii.

Sherman's, *Mandate Days: British Lives in Palestine 1918-1948* offers an interesting account of the social and cultural activities of British personnel stationed in Palestine. Martin Kolinsky's *Law, Order and Riots, 1928-1935* investigates British security policies during and after the Western Wall riots of 1929 and offers a useful understanding of how Palestine fit into Britain's wider geopolitical interests. Each of these books is useful in its own way but none of them, nor the many other books on the Palestine government, investigates the British approach to Islam, for their focus is almost exclusively on how the Palestine government managed the Palestinian-Israel conflict.

In order to understand how Islamic institutions functioned under British rule we need to look at more specialized works. Four works in particular can be recommended, Robert Eisenman's *Islamic Law in Palestine and Israel: a history of the survival of the Tanzimat and Shari'a in British Palestine and the State of Israel* (1978), Yitzhak Reiter's *Islamic Endowments in British Palestine* (1996), Yehoshua Porath's *The Emergence of the Palestinian-Arab National Movement, 1928-1929,* and Uri Kupferschmidt's *The Supreme Muslim Council* (1990). The first two monographs are invaluable for understanding shari'a law and waqf in Palestine under the Ottoman, British, and Israeli rule but are very much geared to specialists. Eisenman and Reiter offer little in the way of analysis of the political context within which these institutions developed and so the reader is left wondering what motivated British or Israeli policies. In contrast, Porath's work delves deeply into the politics of the period. His is the seminal study of Palestinian nationalism and offers perhaps the first detailed account of the SMC's place within the Palestinian nationalist movement. As such, the

work has been useful in my research, alongside Khalidi's *Palestinian Identity* and

Muhammad Muslih's *The Origins of Palestinian Nationalism*, for understanding the

main personalities and organizations in Palestinian politics. And, unlike those other

two works it has also been helpful for understanding how the SMC interacted with

Arab politics. Meanwhile, Kupferschmidt's account of the SMC is unparalleled in its

attention to detail and remains the only major study of the council. It too has been

invaluable for my work. While the accounts of Porath and Kupferschmidt come

closest to giving us an understanding of how Muslim institutions fit within Arab

politics and the role that Britain played in creating these institutions, they ultimately

present a distorted picture of British motivations, as will be made clear in the

following section.

V - Conventional Accounts of Islam under British Rule

The British decision to have Muslims run their own religious affairs has commonly

been viewed by scholars as a simple attempt to mollify Arab frustrations with British

rule. Charles Smith finds evidence of this desire to reach out to Arabs in the first high

commissioner's "conciliatory manner toward those who represented Arab nationalist

feelings."[30] According to Yehoshua Porath this desire to be conciliatory meant that

the

---

[30] Smith, *Palestine and Arab-Israeli Conflict*, 115.

> Government came to feel, it appears, that the gratification of the
> Muslims' wishes in this respect [the creation of the council] and the
> appointment of al-Hajj Amin al-Husayni to the head of a Muslim
> council wielding real power, would placate to some extent the
> opposition to the Zionist aspect of the Mandate and at least prevent the
> outbreak of violence.[31]

Bernard Wasserstein similarly posits that the council was created with the "conscious

intention of conciliating Muslim Arabs and providing them with a form of

representation and a certain autonomy that would compensate to some extent for the

autonomous representative institutions granted to the Zionists."[32]

The frankest language of all is used by Uri Kupferschmidt when he baldly

states that the "establishment of the Supreme Muslim Council was an act of

appeasement towards the Palestinian Muslims, effected by the first, Jewish, High

Commissioner—Herbert Samuel."[33] For him the creation of the council was a

transparent attempt by the British to buy off Muslims that was driven by a vague,

"ever present fear of 'the raising of the religious cry,' with all the adverse publicity

and dangers for Imperial interests which it could possibly entail."[34]

The idea that the creation of the Supreme Muslim Council was a crude attempt

to curry Arab favor is based on two understandable but questionable premises—first,

that the decision to create the SMC broke with the normal colonial practice, which

meant that it was unnecessary and risky, and second, that British policy towards Islam

was driven in some way by feelings of sympathy towards the Arab population or more

---

[31]Yehoshua Porath, *The Emergence of the Palestinian-Arab National Movement 1918-1929* (London: Frank Cass, 1974), 200.

[32] Wasserstein, *British in Palestine*, 132.

[33] Kupferschmidt, *Supreme Muslim Council*, 17.

[34] Ibid.

simply by fear. It is this latter point that has led scholars like Kupferschmidt—mostly writing from a Zionist perspective—to argue that the creation of the council was an act of appeasement, a word that cannot fail to bring up memories of Neville Chamberlain and the Munich Agreement. Before presenting my own understanding of the logic behind British decision-making, it is necessary to consider this style of argument and the assumptions it makes about British thinking.

The first premise was actually argued by a number of people during the mandate. Zionist officials, for instance, complained that the council was a "hybrid institution…never conceived of by Islam in the past."[35] Some British officials also came to see the council as breaking with precedent. Harry Luke (the acting high commissioner 1928-29) lamented after the Western Wall riots of 1929 that the "delegation to the Supreme Muslim Council of jurisdiction so extensive and powers so wide" was "to some extent almost an abdication by the Administration of Palestine of responsibilities normally incumbent upon Government."[36] It is no surprise then to read Kupferschmidt opening his book by stating that, "The Supreme Muslim Council of Palestine was a body unique in the history of those Muslim countries administered by Colonial and Mandatory governments," or to see Porath's argument that the creation of the Supreme Muslim Council represented "a vastly different state of affairs from that in other territories under direct British rule."[37]

---

[35] This quote comes from an undated Zionist memorandum on the SMC, CZA S25/10/373 and is also quoted in Kupferschmidt, *Supreme Muslim Council*, 5.

[36] Harry Luke memorandum enclosed in HC to Secretary of State for the Colonies, June 18, 1929, PRO CO 733/172.

[37] Kupferschmidt, *Supreme Muslim Council*, 1; Porath, *Emergence*, 199.

But the diversity of British approaches towards Islam in their colonies calls this premise into question. In the "veiled protectorate" of Egypt, intervention by British officials into Islamic courts was limited, with Lord Cromer arguing that, "if they are ever to be improved, the movement in favour of reform must come from within. It must be initiated by the Egyptians themselves. Any serious attempt to impose reforms by pressure from without would be most impolitic, and, moreover would probably result in failure."[38] But in neighboring Sudan, Britain feared that Islam might be used as part of an anti-colonial uprising, as had been the case in the successful messianic revolt of Muhammad Ahmad al-Mahdi against Turco-Egyptian rule in the 1880s, a revolt that claimed the life of one of the most celebrated Victorian war heroes, General Gordon of Khartoum. This led British officials, who had been in charge of the country since its re-conquest, to adopt a much more hands-on approach to Islam: they created a Board of Ulama in 1901 and reorganized the Islamic judiciary to favor "representatives of orthodox Islam" over more "popular" religious figures.[39] The government also monitored the remaining Mahdists and worked to cultivate relationships with Muslim leaders who were compliant.[40] These policies followed from Prime Minister Lord Salisbury's call for Britain to take "a predominant voice in

---

[38] Cromer, *Modern Egypt*, 515.

[39] See Kupferschmidt, *Supreme Muslim Council*, 12 and Awad al-Sid al-Karsani, "The Establishment of Neo-Mahdism in the Western Sudan, 1920-1936," *African Affairs* 86, no. 344 (Jul., 1987): 385-404.

[40] Awad Al-Sid al-Karsani, "The Establishment of Neo-Mahdism in the Western Sudan, 1920-1936," *African Affairs* 86, no. 344 (Jul., 1987): 385-404.

all matters connected with the Sudan," a very different position than the one taken by Cromer in Egypt.[41]

In Cyprus, British officials worked alongside local leaders in administering waqf through the appointment of two delegates, one Muslim and one British, to oversee the waqf system. In the Malay States, the British made the local sultans subject to oversight from British residents and introduced the Penal Code but allowed local rulers to retain control over traditional Malay religion.[42] Meanwhile in Northern Nigeria a bifurcated system of British and native (both tribal and Islamic) courts was established, with the British resident having the final right of approval for the appointment of judges and the right to inspect courts and review court cases at any time.[43] The most well known but perhaps the most quixotic approach was taken in India, where a hybrid system called Anglo-Muhammedan Law was put into place, whereby civil courts were given the ability to apply Islamic legal provisions in cases that dealt with the personal status of Muslims or touched on waqf.

This suggests that there was no imperial template for dealing with Islamic institutions and that in each British colony the approach was tailored to the local context. In other words, the uniqueness of the British approach was something rather unremarkable. In fact, I would suggest that the notion that British policy was a break

---

[41] As quoted in William Cleveland, *A History of the Modern Middle East* (Boulder, Colo.: Westview, 2004), 106.

[42] Philip Curtain, *The World and the West: The European Challenge and the Overseas Response in the Age of Empire* (Cambridge: Cambridge University Press, 2000), 104-107.

[43] See Suleimano Kumo, "The Application of Islamic Law in Northern Nigeria: Problems and Prospects," *Islamic Law in Nigeria: Application and Teaching*, ed. S. Khalid Rashid (Lagos: Islamic Publications Bureau, 1986), Ahmad Algazali, *British Administration and the Development of Northern Nigeria 1900-1954* (Master's Thesis: Pittsburgh: University of Pittsburgh, 1967), J. N. D. Anderson, *Islamic Law in Africa* (London: Frank Cass, 1955), 174.

from colonial precedent does not rest on any real historical understanding but on an idealized vision of what colonial control should have been that is heavily influenced by modernization theory. What I mean by this is that these writers, perhaps unconsciously, see the decision to devolve control over religion to local bodies as going against the process of "modernization" that should have occurred with the imposition of colonial rule. It also goes against the expectation of many scholars that imperialism necessarily involved the imposition of colonial order and discipline over most aspects of the lives of the colonized.

As Frederick Cooper and Ann Laura Stoler have rightly warned, "European agency too often remains undifferentiated, assumed, and unexplored," in historical accounts of colonial rule.[44] As a result colonialism often becomes shorthand for the imposition of post-Enlightenment norms or the amorphous concept of "modernity" onto the colonized. But historically things were messier on the ground than is presented by the use of such large terms. This is hardly a profound statement but needs to be considered whenever one confronts the argument that there was one way of doing things in the empire. Philip Curtain has reminded us of this in his basic observation that "the reality of imperial rule was therefore highly variable from time to time and place to place, even within a single colonial empire. Published maps colored appropriately to show British, French, or Portuguese territory merely showed claims to

---

[44] Frederick Cooper and Ann Laura Stoler, "Between Metropole and Colony," in *Tensions of Empire: Colonial Cultures in a Bourgeois World*, eds. Frederick Cooper and Ann Laura Stoler (Berkeley: University of California Press, 1997), 16.

legal sovereignty, not the reality of power exercised on the ground."[45] Especially in

places where colonial bureaucracies and militaries were small, such as in Palestine, the

reach of the state into the lives of its subjects was not nearly as powerful as historians

have sometimes suggested.

Imperialism was also not a process that necessarily involved the wholesale

importation of Western values or political structures to the world outside Europe.

Often the imperial power chose to work through preexisting systems of power, usually

with the result that conquered elites flourished under colonial rule. As Frederick

Cooper has explained "colonial rulers needed to co-opt old elites and generate new

collaborators, but such ties might soften the colonizer-colonized distinction and

strengthen the indigenous social and cultural practices colonial ideology was trying to

denigrate."[46] In short, it should not be assumed that the creation of the Supreme

Muslim Council was illogical or went against the interests of the colonial project in

Palestine.

The second premise that British policy was driven by feelings of sympathy or

fear towards the Muslim community also needs to be reexamined. While it is true that

British officials worried on occasion about the "raising of the religious cry," as

Kupferschmidt puts it, and sometimes wrote about the dangers of pan-Islamic

movements, for the most part they were not particularly moved by these fears. As will

be argued below, officials in Palestine, such as the civil secretary Gilbert Clayton and

---

[45] Curtain, *World and West*, 17.

[46] Frederick Cooper, *Colonialism in Question: Theory, Knowledge, History* (Berkeley: University of California Press, 2005), 28.

the assistant political secretary Ernest Richmond, regarded the threat of a coordinated

Muslim political uprising as remote and saw the idea as a product of the overactive

imaginations of intelligence agents. Officials were certainly not unaware of Muslim

complaints about British policy towards Islam, which centered on the unsuitability of

Islamic affairs, particularly the waqf system, being run by a non-Muslim power. That

officials showed sympathy to these complaints was not driven by a sense of fear or

guilt but by a general acceptance of the underlying contention that religious groups

should have control over their own affairs.

This is not to say that colonial officials were unaffected by Arab nationalism or

concerns about Islam, for throughout the mandate period officials worried about the

destabilizing effects of anti-colonial violence. It is also true that the Palestine

government worked to alleviate Arab political frustrations, at least in the early 1920s,

by attempting to create institutions for the Arab community. But the Supreme Muslim

Council itself was not intended to be one of these institutions, instead it was the 1922

proposal for the creation of a representative legislative council and the later proposal

for the creation of an Arab Agency that were dangled as carrots towards the Arab

community.

This brings us to a final assumption that often frames debate about the creation

of the SMC, namely that its creation was a dangerous concession to a radical Muslim

leader, Hajj Amin al-Husayni. Hussayni's role in the Western Wall riots of 1929 and

his role as the leader of the Arab Higher Committee, the leading political organization

during the Great Arab Revolt of 1936-39, has led many Zionist scholars to portray him as a firebrand responsible for the breakdown of relations between the Arab and Jewish populations. But much more important to this argument was his notorious collaboration with the Nazis during the Second World War in an unsuccessful attempt to recruit Muslims for an army that would liberate Palestine from Jewish and British control. As a result, Hajj Amin has become a monstrous figure in some Zionist and Israeli scholarship, with the British decision to appoint him as mufti in 1921 and as president of the SMC in 1922 presented as the moment that the monster was given life.[47] But, as will be shown in Chapter 4, the idea that Hajj Amin was "evil" when he was appointed is largely an example of hindsight bias. It also makes little sense to see the mufti's appointment as creating a monster (à la Dr. Frankenstein) when the nationalist struggle between Zionism and Palestinian nationalism in the late-1920s and 1930s had a much more profound influence on the political career of the mufti and the SMC. The problem with appeasement argument is that it assumes that the later history of the council was prefigured in its birth, effectively collapsing the history of the council and forestalling any real consideration of how that history was influenced by the larger political conflicts and compromises that were taking place between the Arab, Jewish, and British communities. As Chapter 5 and Chapter 6 will explain, the later history of the council, in particular its emergence as a major political voice in the

---

[47] Probably the most well known recent portrayal of Hajj Amin al-Husayni as the villain of the mandate period can be found in Alan Dershowitz's *The Case for Israel*, where the mufti is described as "a virulent anti-Semite whose hatred of Jews was both religious and racial. He was eventually a close ally and advisor to Adolf Hitler, and an active supporter of the "final solution"—the mass murder of European Jewry." The mufti's connection to Hitler was not as close as Dershowitz argues but what is more problematic is his portrait of the mufti as an anti-Semite in the 1920s, which is not backed up by much supporting evidence. To be sure, the mufti was no great supporter of Zionism but neither was he the same man then as he was in the 1940s. See Alan Dershowitz, *The Case for Israel* (Hoboken, NJ.: John Wiley & Sons, 2003).

Arab community—was heavily shaped by political and social developments in the late-1920s, most notably the nationalist competition between Arabs and Jews over holy space in Jerusalem and the collapse of other forms of Arab political activism.

VI – A Different Argument

I begin this study with the view that the British approach to Islam cannot be understood through the prism of appeasement. The idea that British officials gave in to the Muslim community does not fit with British motivations at the time and seems to reflect much more recent concerns about the possibility of the West or Israel giving in to Islamism and/or Palestinian nationalism.

To avoid such presentism, I believe that we must look at the colonial logic of the period in order to understand what factors governed British policy towards Islam. I argue that British policy towards Islam was influenced by three factors. First, it was shaped by a communalist approach to ruling the local population. The division of the population into three religious communities—Muslim, Christian, and Jewish—was seen as protecting the "natural" divisions in society and preserving the Ottoman policy of the millet system. The viability of this system required the existence of an independent Muslim-run institution, and in the absence of such a body, one had to be created. Second, a general lack of political and material support from London for post-war nation building, the terms of the mandate itself, and the small scale of British settlement ruled out any major colonial intervention into local cultural traditions.

British officials simply had no desire or money to build a state-run religious system as had existed during the Ottoman period or to recreate some version of India's Anglo-Mohemmedan legal system. As a result, the preservation of traditional religious elites was seen as the most efficient and least fractious way to administer religion. This takes us to the final factor, the fact that the creation of the Supreme Muslim Council enabled British officials to rework what Albert Hourani has referred to as the "politics of notables" for their own ends. The council was seen as a good way to elevate a particular notable family—the al-Husayni family—into the position of being an intermediary between the colonial government and the Muslim population. That Hajj Amin al-Husayni came in 1929 and in 1936 to use this arrangement to challenge British colonialism and Zionism should not take away from the fact that this position originally worked as an easy way to devolve power to the Muslim community while placing power in the hands of a family that was beholden to the Palestine government for its position.

Instead of starting with the view that the council was a mistake that should never have been created by the colonial government, I begin with the premise that British officials saw the council as a solution to a specific problem—the difficulty of a Christian power ruling over a predominantly Muslim population in a land that carried a religious significance that made it important throughout the world. In investigating this problematic I will consider British views of Palestinian Islam, the role that officials saw religion playing in society, their views of the Ottoman approach to Islam, and their ideas about the role the Palestine government should play in administering

Islam. I will also consider how events on the ground affected their understanding of these issues. In doing so I hope to figure out how officials worked out the contradiction that was at the heart of their mandatory project—the duty to develop the countries under European tutelage while also protecting their local traditions.

VII - Theorizing Empire and "Tradition"

My view of the British approach in Palestine is informed in large measure by the rethinking of the agenda of colonial studies that informs the 1997 edited volume, *Tensions of Empire: Colonial Cultures in a Bourgeois World*.[48] Frederick Cooper and Ann Laura Stoler open the book with a timely reminder to scholars that work in the field that "Europe's colonies were never empty spaces to be made over in Europe's image or fashioned in its interests; nor, indeed, were European states self-contained entities that at one point projected themselves overseas. Europe was made by its imperial projects, as much as colonial encounters were shaped by conflicts within Europe itself."[49] The articles that follow are thus focused on what Cooper and Stoler call "the contingency of metropolitan-colonial connections."[50] This call to rethink the field came in response to what Cooper has identified in *Colonialism in Question: Theory, Knowledge, History* (2005) as the tendency of scholars involved in the modern fields of postcolonial studies to replicate the same kind of teleological narrative of European colonial hegemony that was central to the modernization theory

---

[48] *Tensions of Empire: Colonial Cultures in a Bourgeois World*, eds. Frederick Cooper and Ann Laura Stoler (Berkeley: University of California Press, 1997).

[49] Cooper and Stoler, "Between Metropole and Colony," 1.

[50] Ibid.

approach that dominated colonial studies from the 1950s to the 1970s.[51] Although the

concept of "modernization" has been supplanted by the idea of "colonial modernity"

and the stultifying influence of Cold War social scientists such as W. W. Rostow has

been replaced by the more innovative approaches of scholars such as Antonio

Gramsci, Michel Foucault, and Edward Said, historical accounts of colonialism have

continued to present a vision of European rule as the steady diffusion of European

post-Enlightenment ideals and techniques of rule to the non-European world. This

kind of narrative breaks down when we look at events on the ground, as Cooper points

out in a long passage that bears quoting in full:

> The most vigorous case for the imposition of modern governmentality
> on colonies comes from historians of India. It hinges on the importance
> British officials attached to institutions that defined the subject in
> relation to the state: the census, the cadastral survey, and more
> generally the collection of knowledge that defines a "population" and
> can be used to maintain surveillance and superintend social change.
> Bernard Cohn's pioneering analyses of knowledge-gathering
> mechanisms convincingly showed that India was as important a
> laboratory for working out such systems in the nineteenth century as
> were the British Isles. But if an Indian history of censuses and
> classifications is supposed to reveal colonial modernity in the
> nineteenth century, then what is one to make of the fact that the first
> census in Kenya that counted indigenous people was conducted only in
> 1948, and that before then officials showed no interest in taking one?
> Colonial states did not necessarily want or need to see individual
> subjects in relation to the state or to classify and enumerate them on
> various axes; they belonged in tribes and could be governed through the
> collectivity. Whereas European governments may have wanted to
> separate populations into the sane and the insane, the criminal and the
> orderly, and to devise institutions that marked their subjects, colonial
> institutions often put more stress on the maladjustment of the

---

[51] See Cooper, *Colonialism in Question*, 113-149.

> collectivity than of the individual, and colonial penology continued into
> the post-World War II era to make use of precisely those punishments
> that from a Foucauldian perspective should have been supplanted by
> modern governmentality—flogging, collective punishment of villages
> and kinship groups, and penal sanctions for contract violations.[52]

Historians who study the mandate period in Palestine will see parallels with Cooper's comments about colonialism in Africa. The colonial concentration on the collectivity rather than the individual and the application of flogging and collective punishment were also part of the British approach in Palestine. There was also a similar reluctance to spread too much civilization to the natives, as shown in the decision by the educational department of the Palestine government to emphasize agricultural training rather than technical or liberal education in government schools, lest such reforms bring about "modern" politically engaged subjects.[53] British officials also clung to seeing the population in terms of the collectivity of religion even though such categories made less and less sense to the population itself.

What is needed to really make sense of British actions in Palestine is to remember one of Cooper and Stoler's central points in *Tensions of Empire*, namely that, "imperial elites may have *viewed* their domains from a metropolitan center, but their actions, let alone their consequences, were not necessarily *determined* there."[54] So while imperialism spread capitalist and liberal values to the colonized, or at least aimed to do so, the imposition of colonial rule required constant compromises with and accommodations to local conditions.

---

[52] Cooper, *Colonialism in Question*, 143.

[53] See Chapter One, fn. 150.

[54] Cooper and Stoler, "Between Metropole and Colony," 29.

One of the local conditions that the colonial authority in Palestine had to accommodate itself to was religion. In the writings of colonial officials we can see a reluctant acceptance that Palestine was a deeply religious space. As the military governor of Jerusalem Ronald Storrs explained in his memoirs, "'Moslems are far more orthodox here than in Egypt,' I had written after my first few weeks in Jerusalem, 'so is everybody, worse luck.'"[55] As will be shown below, this was one factor that led British officials to defend rather than attack religious traditions in Palestine. But this concept of "tradition" needs unpacking, for it was not something that existed out there available for the British to pick up and use. The "traditions" that British officials upheld frequently turned out to be a British versions of past practices, shorn of most of their rough edges and purged of their internal contradictions.

A good example of this comes from the application of Islamic law by British legal officials in India. As Gregory Kozlowski points out in *Muslim Endowments and Society in British India*, judges who worked in the Anglo-Muhammedan legal system saw themselves as upholding traditional Islamic law but in doing so imposed a coherence on the law that had never existed in the past. According to Kozlowski this created a new system that did not conform either to the past or to the lived experience of Muslim in India.

> Though in practice Muslims did not always follow strictly the letter of
> *Quran* or the precepts of classical religious thinkers, Anglo-Indian
> judges assumed that Muslims should comply. Therefore, the judges
> usually insisted on the application of any clear rule they found. *Where
> no such rule existed, as in the case of awqaf, they created one.* In that
> way, the Anglo-Indian courts made judgments supposedly based on

---

[55] Ronald Storrs, *The Memoirs of Sir Ronald Storrs* (New York,: G. P. Putnam's sons, 1937), 346.

> "Islamic law", but which actually bore little relation to the ways
> Muslims lived.[56]

In other words a British discourse of "protecting traditions" produced new reified and distorted visions of those traditions. This observation should be borne in mind when reading the first half of this dissertation, where I talk about the choice that British officials made between the "civilizing mission" and the "protection of religious tradition". From the outset, it should be noted that I do not conceive of these two approaches to colonial rule as representing a choice between nonintervention and intervention but between different types of organizing and domesticating the world of the colonized.

VIII – Chapter Outline

This dissertation is divided into three parts. In the first two chapters, I look at how the British approach to religion in Palestine was informed by their experience of the country before 1917 and by their understanding of the country's Ottoman past. In Chapter One, I argue that British visits to Palestine in the late-nineteenth century led to the development of the idea that the Holy Land was a place that needed to be saved. This led to two discourses about the country: the discourse of the "civilizing mission"—it was the duty of the British to bring development to a desolate and decayed country; and the discourse of the "protection of religious tradition"—it was the responsibility of Europeans to ensure that the holiness of the land and its people

---

[56] Gregory G. Kozlowski, *Muslim Endowments and Society in British India* (Cambridge: Cambridge UP, 1985), 194. Italics added.

were protected. In Chapter Two, I look at the great transformation that was going on in Ottoman Palestine in the late-Ottoman period and indicate how this dynamism was elided in British views of the period, particularly by the British choice to portray Ottoman society as being governed by the status quo and the millet system.

In the second part of my study, Chapters Three and Four, I consider how the British took these ideas and applied them to their general approach to religion (Chapter Three) and to their specific approach to Islam (Chapter Four). Here I argue that the discourse of the "protection of religious tradition," as represented by the concept of the "preservation of the status quo," won out over the civilizing mission, leading to the creation of The Supreme Muslim Council—an institution that made it possible for the British to treat the Muslim community like a millet.

In the final part of the work, I consider how the Supreme Muslim Council was transformed into a political force in Palestine, a development that challenged and ultimately doomed the British approach to institutional Islam to failure. Here the breakdown of a more secular Arab politics (as detailed in Chapter Five) allowed for the development of a space in which the SMC could become more involved in politics. Especially important in the rise to political prominence of the SMC was that the major political contest of the last 1920s took place over religious space (Chapter 6)—an area of Palestinian life that fell solidly within the jurisdiction of the Supreme Muslim Council.

Chapter One

Imagining Palestine, Imagining Palestinians

I – Introduction

An important ancillary part of warfare is selling the war, the business of presenting the war effort as heroic and necessary for the population back home. This is even more important when that effort is not going well, as was the case for the British government at the end of 1917. Progress on the Eastern and Western fronts looked bleak: Britain had effectively lost its Russian ally to the Bolshevik revolution and looked no nearer to breaking through the stalemate of trench warfare than it had been in 1914. But a bright spot was General Allenby's march through the Levant, especially the conquest of Jerusalem two weeks before Christmas. It was no surprise then that the conquest of Jerusalem in December 1917 was presented in the British media and in parliament as a momentous occasion. In truth, the conquest had little military significance—it was less important to the Middle Eastern campaign than the conquest of Gaza, Aqaba, and Damascus—but the British takeover of the Holy City gave the event untold symbolic power. Pregnant with multiple positive storylines— the Christian "re-conquest" of the Holy City, the liberation of Arab lands from Turkish despotism, the reopening of Palestine for Jewish settlement—the event could easily be packaged to different audiences as something greater than a simple military victory.

Mark Sykes in the British Foreign Office was one of the first officials to realize that the conquest made good propaganda for the British war effort around the world. He urged British commanders in the Middle East to send back stirring reports that could appeal to a diverse audience of "English church and chapel folk, New York Irish, Orthodox Balkan peasants and Mujiks, French and Italian Catholics, and Jews throughout the world; Indian and Algerian Moslems."[1] For instance, in a message dated January 15, 1918 to Gilbert Clayton (the chief political officer of the Egyptian Expeditionary Force) he explained that press reports from the troops needed to:

> Rivet [the] British on to [the] Holy Land [of the] Bible and New Testament. Jam [the] Catholics on [their] holy places, [the Church of the Holy] sepulcher, [the] via Dolorosa, and Bethlehem…Fix Orthodox on ditto…Concentrate Jews on [the] full details of [their] colonies and institutes and wailing places [sic.] Vox humana [on] this part…Rally Moslems on [their] absolute control of [the] Mosque of Omar.[2]

In response a series of press messages were drafted in the first half of 1918 that talked up the historical and religious significance of the British conquest. These messages described the British victory as the "liberation of Jerusalem," from the rule of an Ottoman empire that had for four centuries held back the "arts, crafts, [and] prosperity [of] those [who] dwelt within her gates."[3] The British soldier played the role of liberator who had come, unlike his Crusader forebears, "to protect, to save not only the Christians but to free the Arab and Jews as well from the heavy yoke of the Turk."[4] Their Ottoman foes were depicted as "savage Turks," whose destruction of the Middle East could "only find adequate historical parallel in the devastations of

---

[1] This message is a response by Sykes to two telegrams (Nos. 95 and 96) that contained press messages from Clayton that were cabled from Cairo. PRO FO 371/3383/9333.

[2] Ibid.

[3] Sir Reginald Wingate to Foreign Office, January 15, 1918. PRO FO 371/3383/9333.

[4] Wingate to FO, February 15, 1918. FO 371/3383/29296.

their Turanian forefathers Hulagu [and] Jenghiz Khan."[5] Later messages concentrated less on the war and more on vignettes that demonstrated how the religious life of the country thrived under British rule, with articles on the excitement felt by British soldiers celebrating mass in Jerusalem, the awesome experience of Easter in the holy land, the peaceful celebration of the Greek Orthodox Festival of the Holy Fire and Muslim Nabi Musa (Prophet Moses) festivals under the new British administration, and the successful restoration of the Torah of the Sephardic community in Jaffa.[6]

British propaganda thus delivered two somewhat contradictory messages about the importance of British occupation. The first of these was the idea that British occupation, by removing Ottoman tyranny and backwardness, was momentous because it would finally free Palestine to develop into a modern country. The second was the assertion that British rule was significant because it protected the traditional religious life of the country. As we shall see, this tension between reform and preservation would be a central theme of British rule in Palestine and crucial to understanding their religious policy.

It is difficult to tell how much of this propaganda made it directly into the press. Some of these initial messages—written by Ronald Storrs, the military governor of Jerusalem—were considered to be "vile barren stuff" by Mark Sykes and were not distributed, but later messages were sent on by the Foreign Office for

---

[5] Wingate to FO, January 16, 1918. FO 371/3383/9383.

[6] See for instance, "Religious Jerusalem," February 15, 1918, FO 371/3383/29296; "The Western Easter in Jerusalem," April 16, 1918, FO 371/3383/66663; "Easter Ceremonies in Jerusalem," May 13, 1918, FO 371/3391/84653, "Annual pilgrimage to the tomb of Moses (Nabiymusa) [sic]", May 3, 1918, FO 371/3391/78488; "Nabi Musa Pilgrimage," May 24, 1918, FO 371/3391/92045; "Annual Ceremony of the Holy Fire," May 6, 1918, FO 371/3391/79733; "Ceremony of the Holy Fire," June 3, 1918, FO 371/3391/98471; and "The restoration of the Sepheri [sic] Torah," June 6, 1918, FO 371/3391/100452.

integration into articles to be published about Palestine in the English, Indian, and Russian presses.[7]

Even if we cannot directly track how widely this propaganda was distributed, it is clear that messages sent from Palestine were not out of the ordinary. The tropes of liberation, Christian fortitude, British selflessness, and Turkish decadence were also part of a discourse about the conquest in London. This is indicated in the London *Times'* coverage in the days after the conquest of Jerusalem. An editorial on December 11, 1917 (the day that the British formally occupied Jerusalem) boasted that "the deliverance of Jerusalem though its influence on the war may be relatively remote, must remain for all time a most memorable event in the history of Christendom." This extraordinary claim was based on the editorial's argument that the modern crusade against German and Turkish tyranny was another chapter in the historical crusade against the East:

> It has often been said that this war is in truth a crusade for human liberties, and France and Italy of all countries were the lands of the old Crusaders. We, too, played a brilliant part in that wonderful and complex contest between East and West. The countrymen of Richard Couer de Lion and of Edward I dealt many a stout stroke in the struggle.[8]

---

[7] Sykes also accused Storrs of having "no idea of propaganda," in a minuted response to a telegram from Wingate to Foreign Office, January 16, 1918, FO 371/3383/9383.

Sykes was exclusively in charge of British propaganda about Palestine during 1917 to 1918 as indicated by the fact that Sykes oversaw all the press messages that came from Palestine during this period. See also Eitan Bar-Yosef, "The Last Crusade? British Propaganda and the Palestine Campaign, 1917-1918," *Journal of Contemporary History*, Vol. 36, No. 1 (Jan. 2001), fn. 7, pg. 88.

That the later press messages were intended for publication is revealed in the minutes. For example, the "Easter Ceremonies in Jerusalem" report was "being edited for the press"; the two reports on Nabi Musa were given to Reuters "for Indian consumption"; the "Annual Ceremony of the Holy Fire" report was sent to the Russian press, and the "Restoration of the Sepheri [sic] Torah" report was to be given "full press publicity and underlined for Jewish papers." See previous footnote for citations.

[8] *Times*, December 11, 1917.

While most commentators of the period saw the conquest as a victory for Britain and for Christianity, others argued that its primary benefit would be for the native population itself. A letter from the Archbishop of Northampton to the *Times* on December 12th, 1917, highlighted the selflessness of the British victory, a theme that would later be central to official accounts:

> As I write the bells of this Cathedral church are ringing our thanksgiving for a victory deferred for so many centuries. And the thanksgiving is the more heartfelt because we feel no pride of conquest, but a rejoicing that we can give peace and succour and security to the peoples, of the land where the life of Jesus Christ was given for mankind.[9]

Again this could be contrasted with Ottoman savagery, with the Victorian imperialist novelist H. Rider Haggard ("as one who knows and is most deeply interested in the Holy Land") warning in another letter that Jerusalem must never "fall again into the dreadful hand of the Turk."[10]

As a rule, writers back home were more comfortable than officials in Palestine in presenting the conquest as a national religious victory and were more likely to write of the campaign as a crusade. But both groups shared the idea, mentioned above, that the British conquest delivered the native population from the backwardness and tyranny of the Ottomans, a perspective shaped by the widely held view that the "East" was less developed and needed Europe's help. They also shared the view that the British presence in Palestine was beneficial because it alone ensured that the country's sanctity would be protected, a position that saw the values of tolerance and justice to be unique to British imperialism. These two views of the conquest were part of two

---

[9] *Times*, December 12, 1917.
[10] Ibid.

larger discourses that were used throughout the mandate period to justify and guide British policy—the discourse of the "civilizing mission," which held that the modernization of the country depended upon the oversight of a Western power, and the discourse of what I call the "defense of religious tradition," which presented the British as the only people capable of keeping the peace between the warring religious communities of Palestine.

As this chapter will make clear, these two discourses were not invented at the time of the British occupation but had largely developed from Britain's contact with Palestine in the decades before the First World War. I will argue that the experiences of British consuls, missionaries, academics, and tourists in the latter half of the nineteenth century, part of a growing imperial interest in the country, were integral in shaping a vision of the country and its people that affected British actions in the wake of their occupation. This encounter with Jerusalem ended up producing a distorted vision of the country, presenting Palestine as a land that was holy but broken, a territory that had to be saved by a greater British presence.

II – Not Just Another Civilizing Mission

At first glance the language used to describe the British conquest seems to simply recycle the oft-used motif of the Western civilizing mission. The idea that Britain had "liberated" Palestine from Ottoman backwardness and tyranny clearly echoed justifications given for the East India Company's takeover of India from the Mughals and the Crown's later takeover from the Company. The notion that this was an altruistic act meant to benefit the native population reprised Queen Victoria's proclamation to the Indian people that,

> It is our earnest duty to stimulate the peaceful industry of India, to promote works of public utility and improvement, and to administer its government for the benefit of all our subjects resident therein. In their prosperity will be our strength; in their contentment our security, and in their gratitude our best reward.[11]

And the idea that Britain was arriving to save the population fit with Lord Cromer's boast in 1908 that the Englishman had come to Egypt "not as a conqueror, but in the familiar garb of a saviour of society."[12]

Such arguments were part of a by-now familiar orientalist discourse that saw Europeans as ontologically superior to non-Europeans and therefore destined and justified to rule the world. As Edwin Samuel, the son of the first high commissioner for Palestine, argued in an interview years after the end of the mandate, the British could have no regrets about their time in Palestine because ruling was "the white man's burden."[13]

But, victory in Palestine had a millenarian quality absent in other colonial narratives. British victory was viewed by some as a fulfillment of historical and religious destiny. As a telegram from the British forces in Palestine explained in January 1918:

---

[11] Queen Victoria, "Queen Victoria's Proclamation, November 1, 1858," *Imperialism & Orientalism: A Documentary Sourcebook*, ed. Barbara Harlow and Mia Carter (London: Blackwell, 1999), 210.

[12] Earl of Cromer, *Modern Egypt* (New York: MacMillan, 1908), 123.

[13] Edwin Samuel, transcript of an interview for the Thames Television program *Palestine*, which aired on British television in 1978. Thames Television Papers, GB165-0282, Middle East Center Archive, St. Antony's College, Oxford.

For Jerusalem prophecies [have] been uttered and fulfilled that have taxed [the] incredulity of [the most] skeptical. [These] prophecies [are] of equal import to Christian Jew [and] Arab. But whatever measure [of] credence mankind may attribute [to] prophecy and its fulfillment [the] recent taking Jerusalem after four centuries [of[Turkish misrule [is] one of those events which leaves impress on mind [of] man unlike that which has been produced by any of [a] long list [of] military achievements that make [up the] history [of] recent years. This event not only stands [out] from other strategic triumphs for reasons which are obvious but can even be differentiated from similar events in [the] history [of the] City itself—let [it] always be remembered that [the] capture [of] Jerusalem by one conqueror or another is [a] recurrent symptom of world history. [British victory] is unique because it is now [the] intention of those who are now [the] trustees of her prosperity that this [most] recent transformation [in the] fortunes [of] Jerusalem shall unlike [its] predecessors mark [the] definite and enduring emancipation from oppression of a city thrice sacred in [the] hearts [of] civilized mankind, and that in these new circumstances [the] prophecy [of] David shall find noblest fulfillment: "Thou shalt see Jerusalem in prosperity all thy life long."[14]

This argument was echoed back in Britain, with the Lord Mayor of Manchester, arguing that British victory showed that "the vision of the prophet Isaiah would be realized."[15] References to biblical prophecy such as these would soon fade away after the euphoria of conquest wore off. But the deliberate muddying of the boundary between the religious past of Jerusalem and contemporary political events would continue in British discussions about Palestine. Nor was this phenomenon limited to

---

[14] Wingate to Foreign Office, FO 371/3383/9334.

[15] It is perhaps not surprising that this particular mayor would make this statement given the strong Zionist movement in the city. The Manchester School included a number of leading English Jews (Harry Sacher, Leon Simon, Samuel Landman, Norman Bentwich (later Attorney General in mandatory Palestine), Israel Seiff, and Simon Marks) who worked with Chaim Weizmann (a chemistry demonstrator at the University of Manchester) to spread the Zionist message. The city was also home to the *Manchester Guardian,* which took a strong pro-Zionist line thanks to the leadership of C. P. Scott, one of the leading non-Jewish voices in support of Zionism, and the work of Sacher and Herbert Sidebotham, a non-Jew who popularized the idea that imperial and Zionist aims coincided . The quote is found in Barbara Tuchman, *Bible and Sword: England and Palestine from the Bronze Age to Balfour* (New York: Ballantine, 1956), 339.

British views of the country, for Palestinian Arab politicians and Zionists officials also frequently made arguments about Palestine that referenced its biblical past.

It should be noted however that such overt biblical language was not welcomed by all British officials. Members of the Foreign Office complained that too strong an emphasis on Christianity, and in particular on the Crusades, would hurt Britain's standing among its Muslim subjects. This led the Department of Information's Press Bureau to issue a confidential notice in November 1917 imploring the press to avoid all references to a Holy War or crusade. This plea fell on deaf ears since British newspapers and books persisted in using the country's religious past, and in particular the crusades, as a framework for explaining the British presence in Palestine.[16] The reason for this was obvious, it was much easier to sell the occupation by making reference to the Bible than to some vague geo-strategic considerations. In the end, the attempt to limit references to the Crusades itself seems to have been counterproductive. As the historian Eitan Bar-Yossef has argued, "Ironically, the very conscious act of having to suppress the Crusading theme made it seem all the more inevitable. It constructed the Crusade as a known 'secret', shared by all British (Christian) people, against their imperial subalterns."[17]

It would be wrong to assume that this emphasis on religion made Britain's interest in Palestine radically different from their interest in other colonial possessions. As elsewhere in the empire, British interests in Palestine were driven primarily by

---

[16] The use and controversy over the use of this image during the war campaign is discussed in Bar-Yosef, "The Last Crusade?"

[17] Bar-Yossef, "The Last Crusade?"

geo-strategic and economic concerns (though the economic motive was never very strong in Palestine). Nevertheless, allusions to the crusades and the bible are striking in British accounts of their conquest and occupation of Palestine. It is this language that makes the discourse about Palestine different from the discussion of Egypt and India, where religious matters were much less important. It was the religious angle that gave the occupation of Palestine an importance quite out of proportion to its strategic significance. Even if religious considerations were not the prime motivations for British actions in Palestine, it is still important to how this religious approach affected the British approach to Palestine and Palestinians.

III - The Holy Land and the Crusade

How should we understand this link made between Christianity and empire in British discussions of Palestine? Was this a widespread phenomenon within colonial circles? And if so, what did that mean for imperial policy?

It appears that the practice of linking the British conquest to the Crusades was widespread among colonial officials in London and Jerusalem. If the Crusade was a secret, it was an open one, even in Jerusalem. The Jerusalem musician Wasif Jawhariyya observes in his memoirs that the officer in charge of the Palestine campaign, General Edmund Allenby, alluded to the British victory as marking the end of the Crusades in his very first public speech after the conquest.[18] For a Christian

---

[18] Wasif Jawhariyya, *al-Quds al-intidabiyya fi al-Mudhakarat al-Jawhariyya: al-kitab al-thani min mudhakarat al-musiqi Wasif Jawhariyya 1918-1948* [Mandate Jerusalem in the Memoirs of al-Jawhariyya: The Second Volume of the Memoirs of the Musician Wasif Jawhariyya, 1918-1948], eds. Issam Nassar and Salim Tamari (Jerusalem: Institute for Jerusalem Studies, 2005), 280.

taking control of a majority Muslim country such words were, to say the least, ill-chosen. Indeed, Jawhariyya writes of some Muslim leaders walking out in disgust at Allenby's allusion, when otherwise the British occupation was supported by the Arab population of Jerusalem.[19] Allenby's words were no a slip of the tongue, given the fact that during the campaign he had "attempted to identify the sites of his battles (sometimes wrongly) by reference to biblical campaigns."[20] Allenby was not alone in viewing the country through its religious history. Edward Keith-Roach (later the second District Commissioner for Jerusalem) claimed to have dedicated his life to Jerusalem after the discovery of the gravestone of a crusader who was an ancestor of his by marriage, while other officials, such as Ronald Storrs (the military governor of Jerusalem and its first district commissioner) and C. R. Ashbee (the civic advisor for Jerusalem), wrote that Jerusalem's significance to the world was to be found in its religious history.[21] Meanwhile, British command in Palestine boasted in its press propaganda that "two of the commanders who have played a great part in the South

---

[19] Ibid, 280. Indeed throughout the mandate period leading Muslims, such as the Mufti of Jerusalem and the Muslim leaders of the Muslim-Christian Association, would complain about government policies that they saw as religiously motivated, such as the overrepresentation of Christians in the civil service. Indian Muslims, through such organizations as the Khilafat Movement, also consistently expressed outrage at decisions that they regarded as anti-Muslim.

[20] Naomi Shepherd, *Ploughing Sand: British Rule in Palestine 1917-1948* (New Brunswick, NJ: Rutgers University Press, 2000), 6.

[21] See Shepherd, *Ploughing Sand*, 6, Ronald Storrs, *The Memoirs of Sir Ronald Storrs* (New York,: G. P. Putnam's sons, 1937), and *Jerusalem 1918-1920: Being the Records of the Pro-Jerusalem Council during the period of the British Military Administration*, ed. C. R. Ashbee (London: John Murray, 1921).

Palestine campaign are descended from knights who fought in the wars of the

Crusades."[22]

This Crusader past was also emphasized in London, as indicated in the less-

than-imaginative titles of books on British campaigns in the Middle East published at

the time: *Khaki Crusaders* (1919), *Temporary Crusaders* (1919), *The Modern

Crusaders* (1920), *The Last Crusade* (1920), *With Allenby's Crusaders* (1923), and

The Romance of the Last Crusade (1923).[23] Despite the general reluctance of British

officials to offend their Muslim allies, the crusader motif was sometimes promoted by

the government itself. For example, the Department of Information produced a 40-

minute documentary film, *The New Crusaders: With the British Forces on the

Palestine Front* as part of its *The Turk must Go* propaganda campaign during the First

World War.[24]

To be sure, the concept of the crusade had multiple meanings to Britons at this

time. In some cases the Christian aspect was explicit, such as the Bishop of London

Winnington-Ingram's wartime call for a "Holy War," but in many other cases the

---

[22] The quote is from a press message sent by General HQ in Egypt to the Foreign Office: Wingate to
FO, 14 February 1918, FO 371/3383/29296. That message also presented the conquest of Jerusalem as
a stark and seeming eternal contest between the values of Christian Europe and the savagery of the
Turanian and Hun:

> With the Anglo-Celts are their old crusading Allies the Frenchmen of Normandy and Paris, of
> Flanders, Province and all the famous lands which have formed France and the Italian heirs of
> crusading tradition Rome and Sicily, Venice, Genoa and Pisa. Savage Turks from Central
> Asia long ago scattered the bones of the leaders of the old crusading hosts just as only in 1915
> a German Vice Consul and Turkish gendarmerie captain scattered the bones and defiled the
> graves of Napoleon's soldiers who fell at Mount Tabor. But the sword of Godfrey de
> Bouillon is still to be seen by men who care not to massacre as did Godfrey the zealots but to
> protect, to save not only the Christians but to free the Arab and Jew as well from the heavy
> yoke of the Turk [sic].

[23] These are all mentioned in Bar-Yosef, "The Last Crusade?".

[24] Bar-Yosef, "Last Crusade?," 88, 92.

religious aspect was incidental such as in the promotion of the crusader knight as the ideal chivalrous gentleman in Britain's public schools. It was precisely this elasticity in meaning that made the crusade such a powerful image. By invoking the crusade authors could tap into a well of nationalistic, imperialistic, and Christian chauvinistic feeling. But of course in doing so they risked alienating their subject population.

IV - Biblical Imperialism?

For a small group of politicians in Palestine and London religion was an important part of their approach to Palestine. Wyndham Deedes (the country's first civil secretary) and Richard Meinertzhagen (the chief political officer for Palestine 1919-20) arrived in Palestine with deeply held religious convictions.[25] Most importantly, in London, Prime Minister David Lloyd George and Foreign Secretary Lord Arthur Balfour were Evangelicals, who saw the future of Palestine as being linked in some part to its biblical past.[26] Inevitably, this led these important players to become strong advocates for Zionism, as Bernard Wasserstein has pointed out:

> The religious basis of Deedes' Zionism has to be seen in the general context of the concern—a concern so powerful as to merit the title of obsession—of English Puritans and Evangelicals with the fate of the Chosen People. It was this religious stream which debouched in the sentimental philo-Zionism of Lloyd George and Balfour. Most of the early supporters of Zionism among gentiles in England were non-conformist or 'low church'. So were the few undeviating supporters of the idea among British soldiers and officials in the Middle East: men

---

[25] Bernard Wasserstein notes that Deedes was "converted" to Zionism by two "agencies": "first, his fundamentalist religious views which provided soil fertile for the growth of Zionist ideas; and secondly the magnetic effect upon Deedes of the personality of Chaim Weizmann." See Bernard Wasserstein, *Wyndham Deedes in Palestine*, Pamphlet No. 40, (London: Anglo-Israel Association, 1973), 7.

[26] See Tuchman, *Bible and Sword*, 311 and 323.

such as Colonel J. H. Patterson (commander of one of the Jewish battalions in Allenby's army), Colonel Richard Meinertzhagen (who served under Deedes on the intelligence staff in the Palestine campaign) and Orde Wingate (who moulded and inspired the fledgling *Haganah* in the 1930s). Like these men Deedes regarded Zionism as a fulfillment of biblical prophecy and as a prelude to the Redemption, and supported it on that ground.[27]

Richard Meinertzhagen even claimed that King George V supported the conquest of

Palestine for biblical reasons and had "made some remarks about the final crusade,"

although this observation comes with a couple of important caveats—Meinertzhagen

was, to put it kindly, an unreliable witness to the events of his own life, and the King

had little influence on foreign affairs.[28]

Historians who study the mandatory period have tended to avoid discussing the

impact of religion on British policy. Given the diversity of opinions, religious

backgrounds, and political sympathies of British officials in Jerusalem and London, it

is difficult to identify a coherent colonial *Weltanshauung,* let alone one that can be

identified as Christian.[29] Moreover it is not always apparent whether a supposedly

religious argument is in fact that. For example, the *Times'* celebration of the conquest

of Jerusalem as a victory for Christianity could be read as a straightforward example

of Christian chauvinism or it could be interpreted as a rhetorical flourish designed to

sell more papers.

---

[27] Wasserstein, *Deedes,* 7.

[28] Meinertzhagen was strongly pro-Zionist and almost rabidly anti-Arab and his "memoirs" are suspect in places. However, his observations about the king seem probable. Richard Meinertzhagen, *Middle East Diary 1917-1956* (London: Cresset Press, 1959), 11.

[29] The officials mentioned above held a variety of views about Christianity, Arabs, Jews, and the imperial mission. The world-weary cynicism of Ashbee and Storrs, for instance, contrasted greatly with the religiosity of Deedes and Meinertzhagen's zealous support for Zionism, indicating that opinion within the Palestine Government was far from monolithic.

In her 1956 book *Bible and Sword*, Barbara Tuchman argues that there is a

fundamental problem that prevents modern historians from writing about the place of

religion in history: "In our day it has become almost impossible to appreciate justly

the role of religion in past political, social, and economic history. We cannot do it

because we have not got it. Religion is not part of our lives; not, that is, comparably to

its part in pre-twentieth-century lives."[30] But even if historians are guilty of

overlooking religion in their works does this mean that there existed a religious

impulse affecting British policy that is waiting to be discovered?

Tuchman's answer is an emphatic yes. In *Bible and Sword* she argues that the

British did not arrive in Palestine purely for imperial purposes but were driven there

by a religious motive. She contends that Britain had a religious interest in Palestine

before it had an imperial interest and that these two interests ended up being mutually

constitutive. She finds in the writings and pronouncements of various British

intellectual and political leaders evidence of an intellectual and political current in

British history that saw the destinies of Britain and the Palestine as inherently

interlinked. Tuchman focuses specifically on the religious and proto-Zionist views of

a few key British political figures (mostly from the nineteenth and twentieth centuries,

such as Lord Balfour and Lord Shaftesbury, but also going back to Cromwell) and

representatives from Britain's nonconformist sects, all of whom she views as part of a

coherent and continuous "moral motive" that worked alongside the imperial desire for

Palestine.

---

[30] Tuchman, *Bible and Sword*, 181.

Her argument is both ahistorical and tendentious. A fundamental problem is her idea that a coherent "motive" towards Palestine can be constructed from the writings of figures who lived in very different centuries and political situations. Even if the reader can get beyond the stunning anachronism of her project—the full title of her book is *Bible and Sword: England and Palestine from the Bronze Age to Balfour*—the idea that this long relationship can be discovered in the writings of a handful of political figures (however important they were) seems dubious.

A further problem is Tuchman's consistent elision of religious language and moral values throughout the work. The religious attachment of certain officials to Palestine appears as a selfless act that neutralized or at least mitigated the naked self-interest of the imperial project. Her aim here appears to be political: by portraying the British path to Palestine (and in particular the establishment of the Jewish National Home) as being directed in part by the Good Book, Tuchman presents British occupation as not only morally defensible but morally inevitable. This essentially repeats, uncritically, the colonial narrative explored at the beginning of this chapter, except rather than claiming that Britain was justified because of a "white man's burden", she finds justification in Christianity.[31]

What Tuchman fails to consider is the unremarkable fact that the language of the Bible is often exploited for political purposes. We have already seen this in Mark

---

[31] This argument of a British civilizing mission was often repeated during the early years of the mandate by military and civilian leaders alike. Indeed, the entire structure of the mandate system was built upon the notion that former Ottoman territories were "inhabited by peoples not yet able to stand by themselves under the strenuous conditions of the modern world," and needed to be developed by Western mandatory powers, "until such time as they are able to stand alone." See Article 22 of The Covenant of the League of Nations.

Sykes' eagerness to exploit the religious significance of the conquest of Jerusalem for political ends and in the Department of Information's use of crusader imagery in its campaign against the Turks. Tuchman also makes the dubious and unexamined assumption throughout her book that actions motivated by religious belief are more morally upright and selfless than those that are not.[32]

V - Nineteenth-century Imperialism in Palestine

The best evidence against Tuchman's thesis is found by looking at the actual motivations behind British policy in Palestine during the nineteenth century, the period that she herself sees as the most crucial in the relationship between the two countries. Looking at British policymaking during this period, it is clear that British actions were seldom motivated by religious sentiment; instead we find that imperial interest was the factor that drove Britons to Palestine and brought Palestine to the attention of the population back home.

Because of Jerusalem's frequent appearance in news reports today, it is frequently forgotten that at the beginning of the nineteenth century, the city was isolated from the rest of the world and held little interest to Westerners. In her book, *The Zealous Intruders: The Western Rediscovery of Palestine,* Naomi Shepherd notes that for Britons,

---

[32] Cromwell's campaigns in Ireland, for example, show that the relationship between religious devotion and morality are far more complex than Tuchman would suggest. Or to give an example closer to the period under investigation, recent work on nineteenth-century missions to Africa and the Middle East has shown how missionaries were heavily involved in the imperial project and were destructive to local populations.

> Palestine, at the end of the eighteenth century, had been almost terra
> incognita. It had no political frontiers but the shifting historical
> tidelines of biblical, Roman and medieval conquest...Blake's poetry
> might invoke a heavenly Jerusalem, but in his contemporary
> Pinkerston's Modern Geography while Aleppo and Damascus, well-
> known Syrian trading centres, were mentioned, the earthly Jerusalem
> was not.[33]

Most significantly, "Palestine was not even familiar as a place of pilgrimage. By Napoleon's time the tradition of Catholic pilgrimage was moribund."[34]

This state of affairs would change over the course of the nineteenth century, as Britain became involved in a great power struggle that took place in Ottoman Jerusalem. British attention was drawn to Jerusalem in the nineteenth century for two main reasons. For one, Palestine became part of the Eastern Question, the nineteenth-century struggle between Britain, France, and Russia for control over the Middle East and Central Asia. For Britain this competition was intimately tied up with the security of India, which had come under threat with Napoleon's invasion of Egypt in 1798 and Russian expansion into Central Asia in the eighteenth and nineteenth centuries. Throughout the nineteenth century, British foreign policy in the Middle East was dedicated to making sure that France or Russia did not threaten Britain's link to India by gaining a prominent position in the region. This objective was made even more crucial with the opening of the Suez Canal in 1869, and it would be no exaggeration to

---

[33] Naomi Shepherd, *The Zealous Intruders: The Western Rediscovery of Palestine* (London: Collins, 1987), 13.
[34] Ibid.

state that the British takeovers of Egypt in 1882 and Palestine in 1917 were driven by this need to protect the canal.

Another factor that made Jerusalem important in imperial calculations was its emergence as a prize for the imperial powers of Europe. Greater Ottoman investment in the city, as part of the Porte's attempt to centralize power during the nineteenth century, led to an improvement in the city's security and infrastructure. This enabled the city to expand beyond the walls of the old city for the first time and brought modern improvements, such as streetlamps, public parks, and planned neighborhoods.[35] At the same time Europeans—typically consular officials, pilgrims, and missionaries—were drawn to the city not simply as visitors but permanent residents. European settlement and the rush of imperial construction that followed was also spurred on by reforms of the Ottoman Tanzimat period that promoted religious equality and granted foreigners the right to own land throughout the Ottoman Empire. This "opening up of the 'Holy Land' to Europe's political and religious-cultural penetration from the end of the 1830s to the Crimean War," as Alexander Schölch has put it, combined with greater Ottoman investment ended up transforming Jerusalem into an international and cosmopolitan city.[36] This transformation was recognized by the Ottomans in the 1858 decision by

---

[35] See Chapter Three for a greater explanation of these improvements.

[36] Alexander Schölch, "Britain in Palestine 1838-1882, The Roots of the Balfour Policy," *Journal of Palestine Studies*, Vol. 22, no. 1 (Autumn 1992), 40.

the Porte to designate the Jerusalem district as a *mutasarrifiyya*, a special

administrative unit whose governor had to report directly to Istanbul.[37]

These developments helped to transform Jerusalem into a diplomatic

battleground, as the city became part of the larger European competition over the

future of the Ottoman empire. Among the earliest permanent British residents in

Palestine were British consular officials, such as the first consul, William Tanner

Young, and his successor James Finn.[38] Young arrived in 1839, when the British

consulate opened, and was the first official European representative in Jerusalem.

Over the next decade, he was followed by consuls from Prussia, France, Sardinia, the

United States, and Austria, with even more consuls arriving after the Crimean War.[39]

It was typical at the time for the European presence to be justified on the basis

of religious concerns rather than other interests. This was usually done by appealing

to the right of European nations—through the so-called "capitulations"—to protect

their co-religionists in the Ottoman Empire. In practice this led to the construction and

support of local Christian institutions in order to project European power into the city,

through a rapid growth of Christian charities, guesthouses, and churches in Palestine

during the nineteenth century. To be sure, these institutions came to play an important

role in the religious life of the country and were central to the European pilgrim and

---

[37] This was a special type of administrative unit in the Ottoman Empire, for unlike other regions of its size a *mutassarif*ate was a separate administrative unit which was not part of a larger *vilayet* (district) and whose governor reported directly to Istanbul

[38] As Ruth Kark has pointed out, Young was the first official European representative in Ottoman Palestine, see Ruth Kark, *American Consuls in the Holy Land 1832-1914* (Detroit: Wayne State Press, 1994), 94.

[39] Such as those from Spain, Persia, Russia, Greece, Mexico, the Netherlands, and Sweden. Ibid.

tourist trade, but they were founded in the first place because of what Alexander

Shölch has accurately described as the "religious-cultural" competition between

European imperialists.[40]

This is well illustrated in the establishment of British religious institutions in

Palestine. In 1841 the Protestant Episcopate of Jerusalem was established and eight

years later, the first Protestant Church in Palestine, Christ Church, was opened in

Jerusalem.[41] British support for these institutions had little to do with saving souls or

spreading the word of God. In fact, the British consulate had an ambivalent

relationship with British Christians, particularly missionaries, who they often viewed

as being unhelpful to Britain's position in Palestine.[42] These institutions were

important because they gave Britain a place at the table in Jerusalem. If France and

Russia could claim a natural interest in Palestine because of the existence of the

Roman Catholic and Greek Orthodox churches on its soil, then Britain could do the

---

[40] Shölch aptly terms this the "religious-cultural" competition of the nineteenth-century.

[41] The Protestant Episcopate was a joint project of the British and Prussian governments, which contributed equal funding to the Episcopate. The first Bishop was a converted Jew, Michael Solomon Alexander, who was followed by the influential Prussian Bishop Samuel Gobat.

[42] This was made clear in a letter that William Tanner Young sent to the Foreign Secretary in 1842, in which he complained about the Anglican bishop's attempts to convert foreign (i.e. non-Ottoman) Jews. He suggested that London step in to control missionaries, lest they create unnecessary tensions between Britain and the other European powers in Palestine:

> I would humbly suggest these points for Your Lordship's notice, as appearing worthy the consideration of the Authorities in England who have the direction of Religious Mission to their Countries, in order to their being met in a way that would secure a sound and discreet method of carrying on their labours. Without wishing to disparage their pious efforts, it has seemed to me in their zeal, missionaries do not always allow these points to weigh with them; and I would presume to submit to Your Lordship, that in a Country like this it is in vain for them to pretend to the same freedom and privileges in their Calling, as in a Protestant Country, where the circumstances are so widely different.

W.T. Young to Earl of Aberdeen (George Hamilton-Gordon), October 11, 1842 as quoted in Albert M. Hyamson., *The British Consulate in Jerusalem: in relation to the Jews of Palestine 1838-1914*, vol. 1 (London: Edward Goldston, 1939), 47.

same if their was a Protestant presence. This explains why the British pushed the

Porte into allowing the creation of the Episcopate, the construction of Christ Church,

and most importantly the recognition of Protestantism as an official religious

community in 1850.

This push to create a distinct institutional base for Protestantism in Palestine

even led to the creation of a separate Protestant *axis mundi* in Jerusalem. In 1884,

General Charles Gordon (a.k.a. "Chinese Gordon" or "Gordon of Khartoum")

announced that he had found the real location of Golgotha, the location of Christ's

crucifixion and burial, which was not located in the Church of the Holy Sepulchre but

was to be found in the site that is now called the Garden Tomb.[43] Gordon's search for

the "authentic" Calvary came out of nineteenth-century Protestant skepticism (that

coincided with Britain's new imperial interest in Palestine) towards the site's

traditional location, which was and still is controlled by the Orthodox and Roman

Catholic Churches.[44]

The discovery of Golgotha was thus part of a positivist program of using

science (in the application of the survey, the archaeological dig, the ethnographic

---

[43] For a full discussion of the search for the site see Daniel Bertrand Monk, *An Aesthetic Occupation : The Immediacy of Architecture and the Palestine Conflict* (Durham: Duke University Press, 2002), 18.

[44] In this context it is striking that Gordon, a quintessential imperial figure, was the archaeologist who 'discovered' the Garden Tomb. Gordon's work was in turn built on Lieutenant Claude Conder's suggestion that Golgotha (Greek for the "place of skulls") would have to be a rounded skull-shaped hill "on the toponymic assumption that place-names in Jerusalem were not arbitrary but logically had to correspond in form or use to what they designated." It is this hill that Gordon discovered in 1884 and which has become the site Protestants view as the place of Jesus' death and burial. Monk, *Aesthetic Occupation*, 26.

study) to prove the truth of Christian historical texts.[45] But while Gordon and others like him were motivated by strong evangelical beliefs, this new field of biblical archaeology, was driven by imperial interests as Nadia Abu El-Haj has pointed out.[46] The "truth" that Gordon and other archaeologists were finding in Palestine often worked to create a past that was helpful to British imperial interests.

British support for Jews in Palestine was also largely based on imperial interests. As early as 1842, proposals were being drafted for the British to support Jewish colonization in Palestine. In January of that year, the British consul in Jerusalem sent the Foreign Secretary a paper written by a Dr. Benisch, an Austrian Jewish friend of the famous British Jewish philanthropist Moses Montefiore, entitled "Scheme for the improvement of the civil and moral conditions of the Jews of the East." The proto-Zionist proposal called for Britain to help its imperial position by helping Jews settle in Palestine:

> If it be evident that England cannot attain her views by the propagation
> of Protestantism, she must direct her attention to another persuasion
> legally on a par with the resident Catholics and which evinces no
> sympathy with either of the Catholic Powers.—This persuasion is the
> Jewish one.—Scattered over the surface of the whole globe, the Jews
> still form in their religious sentiments an irrefragable unity, and a
> benefit conferred on any of them, fills the hearts of even their ocean-
> separated Brethren, with purely grateful feelings—
> The question now is, how can England acquire their sympathy?
> The answer to this is by supporting the applications about to be made to
> the Porte for the establishment of a Colony in some well situated part

---

[45] For a detailed discussion of British archaeology and imperialism see, Nadia Abu El-Haj, *Facts on the Ground*.

[46] Although he was an evangelical Protestant, it can hardly be said that Gordon's placement of Calvary was determined by belief. There were no specific Protestant traditions about where Christ was buried, and before the advent of the imperial geographer and archaeologist, no real interest in the matter.

of Palestine…The Colony to be under Turkish Government and protection, and England to guarantee the maintenance of the conditions under which the Colony shall be formed.[47]

These proposals resonated with British Evangelicals, such as Lord Shaftesbury, but it was the more pragmatic imperialists, such as Shaftesbury's father-in-law, Lord Palmerston, who decided British policy. For these figures, British support of Jews in Palestine came from the practical consideration that they existed in numbers in Palestine, whereas the Protestant community did not.

In Britain support for the Protestant or Jewish communities was not really about a "religious motive", as Tuchman has put it, or at least wasn't derived primarily from such a motive. Instead we should see this support as part of a political competition over religion that Selim Derengil has described:

> What was at issue was not religion at all, but sovereignty. The Greek man claiming Austria protection, the Georgians being claimed by the Russians, the Greek woman being claimed by the British consul at Preveze [Preveza in modern Greece], the Jew converting to Protestantism and claiming British protection, even the dead body of a convert, all became areas of contestation between rival claims of sovereignty…The convert or apostate became the bone of contention in an international prestige war, in which the Great Powers sought to impose their will on the last remaining non-Christian Great Power, that aberration which rule millions of Christians as a Muslim empire.[48]

---

[47] W.T. Young to Viscount Canning, January 13, 1842 as quoted in Hyamson., *British Consulate in Jerusalem*, 42.

[48] Selim Derengil, "'There Is No Compulsion in Religion': On Conversion and Apostasy in the Late Ottoman Empire: 1839-1856," *Society for Comparative Study of Society and History*, (2000), 42: 567.

VI - Reawakening Interest in the Holy Land

Tuchman's contention that Protestant religious belief determined British policy

towards Palestine is overly simplistic, but this does not meant that religion had no

impact. Where Palestine was religiously significant—and here Tuchman is correct—

was as a symbol. Thomas Friedman has written about the overwhelming attention that

the modern state of Israel has received in the Western media and once asked his

readers to consider "how a tiny country with the population of greater Chicago and the

size of the state of Delaware [can] occupy as much news space as the Soviet Union, if

not more?"[49] Gilbert Clayton (head of the Arab Bureau at the time and later a chief

secretary of Palestine) pondered the same issue at the time of the country's conquest in

1917, when he noted that the conquest of Jerusalem aroused interest, even among

neutrals, "wholly out of proportion with its area, population, wealth [and] strategic

importance."[50]

The reason the British victory in Jerusalem could be exploited in propaganda

was because Jerusalem was "known" to the British population in 1917, as Damascus

and Gaza were not. The victory meant more than the sum of its parts was because

when it came to Palestine/Israel/the Holy Land, as Friedman puts it, "the characters,

the geography, and the themes involved are so familiar, so much a part of our cultural

---

[49] Thomas Friedman, *From Beirut to Jerusalem* (New York: Anchor Books, 1990), 427.

[50] The quote comes from a telegram that was intended for press publication; as such, Clayton's words cannot be taken completely at face value. Nevertheless, at the very least the telegram suggests that victory in Palestine could be exploited like no other British victory in the Middle East: "The poignant and unique position of Jerusalem as a centre of moral force has during last few months received signal illustration from circumstances its recapture an achievement which has elated or depressed friend or foe has aroused interest of neutrals if on such a theme neutrality can be to extent wholly out of proportion with its area population wealth strategic importance an interest greater than that which has centered round any previous event of most eventful period known history [*sic*]."

lenses."[51] This familiarity was a product of the nineteenth century, which was the period in which those lenses were shaped and sharpened by imperial functionaries, missionaries, colonial geographers, archaeologists, and tourists who came to Palestine to find the holy land for Britain.

One of the earliest examples of British popular interest was the 'Panorama of Jerusalem', an outdoor spectacle that opened in London's Leicester Square Pavilion in 1836. Consisting of a set of giant murals of the Dome and the Rock and the Holy Sepulchre, the display covered some ten thousand square feet and was seen by more than 140,000 people. The panorama resulted from an unprecedented visit to Jerusalem in 1833 by a group of English architects and draughtsmen, who had been employed in Egypt by Muhammad 'Ali in restoring ancient Egyptian monuments. Their visit produced a series of architectural drawings and life studies that became the basis for the Leicester Square spectacle.[52]

Two factors had made the visit possible. The immediate cause was the Egyptian takeover of Syria during the 1830s, which, as Alexander Shölch has pointed out, marked a turning point in the history of Palestine by opening the country up to European imperial penetration.[53] But a more fundamental factor was the

---

[51] Friedman, *From Beirut to Jerusalem*, 428.

[52] The principal figures in the group were Frederick Catherwood (who would later become known for his explorations of the Maya civilization in South America) and Joseph Bonomi the Younger. The group's drawings of ancient Egyptian sites were also instrumental in the popularization of Egypt and Egyptian history in Britain during the nineteenth-century. A good account of the Leicester Square Pavilion and the work of these architects can be found in Shepherd, *The Zealous Intruders*, 74-76.

[53] Alexander Schölch observes two key ways in which the Egyptian occupation changed Palestine's foreign relations with Europe: through the abolition of discrimination against non-Muslims and through the acceptance of the establishment of European consulates and missionary activities in Jerusalem. See Schölch, "Britain in Palestine," 40.

modernization of Egypt, which had brought European techniques of discipline and order to Muhammad Ali's domain, as well as European experts, such as these architects, to institute these new reforms.[54] Although they were not part of a British imperial delegation to Jerusalem, their careful cataloguing of Jerusalem's holy sites can be seen as the earliest use in Palestine of what Bernard Cohn calls the "Survey Modality," the investigation by British experts of the natural and social features of the colonized.[55] To be sure, accounts of Syria and the Holy Land had been published by previous European visitors, but this study was new in that it purported to be a scientific study of Jerusalem. It followed the French *Description de l'Égypt*, which had inaugurated the nineteenth century's positivistic search for knowledge of the Middle East, and helped to create, in the words of Edward Said, a "body of theory and practice in which, for many generations, there has been a considerable material investment."[56]

More importantly, the Panorama's financial success demonstrated the commercial value that the 'Holy Land' could command as an exotic curiosity in the British marketplace. This value was further exploited in the many travelogues written by nineteenth century British tourists and adventurers to Palestine and the wider Middle East. Works such as Eliot Warburton's popular *Crescent and the Cross* (1844), Alexander Kinglake's *Eothen: Traces of Travel Brought Home from the East* (1844), and William Makepiece Thackeray's *Notes of a Journey from Cornhill to*

---

[54] See Mitchell, *Colonising Egypt*, 23.

[55] Bernard S. Cohn, *Colonialism and Its Forms of Knowledge : The British in India*, Princeton Studies in Culture/Power/History (Princeton, N.J.: Princeton University Press, 1996), 7.

[56] Edward W. Said, *Orientalism*, 1st ed. (New York: Pantheon Books, 1978), 6.

Cairo (1846) were popular for their picturesque descriptions of trips across continents and cultures.[57] Palestine also began to appear in British novels, such as Benjamin Disraeli's popular mid-nineteenth century novels *Tancred* and *Alroy*.

Around the same time Palestine became an object of scholarly interest, especially in the fields of biblical scholarship, archaeology, and the new discipline of historical (or biblical) geography. The latter field was particularly important in generating interest in Palestine, for it analyzed Ottoman Palestine not in terms of its Arab and Ottoman present but in reference to a biblical past that was familiar to the average Briton. The pioneering figure in this field was the American biblical scholar Edward Robinson, but it was British scholars who became the leading figures in the field, such as George Adam Smith, whose 1894 work *The Historical Geography of the Holy Land* became something of a bible for the field. Also important were scholars attached to the Palestine Exploration Fund (PEF), an organization that studied biblical history through "scientific" techniques such as archaeology, geographical surveying, and ethnography.[58]

---

[57] Warburton's book was particularly successful and ended up being printed in seventeen editions over the next forty-odd years.

[58] The field of historical/biblical geography was started by Robinson in the 1820s. Robinson's work was popular in the United Kingdom and he was the first American to be honored with a Gold Medal from the Royal Geographic Society in 1842. George Adam Smith was a giant of the field at the end of the nineteenth-century. His work *The Historical Geography of the Holy Land* was basically the central text in the field for a century. First published in 1894, the book has had a run of some thirty different editions, the most recent editions having been published in the 1970s.

Founded in 1865 to study Palestine's biblical background, the PEF was active through the mandate period and brought a number of imperial personalities to Palestine such as T. E. Lawrence, Charles Warren, Horatio Kitchener, and the aforementioned Charles Gordon. The fund was run for a time by Lord Shaftsbury and employed leading British archaeologists and orientalists of the day such as William Flinders-Petrie, Claude Conder, Edward Henry Palmer, John Garstang, and Kathleen Kenyon. For more information see Neil Asher Silberman, *Digging for God & Country: Exploration, Archaeology, and the Secret Struggle for the Holy Land, 1799-1917* (New York: Knopf, 1982), John

The surest sign of the country's increased popularity, and almost certainly the greatest generator of knowledge about it, was the establishment of Palestine as a tourist destination during the nineteenth-century.[59] The list of visitors to Jerusalem on the Eastern Grand Tour reads like a Who's Who of the European and American artistic, scholarly, and political elite, with figures like the Prince of Wales (later King Edward VII), Horatio Kitchener, Alexander Kinglake, Robert Curzon, William Makepeace Thackeray, General Charles Gordon, Gustave Flaubert, Alphonse de Lamartine, Gerard de Nerval, Ernest Renan, Crown Prince Frederick of Prussia, Mark Twain, and Herman Melville making the trip eastwards. But the development that made the biggest impact on visits to Palestine was the inauguration in 1869 of Thomas Cook's "Eastern Tours," which opened up the Levant to middle-class British and Western travelers. With their notebooks (and later cameras) tourists became a major source and filter of information about Palestine in Britain. Indeed, by the 1880s hundreds of thousands of commercial photographs of Palestine and scores of travelogues about the country were circulating in Europe and the United States.[60]

Bernard Cohn has argued that the standardization of British tourist routes in India was a means by which the "officializing" procedures of the colonial state were

---

James Moscrop, *Measuring Jerusalem: The Palestine Exploration Fund and British Interests in the Holy Land* (Leicester: Leicester University Press, 2000), and Nadia Abu El-Haj, *Facts on the Ground* .

[59] Before the nineteenth-century there was no real pilgrimage by Europeans to the holy land, let alone a tourist trade. It was only in 1804 that British explorers began to show an interest in visiting Palestine by forming the Palestine Association in London. This body was ineffectual as the journey to Palestine at that time was dangerous and expensive. There are accounts of a few visits to the country by British subjects during the early years of the nineteenth-century (William Turner, Richardson), but it was only in the years after the Egyptian takeover that trips to Palestine by British and European travelers began to occur with any regularity. See Tuchman, *Bible and Sword* and Naomi Shepherd, *Zealous Intruders*.

[60] The bulk of these photographs were produced by professional photographers. Shepherd, *Zealous Intruders*, 191.

extended into the society of the colonized.[61] In Palestine the situation was somewhat

different. The tourist itinerary did not build completely new routes for they relied

upon pilgrim routes that predated the arrival of European imperialism. Where tourism

was important was in defining Palestine for the public back home and by extension

helping to shape the imperial perspective towards the country. As in the India

described by Bernard Cohn, British tourist visits worked to create a repertoire of stock

images and narratives about the country, imposing upon Palestine and Palestinians

what Cohn has identified as "historically specific aesthetic principles [about the East],

such as the "sublime," the "picturesque," the "romantic," and the "realistic"."[62]

This is important for our study because it meant that Palestine was not a *terra

incognita* for Allenby's conquering forces. Soldiers who entered the country in 1917

felt that they were visiting a place that they already knew. As A. J. Sherman has

pointed out, in his study of the lives of the British in Palestine, most Britons came with

"a pre-formed vision of the Holy Land almost invariably shaped by reading and

listening to the King James Bible and the Book of Common Prayer, and influenced by

a tradition of scriptural illustration and Orientalist art seen from earliest childhood,

often vividly recalled."[63] As one soldier put it, "At school...I probably knew far more

about the geography of Palestine than of my own country."[64] This recalls Prime

---

[61] Cohn, *Colonialism and its Forms of Knowledge*, 7.

[62] Ibid.

[63] A. J. Sherman, *Mandate Days: British Lives in Palestine 1918-1948* (Baltimore: Johns Hopkins, 1997), 16.

[64] Ibid. Undoubtedly, this soldier would have been referring to the instruction about the Holy Land that he would have received in R.E. (religious education) classes that were and still are part of the British school curriculum. I can attest from experience that such classes usually include instruction about the geography of biblical Palestine.

Minister David Lloyd George's famous comment to Chaim Weizmann at around the same time that he knew the names of towns in Palestine better than the names of towns on the Western Front.

But the Palestine that Lloyd George and the British soldier (or Weizmann for that matter) were familiar with did not exist. The country they *knew* was a construct shaped by the bible, nineteenth-century travel accounts, orientalist paintings, archaeological digs, and imperial reports. Their Palestine was an old-new land in much the same way it had been for Theodor Herzl, for the country was appreciated almost solely for its biblical past and/or its British/Zionist future. In contrast the present reality of the country held little value for British officials when they arrived in Palestine beyond functioning as a foil against which the past and future could be compared. It was this interest in Palestine for its past religious glory and its future modern development that motivated "the defense of religious tradition" and "civilizing mission" in British policy.

VII - Seeing Past the Country: The "Biblical Gaze"

The tendency of the occupying forces to see the country in terms of its religious past was built upon the "biblical gaze" of their nineteenth century compatriots. What I mean by this is the constant comparison that individuals who visited the country made between the Palestine they encountered and the Palestine they imagined from the bible. The nature of tourist and scholarly visits to Palestine in the nineteenth century made such comparisons unavoidable. British tours to Palestine, which began in 1860, took the form of a religious pilgrimage and featured activities that put tourists in touch with the Bible. For example, tours put on by the famous British tour operator Thomas Cook, "combined visits to the Holy Places, Christian missions and their schools, and 'biblical excavations'; the parties carried not only maps and guide books but bibles and hymn books, and sang as they went."[65] This concentration on biblical artifacts, sites, and place names was also a fundamental part of the fields of archaeology and historical geography, which drew British scholars to Palestine to "uncover" the country's biblical past. The techniques that they employed, such as finding biblical sites through the analysis of local Arabic place names, unearthing biblical artifacts by sifting through (and discarding) hundreds of years of the archaeological record, and preparing biblical maps by transposing the ancient Holy Land onto the features modern Palestine, involved the replacement of the present with the country's Christian and Jewish past.

The biblical gaze led British visitors to look past the predominantly Arab Muslim present of Palestine in order to see its biblical past. This deeply affected the way in which most travelers interacted with the local populace. Traveling well-worn paths on cultural pilgrimages to sites already known, British visitors to Palestine, especially tourists, rarely interacted with the local population besides their hired guides (dragomans), the odd Ottoman functionary, and the exotic bedouin shaykh. The myopia that attended this experience was readily apparent in the work of British painters who came to paint the Holy Land. The work of the artist David Roberts—

---

[65] Shepherd, *Zealous Intruders*, 180.

who became popular in Britain for his skillful reproductions of scenes from Palestine, Egypt, and elsewhere in the Middle East, and whose work is still used to adorn books about Palestine—was indicative of the limited view of Palestine presented in Britain.[66] Roberts' work presented Palestine as a set of biblical and historical sites, with people appearing only for the sake of perspective or aesthetics. Absent was the life of the country; his staged panoramas (like that of the Leicester Square Pavilion) reconfirmed the notion that life in Palestine was ancient, picturesque, and traditional—in a word "biblical". Roberts was not alone, for as Naomi Shepherd has pointed out, "no artist professional or amateur, who visited Palestine ever attempted to show the poverty, the dirt and commercial exploitation of the Holy Places."[67] Instead Palestine was marketed as a set of pristine orientalist images that revealed little about the lives of its Arab majority and nothing about the Ottoman regime.

The arrival of photography to Palestine, which coincided with the advent of the tourist industry but was mostly a commercial enterprise, did little to change this presentation. Introduced as a more accurate means for capturing the true essence of Palestine's monuments and landscapes, photography fell into cliché as it became a commercial industry. "The result was thousands of photographs of Jerusalem from the Mount of Olives, the Dome of the Rock, the Pool of Bethesda, Rachel's Tomb and the Holy Sepulchre, which were easy assignments. Even the angle from which they were

---

[66] Linda Osband's *Famous Travellers to the Holy Land* contains a number of reproductions of his lithographs. See Linda Osband, *Famous Travellers to the Holy Land: Their Personal Impressions and Reflections* (London: Prion, 1989).

[67] Shepherd, *Zealous Intruders*, 105.

seen varied very little."[68] As in painting, the local population tended to be of

secondary importance to the land and its religious sites, with people most often used as

props to confirm the exoticness and timelessness of the place. According to Shepherd

this led to a rather distorted picture of the demographic makeup of the country, for

"rarest of all were portraits of Turkish officials and soldiers, or Moslem notables in the

towns—though artisans and shopkeepers in the bazaars, anxious to please clients, were

willing sitters. Armenian priests, Samaritans, Bedouin, and Russian peasants were

photographed frequently…The Jews of Jerusalem were also captive subjects."[69]

It can be argued that the tendency of the photographer to distort the image of

Palestine was even more problematic than that of the artist. Not only did the

photographer have a much greater impact on the way Palestine appeared back home

because of the much greater number of images he or she produced, but more

importantly the photograph unlike the painting was (and continues to be) treated not as

a mere artist's rendition but as a cold, unfiltered reproduction of nature by the

camera's unflinching eye.[70]

The great irony then of the late-nineteenth century scientific and documentary

presentation of Palestine was that it reinforced an image of the country that was

timeless, when in fact the country was undergoing considerable political and social

change (as explained in the next chapter). The Leicester Square Pavilion's spectacular

---

[68] Shepherd, *Zealous Intruders*, 186.

[69] Shepherd, 190.

[70] Louis Daguerre, the inventor of the first photographic process, had himself boasted to investors in 1838 that his "daguerreotype is not merely an instrument which serves to draw nature . . . [it] gives her the power to reproduce herself." Quoted in Susan Sontag, *On Photography* (New York: Dell, 1977), 188.

panoramas may have been replaced by actual photographs of the place but the British

portrait of Palestine remained fixated on the timelessness of the country's biblical past.

As Shepherd has put it,

> Hundreds of thousands of photographs of the Holy Land were taken by the
> 1880s. Many came to resemble the 'phantasmagoria' and panoramas of the
> early years of the century; they were touched up, tinted and made into
> montages and lantern slides, and the stereographic techniques invented in the
> 1850s gave the illusion of three dimensions to photographs shown in Sunday
> schools in Europe and America from the 1860s onward; from the 1870s, card
> series were being sold from door to door.
>
> Before long, the popular and selective view of Palestine had made its way
> over millions of doorsteps. Ironically, the medium, which had promised truth
> and accuracy in the depiction of a country which more often than not
> defeated the descriptive skills of both painters and writers, had produced the
> most distorted image of all.[71]

Again this important to our study because of the profound effect that this selective

view had on the way in which the British occupiers saw the country. As A. J.

Sherman notes,

> Expecting Palestine to look "Biblical", they were often thrilled to see their
> imaginations confirmed: actual shepherds tending their flocks of sheep,
> camel caravans, olive groves, the rock-strewn slopes of the Judean hills, all
> somehow familiar, often evoking specific passages from Scripture. The
> names of towns, hills, rivers were for the most part known, each with its web
> of associations, sometimes tied to a specific Biblical episode or parable, or a
> well-remembered phrase.[72]

---

[71] Shepherd, 191.

[72] Sherman, *Mandate Days*, 16.

Not all visitors had this reaction. Other arrivals were disappointed when the country could not measure
up to their imagination. Ronald Storrs, for instance, wrote that "Many were "disappointed with
Jerusalem" because "it was so different to what they had expected". The roads were even worse than
the hotels and in place of the Holy City they found—a smell." But the "thrill" described by Sherman
and the "disappointment" observed by Storrs came from the same place, the emotional response Britons
had when comparing the observed state of Palestine with the biblical aesthetic of their imagination. See
Storrs, *Memoirs*, 324.

VIII - Backwardness and Decay

Palestine's biblical past was not the only part of its history that interested British officials. They were also interested in the country's Ottoman past, which became the baseline against which they could measure the reforms they brought to the country. As we saw above, Ottoman Palestine was described in press messages as hopelessly backward. The desperate condition of Jerusalem when the British took over in December 1917—the city and surrounding region faced famine— was presented as resulting from four centuries of Ottoman neglect, rather than from the obvious destructiveness of the First World War.[73] For British propagandists this neglect came from the fact that the Turks were tyrants who were scarcely better than "their Turanian forefathers Hulagu and Jenghiz Khan."[74]

This wartime propaganda was of course hyperbolic, but the notion that Ottoman rule had spoiled Palestine was also found in internal official reports. Writing in 1915, five years before he became Palestine's first high commissioner, Herbert Samuel argued that "under the Turk, Palestine has been blighted. For hundreds of years she has produced neither men nor things useful to the world. Her native population is sunk in squalor. Roads, harbours, irrigation, sanitation are neglected."[75] Likewise, *The Syria and Palestine Handbook*, a publication produced in 1919 by the Foreign Office to educate British officials about the Levant, described the native

---

[73] FO 371/3383/9333.

[74] FO 371/3383/9383.

[75] Samuel, "The Future of Palestine", printed for the Cabinet, January 1915. Herbert Samuel Papers, GB165-0252, Middle East Centre Archive, St. Antony's College, Oxford.

population of Palestine as having "for centuries been ground down, overtaxed, and bullied by the Turk, and still more by the Arab-speaking Turkish minor official and the Syrian and Levantine landowner."[76]

This portrait of Palestine as underdeveloped and uncivilized fit with widely held beliefs about the non-Western world and supported the popular notion that Britain as the "morally and economically" superior society had a right to decide, to quote the Earl of Cromer (who was writing about Egypt), "by the light of western knowledge and experience tempered by local considerations, [what] we conscientiously think is best for the subject race."[77] Samuel's 1915 report reads like a cribbed version of Cromer's work, for after he describes the squalor of Arab living conditions and the disrepair of the country's infrastructure, he assures the cabinet that "under British administration this will be quickly changed," and that "England should assume control of the country because by that means she can forward the purpose for which, at bottom the British Empire in the tropics and sub-tropics exists."[78]

But of course Samuel's paternalistic argument could only make sense if the local population were shown as helpless. Since there already was a tradition of ignoring or downplaying the country's Arab Muslim present, it was not difficult for people to accept Samuel's argument at face value. As Beshara Doumani has written, European visitors to Palestine in the nineteenth century had an "amazing ability to discover the land without discovering the people," a selective vision that undoubtedly

---

[76] FO 373/5/3 Historical Section of the Foreign Office, *Syria and Palestine Handbook*, 57.

[77] Earl of Cromer, "The Government of Subject Races," *Edinburgh Review*, No. 423 (Jan. 1908), 2.

[78] Samuel, "The Future of Palestine", printed for the Cabinet, January 1915. Herbert Samuel Papers, GB165-0252, Middle East Centre Archive, St. Antony's College, Oxford.

contributed to Britain's eventual support for the Jewish National Home.[79] As

mentioned, the "biblical gaze" was a significant factor here. The French traveler

François-René de Chateaubriand had observed at the beginning of the nineteenth-

century that Arabs of Palestine were "the descendants of the primitive race of

mankind; I beheld them with the same manners which they have retained ever since

the days of Hagar and Ishmael; I beheld them in the same desert that was assigned to

them by God for their inheritance..."[80] This idea was later given "scientific" backing

by the work of the Palestine Exploration Fund, which saw the Palestinian peasantry

(fellahin) as "the modern representatives of those old tribes which the Israelites found

settled in the country, such as the Canaanites, Hittites, Jebusites, Amorites, Philistines,

Edomites, etc."[81]

This quixotic view of the Palestinian fellah came out of the PEF's efforts to

discover the location of biblical sites, a project that superimposed a biblical map onto

the territory of Palestine by replacing the names of modern Arab villages with their

Hebrew names. Ironically, this project depended heavily upon the Arab peasantry's

indigenous knowledge, as Nadia Abu el Haj has pointed out.[82] For the PEF, the

peasant thus came to be seen as a reservoir for the past and the ideal native. The Arab

townsperson by contrast was viewed as a hybrid "Levantine" personality, which made

him or her unworthy of scholarly attention since they could not easily be traced to the

---

[79] Beshara Doumani, "Rediscovering Ottoman Palestine," *Journal of Palestine Studies*, Volume 21, No. 2 (Winter 1992), 8.

[80] Quoted in *Famous Travellers*, 33.

[81] Charles Clermont-Ganneau, "The Arabs of Palestine," *Palestine Exploration Fund Quarterly* (1875), 208 as quoted in Abu el-Haj, *Facts on the Ground*, 38.

[82] Abu el-Haj, *Facts on the Ground*, 35-38.

biblical past. Such race theories remained important in the 20th century as shown by the *Syria and Palestine Handbook*'s statement that the "people west of the Jordan are not Arabs, but only Arab-speaking,"[83] and the observation by one official that "the people here are not Arabs nor do they have anything in common with the 'mystic East', with the sole exception of their great dislike of any kind of work. They are simply Arabic-speaking Levantines."[84]

Another factor that made the indigenous population of Palestine appear backward to nineteenth century visitors was the "foreignness" and timelessness of their practices and traditions. The novelist William Makepeace Thackery described the bazaar in Jaffa as full of gambling, story-telling, and water-pipe smoking. He viewed these activities as fundamental to making the local population blissfully ignorant to the outside world and the concept of progress:

> The devotion and energy with which all these pastimes were pursued
> struck me as much as anything. These people have been playing
> thimble-rig and casino; that story-teller has been shouting his tale of
> Antar, for forty years; and they are just as happy with this amusement
> now as when they first tried it. Is there no ennui in the Eastern
> countries?[85]

Local religious festivals were also often used to illustrate Arab backwardness and irrationality. In 1849, the British diplomat and traveler Robert Curzon wrote a famous account of the annual Greek Orthodox Holy Fire celebration in Jerusalem, which

---

[83] FO 373/5/3 Historical Section of the Foreign Office, *Syria and Palestine Handbook*, 56.

[84] Stewart Perowne to father, May 26, 1926. Perowne Papers, GB165-0228, Middle East Center Archive, St. Antony's College, Oxford. Perowne was the secretary to the Anglican Bishop in Jerusalem at the time and would later serve in the Palestine government's Education Department and as the Private Secretary to the High Commissioner.

[85] Quoted in *Famous Travellers*, 127.

emphasized what he saw as the animalistic and exotic nature of the celebration. "At

one time," Curzon wrote, "before the church was so full, they made a race-course

round the sepulchre; and some, almost in a state of nudity, dance around with frantic

gestures, yelling and screaming as if they were possessed." For this reason, he

described the celebration to his readers as being comparable to a performance at

Astley's Royal Amphitheatre, the site of the London Circus.[86] Muslim festivals, such

Nabi Musa (the festival of the Prophet Moses), were similarly regarded as unruly and

potentially dangerous. An account by two members of the Palestine Exploration

Fund, a British archaeological and geographical society, for example, dwelt the unruly

nature (in the eyes of the British) of Nabi Musa:

> …dervishes from all part of the land, each sect with its special banner,
> and their drums decorated with calico of the same colours as their
> banners. Each man has a sword suspended from his neck, and a spear
> in his hand. They also carry tambourines and cymbals, and the shout
> "Allahū akbar!" (God is most great) and flourish their swords. Behind
> these are the shabāb (young men) of Jerusalem with their banner in
> their midst, carried by…the Sheikh esh-Shabāb and they, too, make
> play with swords and knives and revolvers, which they fire into the
> air…at the end of the procession come young men accompanying the
> Mufti, and assisting him to carry the banner of Nebi Mūsa.[87]

These exotic elements of the festival were highlighted because they conflicted with

British notions of proper religious decorum. The Nabi Musa festival or the Greek

Orthodox Ceremony of the Holy Fire were viewed as exotic, loud, and almost

primitive religious rituals when compared with the sober Protestant liturgy and

---

[86] Curzon witnessed the festival of the Holy Fire as part of a Grand Tour to Egypt, Syria, Turkey, and
Greece in 1833-4, an experience described in his book *Visits to Monasteries in the Levant*, published in
1849. See *Famous Travelers*, 37.

[87] This passage is quoted in Halabi, "Transformation of the Festival," 91. The original can be found in
E. Masterman and R. Macalister, "Occasional papers on the modern inhabitants of Palestine," *Palestine
Exploration Fund*, Quarterly Statement, (1915): 176-177.

practice, and were held to be evidence of the backwardness and fanaticism of the local population.

The layout of Arab cities, which appeared chaotic to British visitors, and Arab agricultural practices, which appeared medieval, were also considered signs of Arab backwardness. The winding alleyways of Jerusalem, as compared to the structured street-planning of modern European cities, were interpreted as an example of what Lord Cromer had described in Egypt as the "want of accuracy" in the Oriental mind.[88] Meanwhile the indigenous farming techniques of the Arab population were denigrated, as officials, such as Laurence Oliphant and Herbert Samuel, heaped praise on the farms of Jewish immigrants, which were more familiar to British officials. In doing so, the low success rate of these early Zionist enterprises and their reliance on heavy subsidization were conveniently ignored.[89]

Related to this concept of backwardness was the theme of corruption. The demonization of the Ottoman regime, which was so important in British wartime propaganda, was built on the view that the Oriental was not only backward but corrupt. Arabs were also presented as duplicitous and untrustworthy in British

---

[88] Cromer, *Modern Egypt*, 146.

[89] For a discussion of these early Zionist settlements see Shafir, *Land, Labor and the Origins of the Israeli-Palestinian Conflict, 1882-1914.*

To be fair, Edwin Samuel, son of Herbert Samuel, recognized British ignorance when it came to agricultural practices:

> 'Clear your lands [of rocks]!' I yelled at my lazy serfs. 'It will be so much easier to plough. Pile up the rocks into dry-stone walls around your fields and keep wandering beasts from grazing on your ripening crops!' It was all so beautifully logical—and so wrong. Soil experts have now discovered that, at night in summer, dew condenses on the cold surface of rocks and drips onto the surrounding soil.

Edwin Samuel, *A Lifetime in Jerusalem: The Memoirs of the Second Viscount Samuel* (London: Vallentine, Mitchell, 1970), 77.

accounts of Palestine. References to baksheesh were *de rigueur* in British travel accounts of the nineteenth-century, and, added to the many shocked descriptions of the commercialism surrounding the holy sites, created the notion that Arabs were more interested in exploiting Europeans than taking care of Palestine. "In Jerusalem and Bethlehem one sees greater disregard for all the great principles common to all faiths than anywhere I've ever been. It is absurd to talk of the brotherhood of man here," one soldier explained, because, "Everyone has to make money out of religion here, either by fair means or foul and one is thoroughly disgusted by the tricks that are resorted to."[90] For the English headmistress for the Jerusalem Girls' High School during the early years of the mandate, this corruption came from Turkish (Ottoman) rule: "there is no section of the community which you could trust to rule at all, and the country has lived for so long under the Turks, that it will take ages to instill into the people any idea of public service, or truthfulness, or cleanliness."[91] But for others the nature of the Arab population was a product of its environment. As the pro-Zionist political intelligence officer Richard Meinertzhagen explained to Prime Minister Lloyd George, the Arab was "stupid, dishonest, and producing little beyond eccentricities influenced by the romance and silence of the desert."[92]

To be sure, few officials were as actively anti-Arab as Meinertzhagen. We also must not forget that there were a number of voices that were sympathetic towards the Arab and Muslim cause, both within the Palestine government itself and also back

---

[90] H. D. Myer to parents, January 5, 1919 as quoted in Sherman, *Mandate Days*, 39.

[91] S. P. Emery, Diary, Emery Papers, GB165-0099, Middle East Center Archive, St. Antony's, Oxford.

[92] Meinertzhagen to Lloyd George, March 25, 1919, Meinertzhagen Papers, GB165-0202, Middle East Center Archive, St. Antony's, Oxford.

home in London. Ernest Richmond, the assistant secretary for political affairs 1920-24, was the Palestine government's political liaison with the Arab political and religious elites, and was well known (infamous in Zionist circles) for his championing of the Arab cause. C. R. Ashbee, Jerusalem's civic advisor at the beginning of the mandate, and Ronald Storrs, the first British governor of Jerusalem, were also respectful of Arab culture, having lived and worked in other Arab countries before arriving in Palestine. A. J. Sherman has even claimed that British officials and soldiers saw the Arabs as the "good" tribe in Palestine and the Zionists as the "bad" tribe, a perspective largely shared by Bernard Wasserstein.[93] The situation was more complex than that because the Palestine government was not monolithic in its views of the local populace. But even if some officials sympathized with the Arab position this did not preclude them from perpetuating the notion of Arab backwardness. For example, Jerusalem's civic advisor, C. R. Ashbee, respected Arabs for their conservatism and connection to the past, which appealed to his Arts and Crafts aesthetic.[94] The same was true about Ronald Storrs' friendship towards the Palestinian Arab notability, who he saw as useful partners in his effort to preserve the past of the Jerusalem district he governed. Even Ernest Richmond, the greatest advocate for the Arab cause, tended to view the Arab community's value to the British and to Palestine

---

[93] Sherman, *Mandate Days*, 16.

[94] During his time as the civic advisor, Ashbee wrote a long and detailed report on the arts and crafts of the Jerusalem district, in which he was a passionate advocate of traditional native crafts as opposed to the importation of modern commercial European products. As secretary of the Pro-Jerusalem Society he pushed for the encouragement and even the re-introduction of traditional crafts, such as weaving, tile-making, and glass-making. This fit with his training in the Arts and Crafts tradition of William Morris. For a more detailed study of Ashbee see Inbal Ben-Asher Gitler, "C. R. Ashbee's Jerusalem Years: Arts and Crafts, Orientalism, and British Regionalism," *Assaph*, Volume 5 (2000): 29-52.

in terms of its historical and cultural institutions (such as their religious monuments) rather than its economic or social potential.[95] Tellingly, no British officials made much of an effort to champion political and economic causes that were important to the community itself, such as the re-establishment of municipal councils or the establishment of an Arab land fund.

In the same way, officials back home that were sympathetic towards or at least cognizant of the Arab position in Palestine, such as Edwin Montagu and Lord Curzon, did little to refute the notion that the 'backward' Arab community was incapable of running a modern nation by itself. Like their counterparts in Palestine they did not take the time to analyze the economic and political situation in Palestine, or else they would have seen a local economy that had modernized and opened up to the world economy in the years before the First World War and an Arab population had begun to think of an independent future.[96] Instead, their focus was squarely on Britain's national and imperial interests, and their concern for the fate of the Arab community was really a concern about the fact that Britain was failing to conform to its customary role as the pater familiaris.[97]

---

[95] For more details about Richmond's position see Bertrand Monk, *Aesthetic Occupation*.

[96] For a discussion of the economic history of Ottoman Palestine see Alexander Scholch, *Palestine in Transformation, 1856-1882: Studies in Social, Economic and Political Development* (Washington, DC.: Institute for Palestine Studies, 1993) and Roger Owen, *The Middle East in the World Economy, 1800-1914* (London: I.B. Tauris, 1993), 173-179. The best accounts of the rise of nationalism in Palestine are Rashid Khalidi, *Palestinian Identity: The Construction of a Modern National Consciousness* (New York: Columbia University Press, 1993) and Muhammad Muslih, *The Origins of Palestinian Nationalism* (New York: Columbia Press, 1988).

[97] In short both Curzon and Montagu argued that if the British supported the Jewish National Home they would not be fulfilling their duty to protect the native population. For a good analysis of Curzon's opposition to the Jewish National Home see David Gilmour, "The Unregarded Prophet: Lord Curzon and the Palestine Question," *Journal of Palestine Studies*, Vol. 25, No. 3 (Spring 1996), 60-68.

IX – A Distorted Policy

This discourse about Palestine and Palestinians would have a significant effect on

British policy in Palestine even before the conquest of Jerusalem. As is well known,

British officials and soldiers arrived in Palestine with a policy—the Balfour

Declaration—that promised British assistance in the establishment of a Jewish

National home in Palestine.

> Foreign Office,
> November 2nd, 1917
>
> Dear Lord Rothschild,
>
> I have much pleasure in conveying to you, on behalf of His Majesty's
> Government, the following declaration of sympathy with Jewish
> Zionist aspirations which has been submitted to, and approved by, the
> Cabinet: "His Majesty's Government view with favour the
> establishment in Palestine of a national home for the Jewish people,
> and will use their best endeavours to facilitate the achievement of this
> object, it being clearly understood that nothing shall be done which
> may prejudice the civil and religious rights of existing non-Jewish
> communities in Palestine, or the rights and political status enjoyed by
> Jews in any other country". I should be grateful if you would bring this
> declaration to the knowledge of the Zionist Federation.
>
> Yours sincerely
> Arthur James Balfour

The declaration had been issued only a month before the conquest but had come out

of plans for Palestine's future that had been developing in British policymaking circles

since at least 1915. In official discussions about the country's future, which were

heavily influenced by Zionist politicking, the concept of native backwardness was

---

Montagu's position towards the Balfour Declaration is reproduced in chapter 13 of *From Haven to Conquest*, ed. Walid Khalidi (Washington DC: Institute for Palestine Studies, 1987), 143-152.

used to promote Zionist immigration on the grounds that Palestine could only develop with an infusion of European dynamism and know-how. This vision of Palestine's future fit well with the notion that Britain's imperial duty was the colonizing mission. But the Balfour Declaration also pledged that "the civil and religious rights of existing non-Jewish communities in Palestine," would not be prejudiced by British support for the establishment of the Jewish National Home. And so the "defense of religious tradition" also became part of Britain's vision for Palestine's future.

Various reasons for the issuance of the declaration have been given. Some scholars have argued, following Lloyd George's own explanation, that the declaration was a reward to the Zionist leader Chaim Weizmann for his wartime assistance; others see it as an appeal that was made to Jews around the world for help during the war; others claim that it resulted from Zionist influence upon Whitehall, that it was a product of the evangelical beliefs of the British foreign and prime ministers, or that it was a cynical use of the Jewish cause to bolster British claims to Palestine. The latter motivation—the creation of a Jewish Ulster—was the most likely, but whatever the reason it remains clear that the declaration was made possible because it resonated with preexisting notions about the country and its people.

In this respect I agree with Barbara Tuchman's argument that the Balfour Declaration was a product of British attitudes towards Palestine. But whereas Tuchman sees these attitudes as being determined by their moral (read: religious) respect for the country, I see them as developing out of a colonial agenda that used a biblical narrative for its own ends. If C. R. Ashbee could charge Zionists in 1923 for their cynical use of the biblical past—"The Jewish members of the Pro-Jerusalem Council do not kiss the Wailing Wall but they know its value for purposes of propaganda"—the same accusation could be leveled against the British administration throughout the mandate.[98] Indeed, what made the Balfour Declaration so attractive to both the Zionists and the British government was the opportunity it gave both parties to use that past for their own ends.

The impact of British theories about Arabs upon the British support for the Jewish National Home is apparent in two influential papers explaining the benefits of a Jewish Palestine, Herbert Samuel's, aforementioned 1915 paper, "The Future of Palestine," and Herbert Sidebotham's "British Interest in Palestine, 1917." The first was a secret report to the Cabinet written five and half years before Samuel became the first high commissioner of Palestine. The second was an essay from a prominent journalist with the *Manchester Guardian* (the newspaper most sympathetic to English Zionism) penned before the promulgation of the Balfour Declaration in 1917. Both were pro-Zionist pieces that presented the Jewish state as crucial for the protection of British interests and the spread of modern (Western) civilization in the Middle East. Although both authors mention the importance of helping the Jewish race, this is de-emphasized in order to make the argument that a Jewish state in Palestine would be the engine for developing a British Palestine.[99]

---

[98] C. R. Ashbee, *A Palestine Notebook, 1918-1923* (New York: Doubleday, Page, and Co., 1923), 147.

[99] This was especially true in Sidebotham's piece which concentrates almost exclusively on British interests. The Samuel paper is more eloquent about the need to help the Jewish race but as Bernard Wasserstein has pointed out, the lyrical passages about Jewish hopes were removed from a revised version of the paper that concentrated more on "*realpolitik* considerations," which was released in March 1915. Sidebotham's essay was eventually published in Herbert Sidebotham, *England and*

Interestingly, neither author mentions Britain's protection of the Jewish

community during the nineteenth century, which would seem to be a useful precedent

to reference. But this is understandable when one considers that their interest lay with

the potential of the modern Zionist immigrants and not with the old *yishuv,* the

traditional Jewish "settlement" in Palestine. It is well known that the yishuv was

viewed in Zionist circles as being irretrievably backward and useless in their

nationalist struggle but this view of the orthodox Jews of Jerusalem—the bulk of who

were non-European Jews—was also part of British reports on Palestine. For example,

in the Foreign Office's *Syria and Palestine Handbook,* the Jews of Jerusalem are

described as men, "whose physical development is almost atrophied and whose

intellectual development is abnormally strained. They are intensely bigoted, and are

always ruled by the rabbis; the Jerusalem rabbinate is large and contains few men of

distinction or even of striking personality."[100]

In Samuel's and Sidebotham's accounts, the Mizrachi (Eastern) Jew and the

Muslim or Christian Arab were presented as "traditional" and thus unqualified to

contribute to the modernization of Palestine. This built upon nineteenth century

British views of the local population and indicates that the religion of the local

---

Palestine: Essays Towards the Restoration of the Jewish State (London: Constable and Company,
1918) and is reprinted in *From Haven to Conquest,* 125-134. The Samuel Cabinet paper can be found
in the Herbert Samuel Papers, GB165-0252, Middle East Centre Archive, St. Antony's College, Oxford.
A good account of his thinking at the time, which was influenced to a certain degree by discussions
with leading Zionists Chaim Weizmann, Nahum Sokolow, Lord Rotschild, and Moses Montefiore, is
found in Bernard Wasserstein, *Herbert Samuel, a Political Life* (Oxford: Clarendon Press, 1992), 200-
240.

[100] *Syria and Palestine Handbook,* 61.

inhabitant made little difference in their backwardness vis-à-vis the European.[101] In

short, the indigenous Palestinian Arabs and immigrant European Jews belonged to

different eras and the future development of the country could be secured only by

relying on the enterprising immigrants. For Samuel, this meant that the Arab

community could not assist in developing the country and he warned that the Arab

community's demographic size could be an impediment to the "dream of a Jewish

State, prosperous, progressive, and the home of a brilliant civilization."[102]

Sidebotham, who doesn't even mention Arabs by name, similarly dismisses them as

potential agents for development:

> The Turks are an alien oligarchy in almost all parts of their Empire, and even
> if their rule had been enlightened and progressive no violence would be done
> to the population in dispossessing them. Indeed the principle of nationality
> requires their dispossession. Nor is there any indigenous civilization in
> Palestine that could take the place of the Turkish except that of the Jews,
> who, already numbering one-seventh of the population, have given to
> Palestine everything that it has ever had of value to the world.[103]

X - The Balfour Mentality

This dismissal of the Arab community would soon find its way into the Balfour

Declaration, which Samuel helped to write. In the declaration the Arab community is

---

[101] This style of thinking about different peoples occupying different ontological positions along a continuum of development has been ably explored in Johannes Fabian's *Time and the Other*. In his introduction to the first edition of *The Handbook of Palestine and Trans-Jordan* (1934), Samuel makes an explicit reference to this continuum when he contrasts Arab villages living under "mediaeval conditions" with the new Jewish immigrants from Eastern and Central Europe, and from America, who "bring with them the activities of the twentieth century, and sometimes perhaps, the ideas of the twenty-first." Herbert Samuel, "Introduction," *The Handbook of Palestine and Trans-Jordan*, first edition, ed. Harry Luke and Edward Keith-Roach (London: MacMillan, 1922), xv.

[102] Samuel, "The Future of Palestine."

[103] Sidebotham, "British Interests in Palestine, 1917," in *From Haven to Conquest: Readings in Zionism and the Palestine Problem until 1948* (Washington DC: Institute of Palestine Studies, 1987), 125.

again not named but referred to by the condescending referent "the non-Jewish inhabitants of Palestine." These inhabitants were guaranteed in the declaration to have their "religious and civil rights" protected, a clause that denied Arabs any political or national rights in the country. This guarantee also established the notion that it was the religious traditions of the native population that were worthy of protection, an official endorsement of the "defense of religious tradition" discourse.

This dismissal of the Arab right to self-determination was confirmed by the wholesale inclusion of the terms and wording of the Balfour Declaration into the Mandate for Palestine. This established a political system that was unique among the mandates created by the League of Nations, in that any potential Arab independence was compromised by the British commitment to the Jewish National Home. To be sure, the imposition of the mandate system upon the Middle East meant that President Woodrow Wilson's call for national self-determination was ignored across the region, but the situation in Palestine was *sui generis* with the British supporting the national rights of a largely immigrant community over that of the local population. This position would be made clear in Article 4 of the mandate which guaranteed a role for a Jewish agency as advisor and partner to the Palestine Government but provided nothing similar for the Arab community.

I do not want to suggest that the terms of the Balfour Declaration and the Mandate for Palestine were the only considerations that influenced British policy. The legacy of four centuries of Ottoman rule and the terms of mandatory rule played an important role in policymaking, as will be shown in the following chapters.

Moreover, most officials, including High Commissioner Herbert Samuel, found that assisting too much in the establishment of the Jewish National Home to be impracticable in a country with an overwhelming Arab majority. But the ideas behind the declaration undoubtedly had an impact on how Arabs and Jews were treated by the colonial government. Economically, this was shown in the very different economic relationship that the Palestine government had with the Jewish community and the Arab community. As detailed in Barbara Smith's *The Roots of Separatism in Palestine*, the British authorities consistently intervened in the marketplace to subsidize, protect, and cooperate with Jewish industries, on the grounds that these industries were crucial for Palestine's development. Meanwhile, the government did very little financially to support Arab companies, except in sectors that were traditional: such as in agricultural and crafts industries.[104] Arab industrial enterprises were not promoted and in some cases were actively discouraged.[105]

British stereotypes about Arabs also had an effect on politics. Shortly after the British occupation, officials were complaining that Arabs were not culturally developed enough to properly participate in the political process. The military

---

[104] This was shown in the agricultural bias in the educational curriculum, which was typically used in British colonies to protect the country from an overproduction of intellectuals who were feared for their nationalist potential. This bias was detailed by the Director of Education, Humphrey Bowman, before a Royal Commission in 1936. See Bowman Papers, GB165-0034, Middle East Center Archive, St. Antony's, Oxford. The standard work on the Palestine educational systems (for there were parallel government and Zionist systems) is A. L. Tibawi, *Arab Education in Mandatory Palestine: A Study in Three Decades of British Administration* (London, Luzac, 1956). See also Abdulqadir Mohammad Yusuf. "The British Educational Policy in the Arab Public Schools of Palestine During the Mandate." Ph.D. Diss. University of Indiana, 1956, and Judith Wolf. "Selected Aspects in the Development of Public Education in Palestine 1920-1946." Ph.D. Diss. Boston College, 1981.

[105] The belief that Arabs had little economic potential was baldly shown in the Palestine Pavilion at the Empire Exhibition of 1924, which portrayed Palestine almost solely as a collection of British and Zionist industrial concerns. See Nicholas Roberts, "Palestine on Display: the Palestine Pavilion at the British Empire Exhibition of 1924," *Arab Studies Journal*, vol. 25, no. 1 (Spring 2007): 70-89.

governor of Jaffa wrote to his superiors in Jerusalem that "freedom of speech is not understood in this country, and the privilege is invariably abused."[106] The fact that his complaint was directed at the propaganda activities of a political society (the *Muntada al-Adabi*), made up of members of the Arab elite who had been given a modern Western-style education, indicates just how pervasive this stereotype was. Allied to this was the widespread notion that Arab political activity, especially if it took the form of a protest or strike, was a manifestation of a pre-modern mob mentality or a form of racial hatred. As chapter five will make clear, this led British officials to consistently underestimate the nationalist feelings and political intelligence of the Arab population. Viewed as a passive population, local Arabs were seen as being incapable of having political grievances or nationalist aims. Instead for many years they were seen as little more than sheep incited to action by foreign *agents provocateurs* or local religious preachers.

This was a self-serving argument of course because the British presence was based upon the logic of mandate rule: the notion that the local population was unable to stand up to the rigors of the modern world and needed European protection. Although there was some internal debate about the economic and political capabilities of the Arab population, British policy as a whole treated the Arab population as incapable of being a force for modern development. Consequently, whether in the field of education, politics, economics, or medicine, the Palestine government took upon itself the role of protector of the Arab community. This role was enshrined in

---

[106] Lieutenant-Colonel H. H. Postlethwaite to Civil Secretary Wyndham Deedes, May 29, 1919. Chief Secretary's Files, Record Group 2, CS 5/155, Israel State Archives.

the terms of the Mandate for Palestine and was zealously defended by the Palestine

government throughout the mandate even in the face of Arab nationalist petitions,

protests, and violence. As Bernard Wasserstein put it, because of their disdain for the

Palestine Arabs, British officials adopted "a paternalistic conception of themselves as

Platonic guardians entrusted with the duty of managing affairs and defending the

interests of the "bemused" Arab peasants who (unlike the Jews) 'obviously

couldn't…manage their own affairs satisfactorily.'"[107]

XI – Conclusion

Ronald Storrs' observation that his staff in Jerusalem was made up of a rag-tag group

of individuals with little or no colonial experience has been used by some scholars,

Wasserstein among them, to argue that the British administration that arrived was

politically naïve.[108] This fits with the uniquely British idea that their empire had been

acquired in a "fit of absence of mind," a narrative that absolved Britons of their

responsibility for the excesses involved in its creation.[109] According to this line of

---

[107] Wasserstein, *British in Palestine*, 54. This statement includes a quote from G. S. Symes, who was the District Governor of Galilee and Samaria, 1920-25, and Chief Secretary of Palestine, 1925-28.

[108] Storrs explained in his memoirs that the group was made up of:

> a cashier from a bank in Rangoon, an actor-manager, two assistants from Thos. Cook, a picture-dealer, an Army coach, a clown, a land valuer, a bo'sun from the Niger, a Glasgow distiller, an organist, an Alexandria cotton-broker, an architect (not in the Public Works but in the Secretariat), a Junior Service London postal official (not in the Post Office but as a controller of Labour), a taxi-driver from Egypt, two school-masters and a missionary.

Storrs, *Memoirs*, 8.

[109] The ardent imperialist Sir John Seeley had argued in his 1883 work *The Expansion of England* that the British empire had been acquired in a "fit of absence of mind" as a criticism of British imperial policy, which he argued should have been more coherent and directed. But for others this idea was attractive for presenting the expansion of the British empire as less deliberate and therefore less rapacious than other European empires.

thinking British rule in Palestine was compromised by the use of incompetent individuals, a contributing factor in the poor administration of the country. I would argue that individual incompetence was a relatively minor factor. What was more problematic is that the British didn't understand Palestine. This was not due to a lack of knowledge about the country; to the contrary, they arrived with a storehouse of information about Palestine and Palestinians. The problem was that this knowledge was generally unreliable since it was too heavily influenced by British imperial prejudices.

This chapter has argued that the British experience in Palestine over the course of the nineteenth century led to the development of the belief that the country was broken from centuries of Ottoman rule and Arab backwardness. As we shall see in the next chapter, this was a myopic view of the country that ignored its history of modern development under the last years of the Ottoman empire. But the idea that the Holy Land had fallen into disrepair made the country available for salvation by an imperial power. The British saw their occupation as bringing the benefits of civilization long denied to the local population, while at the same time that occupation protected and polished the religious heritage of the country. This confidence in the imperial project to redeem Palestine carried over into an expectation that British rule would naturally be accepted by the benighted Arab population. To the modern reader this naturally appears as a rather naïve and self-serving view of imperialism and its reception by the native population. But it would take a better part of a decade for the British to realize the gap between their expectations and the reality of the imperial situation in Palestine.

Chapter Two

Using the Past

I – Introduction

According to Pamela Ann Smith, "so great was the devastation [of the First World

War on Palestine] that it was not until the early part of 1919 that the military

administration could turn its attention away from the immediate problems of feeding,

clothing and heating the population to the urgent task of setting up a new government.[1]

But we know from British records that in 1918 the military authorities had already

commissioned a report on the arts and crafts of the Jerusalem district and an

engineering study of the Dome of the Rock, the latter being carried out when the First

World War was still ongoing. Why study arts and crafts or the Dome of the Rock

when there were much more pressing tasks at hand? For C. R. Ashbee, the author of

the arts and crafts study, this work was justified because it was useful—"The object of

this report is practical. It is the application of the new civic ideas or a certain portion

of them to a particular city and its environments. Its purpose is to show how under

given conditions certain things can be done."[2] These studies would be followed by a

---

[1] Pamela Ann Smith, *Palestine and the Palestinians 1876-1983* (London: Croom Helm, 1984), 37.

[2] Ashbee was the civic advisor for Jerusalem from 1918-1923, a position created by the governor of
Jerusalem Ronald Storrs. The quote comes from the introduction to an unpublished report, entitled "A
Report by Mr. C. R. Ashbee on the Arts and Crafts of Jerusalem District." Jerusalem Municipality
Archives, Ashbee Files, Box 361.

      The report on the Dome of the Rock was compiled by Ernest Richmond, who once had been an
architect in the Egyptian Department of Public Works and was brought to Jerusalem by his former
colleague Ronald Storrs.   Richmond would go on to be active in restoring the Dome of the Rock, a job
that was later detailed in his book Ernest Richmond *The Dome of the Rock in Jerusalem: A Description
of its Structure and Decoration* (Oxford: Clarendon Press, 1924). Richmond also held the position of
Assistant Civil Secretary (Political) in the civilian administration from 1920-1924, where he was

98

series of reports on Palestine's history and culture: J. B. Barron's book on Palestinian

awqaf (1922), Archer Cust's analysis of religious rights in Palestine (ca. 1925),

various town plans and surveys of Jerusalem (1919-1925), as well as a host of works

produced by the Pro-Jerusalem Society, the Palestine Oriental Society, and the

Palestine Exploration Fund throughout the mandate.[3]

The study of local practices and beliefs was typically driven by administrative

needs. Richmond's report was commissioned in order to study the feasibility of a

British renovation of the Dome of the Rock, a project designed to generate good will

in the Arab community; the study of *awqaf* was undertaken by Barron, the

government's director of revenues and customs, to help the Palestine government deal

with land ownership issues; and Cust's report was an attempt to understand the

---

criticized by Zionists for his pro-Arab views. Richmond tendered his resignation in 1924 as a protest against the government's pro-Zionist policy, although he would later serve as Director of Antiquities from 1927-37.

[3] Cust's work was an unpublished government report that became the standard colonial interpretation of religious rights at the holy places of Palestine. Barron's report also began as an internal government report on Muslim endowments in Palestine but was eventually published by a local publishing house, it too became a standard text in colonial policymaking. Richmond's report guided the Palestine government's renovation of the Dome of the Rock, which was completed in conjunction with the Supreme Muslim Council. See L. G. A. Cust, "The Status Quo at the Holy Places," PRO CO 733/132/2, J. B. Barron, *Mohammedan Wakfs in Palestine* (Jerusalem: Greek Convent Press, 1922), and Ernest Richmond, *The Dome of the Rock in Jerusalem: Description of its Structure and Decoration* (Oxford: Clarendon Press, 1924).

The Pro-Jerusalem Society (PJS) was an urban preservation society that was founded in 1918 by Ronald Storrs. It was the main urban planning body in British Palestine during Storrs' time as governor of Jerusalem from 1918-1926. The society was technically a private body but since its most active members were British government officials, such as Storrs and Ashbee, it functioned as an extension of the Palestine government. The PJS produced various studies, exhibitions, and reports on the architecture and crafts of Jerusalem.

The Palestine Oriental Society was established in 1920 and existed until the end of the mandate in 1948. Its purpose was to produce scholarship on the archaeology, history, and anthropology of Palestine. The society produced *The Journal of the Palestine Oriental Society* which was first published in 1921.

The Palestine Exploration Fund, as mentioned in the last chapter, was founded in 1865 and continued to conduct archaeological digs during the mandatory period and still exists today. Its activities are detailed in the *Palestine Exploration Fund Quarterly.*

complex unwritten religious rights that operated in Palestine, in the hopes of codifying them for use by British officials.[4]

The importance of scholarship for colonial administration has famously been explored by scholars such as Bernard Cohn and Edward Said, who have described the production and control of knowledge as a central tool in colonial hegemony. In a vein similar to that of Michel Foucault, Cohn has pointed out that the modern state's control of knowledge was part of its "extension of 'officializing' procedures that established and extended [its] capacity in many areas."[5] Knowledge about history was particularly important, for the "establishment and maintenance of…nation states depended upon determining, codifying, controlling, and representing the past."[6]

In this way, the "discovery" of knowledge in the colonial context was closer to the production of "actionable intelligence" than some positivist search for truth. As Cohn has ably put it, "knowledge was to enable the British to classify, categorize, and bound the vast social world that was India so that it could be controlled."[7] The same was true in Palestine, where British experts translated aspects of the local religious and

---

[4] To a certain degree, this close relationship between scholarship and imperialism had been anticipated by the work of British experts in Palestine in the nineteenth century. For example, the work of the Palestine Expeditionary Fund (PEF) was very useful to the imperial mission in Palestine, in providing maps and surveys of the country that could be used for military purposes. Indeed the maps used by Allenby when he invaded Palestine were those made by the survey. But whereas in the nineteenth century the objective had been largely to establish a scholarly (and imperial) claim on Palestine, the use of scholarship in British Palestine was intended to make British rule easier. For more information, on the PEF's role in advancing Britain's political interests see Silberman, *Digging for God*, Abu El Haj, *Facts on the Ground*, and

Meron Benvenisti, *Sacred Landscape : The Buried History of the Holy Land since 1948* (Berkeley: University of California Press, 2000), 28.

[5] Cohn's approach is not manifestly Foucaultian as Said's was, nevertheless his argument has many parallels with that of the French post-structuralist. Cohn, *Colonialism and its Forms of Knowledge*, 3.

[6] Ibid.

[7] Cohn, *Colonialism and its Forms of Knowledge*, 4.

political environment into a bureaucratic language that policymakers could understand.

The past that British administrators were translating was of course the Ottoman past. Despite Herbert Samuel's claim that "you cannot pour new wine into old bottles," British policy was based on the principle that British Palestine would be built out of the traditions of the past. This approach was determined by the terms of the Hague Convention of 1907, which required the occupying forces to respect the existing religious and civil rights of the population. As we have seen this respect for local traditions was also part of the British understanding of their mission in Palestine and had been incorporated into the Balfour Declaration as a pledge to make sure that nothing would be done to compromise the religious and civil rights of Palestine's non-Jewish inhabitants. Finally, this approach was determined by the terms of mandatory rule as established by the Permanent Mandates Commission of the League of Nations.

But British respect for Ottoman precedent was most importantly a consequence of their style of colonial rule. Although there was no one approach in British colonies, it is true that British rule tended to lean heavily upon traditional elites and institutions in their colonies, protectorates, and mandates. Rather than replacing existing elites, officials throughout the empire attempted to graft British rule onto existing hierarchies. What this meant in Palestine and throughout the empire was that despite the presence of the civilizing mission, colonial rule tended to be conservative, especially when it came to cultural and religious matters.[8]

Palestine was no exception to this practice. The chapters that follow this one will show how religious traditions and hierarchies from the Ottoman period were preserved and integrated into the system of British rule. But before doing that, it is necessary to discuss this Ottoman past and in order to see how it was (mis)understood by the British. This chapter investigates Palestine under Ottoman rule, with a particular focus on how Islam was organized. My aim is to outline the state of Islam at the time of the British arrival and to explain how it had come to take that particularly form. In discussing Islam, I do not intend to describe all aspects of the religion. What I am interested in is a more limited investigation of the institutional form that Islam took under Ottoman rule because it was the institutions of Islam—the *waqf* system, the *shari'a* court system, the muftiships and qadiships—that were important to British policymakers. This sets the stage for the next chapter in which I detail how the British dealt with the Ottoman religious system in constructing the parameters for their own treatment of Islam.

II - Ottoman Palestine

---

[8] To be sure, some local traditions were abolished by the British authorities, such as *sati* in India, but even then British efforts to outlaw such practices tended to be slow and hesitant. Besides these interventions were exceptions to the general practice of nonintervention into the religious and cultural affairs of the colonized. It could be argued that the impact of British missionary activity on traditional practices was more profound, though it easy to overestimate the impact of this intervention on colonial societies. It must also be pointed out that this missionary activity was frequently at odds with the objectives of the central government and was often opposed and on occasion outlawed by colonial officials.

Palestine did not formally exist during the Ottoman period. The territory that became

mandatory Palestine was never ruled as a separate administrative unit but was instead

divided between different provinces (*eyelets* or *vilayets*) or administrative districts

(*sanjaks*). In the seventeenth and eighteenth centuries, the land had been divided

between the province (*eyalet*) of Sham (Syria) governed from Damascus, and the

eyalet of Sidon, but after provincial reforms in the nineteenth century, which were

designed to centralize the power of the state, the area became part of a single Syrian

province. This province (now termed a *vilayet*) was further subdivided into the district

of Acre (which also included Haifa, the Sea of Galilee, Safad, and Tiberias), the

district of Nablus (which also included Beisan, Jenin, and Qalqiliya), and the district

of Jerusalem (which also included Bethlehem, Jericho, Jaffa, Gaza, and Hebron).[9] A

further reorganization of the territory occurred in 1874, when the vital Jerusalem

district became an independent district (*mutasarifiyya*), with its own governor who

reported directly to Istanbul. And finally, in 1878 the districts of Nablus and Acre

were removed from the oversight of Syria, to become part of the newly created

province of Beirut.

Ottoman interest in these provinces was highest at the beginning and end of

their rule, when Jerusalem was symbolically and politically important. The Ottomans

conquered the city from the Mamluks in 1517, a victory that enhanced the prestige of

the Ottoman dynasty, for it brought the third holiest city in Islam under the control the

---

[9] Palestine's inclusion in the *vilayet* of Damascus came out of the laws of provincial administration of
1864 and 1871. These laws also consolidated the districts (*sanjaks*) of the region from the districts of
Gaza, Jerusalem, Nablus, Lajun, Safad, and Acre into the three larger districts of Acre, Nablus, and
Jerusalem.

Sublime Porte.[10] Jerusalem was soon included (next to Mecca and Medina) as one of the prominent places ruled by the Sultan Suleyman in a list of his titles that accompanied a letter to the French King Francis I in 1536 and became the site of significant Ottoman investment.[11] To harness Jerusalem's religious power the Ottomans worked hard after their conquest to rebuild the city's religious sites. As Robert Hillenbrand's excellent work *The Architecture of Ottoman Jerusalem* points out, "public architecture of the Ottoman centuries in Jerusalem was almost unswervingly dedicated to religious purposes," in contrast to the secular architecture that prevailed in Homs, Damascus, Aleppo, or other cities in the empire's Arab provinces.[12] Although this architecture tended to be more modest when compared to the monumental buildings of the preceding Umayyad and Mamluk periods, "taken all together, that architecture makes a powerful cumulative impact as the physical record of centuries of unpretentious devotion to the Holy City and to the Muslim religious life practiced there."[13] The Ottoman preference for functional religious architecture—the provision of *sabils* (public drinking fountains), prayer platforms, and open-air

---

[10] The Ottomans conquered Palestine as part of their campaign against the Mamluks in 1516-17, which brought the Ottomans control over the Levant, Egypt, the Hijaz, and parts of Yemen.

[11] The letter's introduction began with an impressive boast about the Sultan's power

> I, who am the sultan of sultans, the sovereign of sovereigns, the dispenser of crowns to the monarchs on the face of the earth, shadow of god on earth, the sultan and sovereign lord of the Mediterranean and the Black Sea, of Rumelia and Anatolia, of Karamania and the land of Rum, of Zulkadria, Diyarbakir, of Kurdistan, of Azerbaijan, Persia, Damascus, Cairo, Aleppo, of the Mecca and Medina, of Jerusalem, of all Arabia, of the Yemen and many other lands, which my noble forefathers and my glorious ancestors - may God light up their tombs - conquered by the force of their arms and which my august majesty has made subject to my flaming sword and victorious blade, I, Sultan Süleyman Han, to thee, who art Francis, king of the land of France ...

[12] Robert Hillenbrand, *The Architecture of Ottoman Jerusalem: An Introduction* (London: Altajir World of Islam Trust, 2002), 11.

[13] Ibid.

mihrabs (wall niches indicating the direction of Mecca)—was balanced by two spectacular public work projects of the 1530s: the construction of the walls around the Old City and the retiling of the Dome of the Rock. The latter project was unnecessary and aesthetically questionable, for it replaced undamaged and unique Umayyad mosaics with generic, although beautiful, glazed tilework.[14] But, along with the construction of the walls of Jerusalem, the project was a political rather than an aesthetic statement. The construction of Jerusalem's walls and the retiling of the Dome of the Rock told local inhabitants and visiting pilgrims that the city was under the control of a strong and self-confident Muslim empire.

This period of architectural fluorescence and imperial interest did not last long as Ottoman attention was soon diverted to other parts of the empire. In contrast to the unwavering political significance of Palestine and Israel in the twentieth and twenty-first centuries, for most of the Ottoman period the territory was a political backwater. Underpopulated, poor, and strategically insignificant, the area was a rather minor imperial possession as compared with the economically productive European provinces, the greater religious prize of the Hijaz, or the strategically vital border region of the Mesopotamian plain. It wasn't until the late-nineteenth century that the territory's fortunes changed, with the competition between European powers for preeminence in Jerusalem. As mentioned above, this led the Ottomans to take a more active role in the administration of the Jerusalem district, leading in 1874 to the creation of the Jerusalem *mutasarifiyya.*

---

[14] Hillenbrand, *Architecture*, 15.

Like other peripheral parts of the empire, the Ottoman military and
administrative presence in the area was light, at least until the centralizing
administrative reforms of the nineteenth century. This enabled regional warlords
(such as Zahir al-Umar, and Ahmad al-Jazzar), bedouin chiefs, and local sheikhs to
exercise military control over the territory during long periods of its history. It also
meant that the central government exercised little direct administrative oversight of the
territory. Instead many prominent administrative functions, such as tax collection or
the supervision of the waqf system, were farmed out to prominent notable families
(such as the Husaynis, Nashashibis, Khalidis, Alamis, and Nusaybas), who were—to
use Pamela Ann Smith's designations—members of the intellectual aristocracy
(*ashraf*) and/or the great landowning families ('*ailah*) of the area.[15] As such, the local
administration of Palestine conformed to Albert Hourani's "politics of the notables,"
in which the landed provincial elites acted as middle-men between the local
population and the Ottoman government.[16]

III - Local and Regional Identities

The division of the territory into separate districts meant that local identities were built
around sub-state loyalties and regional identifications. Local inhabitants identified
themselves with their villages, their families, their clan (*hamula*), their religious
community, or their occupations. A Syrian (*shami*) identification was also strong
among the intellectual and commercial elite due to the area's inclusion in the province

---

[15] Pamela Ann Smith, *Palestine and the Palestinians*, 18.

[16] Hourani, "Ottoman Reform and the Politics of Notables."

of Syria until the late-nineteenth century, as well as to the area's economic ties to

Damascus. This helps to explain why so many Palestinian politicians and intellectuals

promoted Palestine's union with Syria during the first two years of British rule.[17]

This did not mean that there was no concept of Palestine during the Ottoman

period. As Rashid Khalidi points out in his seminal work *Palestinian Identity*, Najib

'Azuri, a former Ottoman official in Palestine, argued in 1908 that "the progress of the

land of Palestine depends," upon the expansion of the district of Jerusalem northwards

to include the northern regions of the country.[18] Three years later the newspaper

Filastin (Palestine) was first published in Jaffa, which would take a strong Palestinian

nationalist and anti-Zionist stance throughout the mandate period. But this

identification with Palestine came very late in the Ottoman period, even if we accept

Khalidi's and Alexander Schölch's contention that this was based upon preexisting

religious notions of the holy land.[19] Also, the fact that there existed some notion of a

territory called Palestine did not equate to a shared sense of Palestinian nationalism

even among the educated and politically motivated elite. Nor should it have. As long

---

[17] This position was also heavily influenced by Faysal's apparent success in establishing an Arab kingdom in Syria.

[18] Khalidi, *Palestinian Identity*, 28.

[19] As Rashid Khalidi and Alexander Schölch have both pointed out this religious concept of Palestine existed among both Christians and Muslims in the area. For the former the holiness of the land was attached to biblical stories from the Old and New Testaments which recognized the 'holy land' as running from Dan to Beersheba. For Muslims the territory's holiness was tied to the religious significance of Jerusalem, the first qibla (direction of prayer) of Islam, known in Arabic as *al-Quds* ("The Holy"). The Muslim concept of Palestine's holiness was expressed in the *fada'il al-Quds* literature which is discussed by Khalidi and Schölch. See Khaldi, *Palestinian Identity*, 30.

as the Ottoman Empire existed it was difficult to conceive of a separate Arab 'nation'
let alone the series of Arab nations that emerged as a result of the First World War.[20]

In the pre-mandate period the inhabitants of the country had multiple and
overlapping loyalties with "the Ottoman state, the Arabic language, and the emerging
identity of Arabism, as well as their country and local and familial foci."[21] Such
identifications were not mutually exclusive and could co-exist with new notions of
Palestine, as Khalidi has pointed out. This fact was made clear to the British
authorities shortly after their occupation when they received petitions from petitioners
who chose to identify themselves in a multiplicity of ways—"The Representatives of
Ramla", "The Muslims of Nablus", "butchers, merchants of cereals and
manufacturers"—but who shared a common concern with "our country" (*biladna*)
which was nearly always referred to as Palestine.[22] Indeed, at a time when the nation-

---

[20] Because of this it is pointless to engage with the common assertion in Zionist polemics that
Palestinian nationalism is artificial since it is a modern construction, most famously expressed by Golda
Meir's infamous comments that "there was no such thing as Palestinians". This assertion has also
found its way into "scholarship", such as the infamous Joan Peters, *From Time Immemorial: The
Origins of the Arab-Israeli Conflict* (New York: Harper & Row, 1984) and Alan Dershowitz, *The Case
for Israel* (Hoboken, N.J.: John Wiley & Sons, 2003).

    The problem with this assertion is that is based on the assumption for nationalism to count it
has to be long-lived. This is inherent to the logic of nationalism which asserts that the nation is natural
and eternal. In actuality all nationalisms are modern, nationalism as a political movement was basically
unheard of in much of the Middle East up until the twentieth century; indeed, most European
nationalisms (including Zionism) only began in the last two or three decades of the nineteenth century.
Insisting that the Palestinian and Zionist identities are ancient is ahistorical and dangerous because it
suggests that the present nationalist contest between Palestinian Arabs and Israeli Jews is eternal.

[21] Khalidi, *Palestinian Identity*, 6.

[22] In these petitions we find locals identifying themselves according to their hometowns—"the
representatives of Ramla," "the inhabitants of Tul Karem,"—their religion—"the Muslims of Nablus,"
"the leading Muslims and Christians of Jaffa,"—or their occupation—"butchers, merchants of cereals
and manufacturers." Despite their disparate backgrounds these petitioners saw themselves as part of a
larger Palestinian identity. One petition from "the chiefs of the bedouin tribes residing in al-Jazira," for
example, states that "we join our countrymen in their protests and confirm them and add to them the
protests of the inhabitants of the desert..." It is to be noted that even when petitioners lobbied for their

state was not yet the norm, it is useful to bear in mind Eric Hobsbawm's sage reminder

that "men and women did not choose collective identification as they chose shoes,

knowing that one could only put on one pair at a time."[23]

Among the more important identifications for local inhabitants was religion.

As Donald Quatert writes, "One's religion—as Muslim, Christian, or Jew—was an

important means of differentiation in the Ottoman world."[24] Throughout the empire,

where people worshipped, whom they married, how they married or got divorced,

their rights of inheritance, who they associated with, where they lived, and in certain

periods even what clothes they wore were affected by their religious identity. The

holiness of Jerusalem probably enhanced this identification, since the city was a

significant destination for Christian and, to a lesser extent, Muslim pilgrimage and

contained religious sites that were among the holiest sites of the three major

---

land to become part of Syria, they referred to that land as Palestine. For a collection of these petitions
see ISA, 2/1/30 Files I and II, as well as 2/5/131.

[23] Eric Hobsbawm, *Nations and Nationalism since 1780* (Cambridge: Cambridge University Press,
1992), 123.

One of the factors that has made nationalism so powerful in the modern world is the fact that the
discourse of nationalism has naturalized the idea that local identities, economies, languages, and
collective memories necessarily submit to the nation *and* more perniciously that they have always
submitted to the nation.

It has to be remembered that even in the birthplace of nationalism, France, the process of
producing national citizens took a long time to achieve as noted in Eugen Weber's famous work,
Peasants into Frenchmen: The Modernization of Rural France, 1870-1914 (Stanford: Stanford UP,
1976). More recent work by scholars, such as Manu Goswami, *Producing India: From Colonial
Economy to National Space* (Chicago: University of Chicago Press, 2004), has tracked the process of
national identity formation in the colonial and subaltern context. The general and somewhat generic
processes involved in forging national identity—the spread of print-capitalism, the secularization of
culture, the state's control over statistics and map-making, etc.—has been the subject of a number of
important studies, such as Benedict Anderson's *Imagined Communities: Reflections on the Origin and
Spread of Nationalism* (London: Verso, 1991), Eric Hobsbawm, *Nations and Nationalism since 1780*
and Ernest Gellner's *Nations and Nationalism* (Ithaca: Cornell UP, 1983).

[24] Donald Quataert, *The Ottoman Empire, 1700-1922* (Cambridge, UK: Cambridge UP, 2000), 173.

monotheistic religions.[25] The Palestinian calendar was also full of festivals that

brought members of individual religious communities together in private and

communal gatherings, such as in the Jewish festivals of Purim and Yom Kippur, the

Christian festivals of Easter, Christmas, and the Orthodox celebration of the Holy Fire,

and Muslim holy celebrations such as Ramadan, the birthday of the Prophet

Muhammad, and the festivals of Nabi Musa and Nabi Saleh.[26]

IV- Jews, Christians, and the Millet System

The Ottoman conquest of the Mamluk empire did little to change the religious status

of local Jews and Christians, who had been allowed to freely practice their faith since

the conquest of Jerusalem by the Caliph Umar ibn Khattib in 638. Conversion was

---

[25] For Jews "Eretz Israel" (Palestine) is the holy land promised to Abraham and his descendants by God. Jewish holy sites include the Western Wall in Jerusalem, which is the last remaining ruins of the Second Temple and the holiest site in Judaism, the Tomb of the Machpelach (Patriarchs) in Hebron, and Rachel's Tomb near Bethlehem. For Christians Palestine/Israel is tied to the biblical story of Jesus and consequently Christian sites are tied to his life history in Bethlehem, Jerusalem, and the Galilee. Muslims consider Palestine to be holy because Jerusalem was the first *qibla* (direction of prayer) in Islam before Muhammad had a revelation stating that the direction of prayer should be Mecca. Jerusalem is also the site of the "Farther Mosque" (identified today with the al-Aqsa Mosque) mentioned in the Qur'an as the place where Muhammad started his night journey to heaven. Major Muslim holy sites include the Dome of the Rock, the al-Aqsa Mosque (which together make up the *Haram al-Sharif*) the tomb of Nabi Musa in Jericho, the shrine of Nabi Samwil north of Jerusalem, and Rachel's Tomb near Bethlehem.

The country was also full of numerous minor places of worship, such as the many local Muslim *zawiyas* (saints' shrines) that dotted the countryside. The most complete account of these shrines is by Tawfiq Canaan an Arab member of the Palestine Oriental Society, see Tawfiq Canaan, *Mohammedan Saints and Sanctuaries in Palestine* (London: Luzac & Co., 1927).

[26] The festival of Nabi Musa is a Muslim festival that celebrate the Prophet Moses who Palestinian Muslims (as opposed to Christians and Jews or Muslims in other places) believe crossed the Jordan river and died in Palestine. The shrine commemorating the place of his death lies near Jericho just off the main road connecting Jerusalem and Jericho. The festival brought together Muslims throughout the country in the last years of Ottoman rule and during the mandate period became a nationalist festival that was attended by Christians as well as Muslims. The festival of Nabi Saleh is more regional in scope and commemorates a pre-Islamic Arab prophet in the village of Nabi Saleh near Ramallah.

simply not a major part of Ottoman religious policy as Selim Derengil has explained.[27]

That policy was based upon the Qur'an's injunction that "there is no compulsion in

matter of faith," and the recognition in Islamic law that Jews and Christians were

'People of the Book,' (*Ahl al-Kitab*), who should not be persecuted.[28] In practice this

meant that conquered non-Muslims took on the formal status of *dhimmi*s (*zimmi*s in

Ottoman Turkish) who were entitled to security of the person and property, freedom to

practice their own religion, and a degree of internal communal autonomy in exchange

for submission to the Islamic state. As an element of shariʿa law, this compact was a

binding principle of Ottoman law, helping to ensure that "for many centuries, persons

who were of minority status enjoyed fuller rights and more legal protection in the

Ottoman lands than, for example, did minorities in the realm of the French king or of

the Habsburg emperor."[29]

This did not mean that non-Muslims enjoyed an equal standing with the

Muslim community. Up until the *Tanzimat* reforms of the nineteenth century, the

notion of religious or any other form of social equality in Ottoman society (as in other

pre-modern societies) was unknown.[30] Although practices changed over time and

---

[27] According to Derengil, "The Ottoman attitude to conversion is nowhere near as clear as that of the Spanish and Portuguese in South America, or the Russians in their expansion southwards into the Don-Volga region. The "saving of souls" was not an integral part of Ottoman Imperial policy as it was in the Christian empires." Derengil, "There is No Compulsion in Religion", 551.

[28] See al-Qur'an 2:256: "There is no compulsion in matter of faith. Distinct is the way of guidance now from error. He who turns away from the forces of evil and believes in God, will surely hold fast to a handle that is strong and unbreakable, for God hears all and knows everything." *al-Qur'an*, trans. Ahmed Ali, (Princeton: Princeton University Press, 1990), 45.

[29] Quataert, *Ottoman Empire*, 175.

[30] As with all pre-modern empires, the Ottoman Empire was built upon a hierarchical ordering of society, with the monarch enjoying both supreme political and religious legitimacy—the Ottoman Sultan was recognized both as the *padishah* ("lord of kings") and the caliph.

differed according to the local context, religious hierarchies were built around Islamic norms, which held that although the people of the book were to be respected, they could also be treated as second-class subjects in a Muslim state. This inferior position had been shown in a number of ways through the centuries: the payment of tribute to the state in the form of the *jizya* tax, the promulgation of clothing laws which restricted the colors and types of clothing that *dhimmis* could wear, periodic bans on their right to bear arms, and restrictions on the ringing of church bells. It was also shown in the fact that Islamic law took precedence over other religious laws, as in court cases involving both Muslims and non-Muslims, which were always adjudicated in the court of the local qadi.

Quite apart from religious law, the practicalities of ruling large minority communities made religious tolerance a rational approach for the Ottomans to adopt. The Ottomans ruled over a vast empire with a significant Christian component, with some areas, like the Balkan provinces, in which Christians were in the majority. Given the sheer number of non-Muslims, forced conversion would have been difficult and destabilizing (even if it wasn't already banned according Islamic law). Economically it also made sense to leave these subjects unconverted, since the Ottoman state could collect extra taxes from non-Muslims, in the form of the *jizya* tax. Furthermore, as Justin McCarthy has asserted, the devolution of powers to the empire's religious communities fit with the Middle Eastern traditions of having religious institutions provide "many of the public services that modern citizens expect of the state."[31] As a result, the empire's schools, courts, and systems of social welfare

were largely run by religious groups until the state took a more active role in society

during the reforms of the nineteenth century.

The arrangement that made all of this possible was the *millet* system, whereby

various religious communities were recognized as *millet*s (literally 'nations') by the

Ottoman government.[32] Recognition gave the religious community the right to a

modicum of self-government: the *millet* was in charge of the education, welfare, and

personal law of its members. As McCarthy points out, the system was not uniform in

its treatment of minority religions. For example, the position of Greek Orthodox

millet was officially recognized by law, whereas that of the Jewish community was

only recognized by tradition.[33] This suggests that the traditional scholarly portrait of

the *millet* system as a rigid system of legally recognized communities needs revisiting.

Recent scholarship has indeed begun to revise the idea that the political differentiation

of the *millet* system translated into a social division of society along religious lines.

Donald Quataert, for one, has argued that the term *millet* was not used to designate

Ottoman non-Muslims until the early nineteenth century, and views this as a sign that

Ottoman society was not as religiously divided as scholars have presumed.[34]

---

[31] It can of course be argued that this was a tradition in most pre-modern empires. Justin McCarthy, *The Ottoman Turks: An Introductory History to 1923* (London: Longman, 1997), 127.

[32] McCarthy's book offers a good overview of the main *millet*s—the Greek Orthodox, the Armenian Gregorians, the Jews—and other groups he terms *de facto millets*—the Nestorians, Syrian Orthodox, and Maronites. McCarthy, *Ottoman Turks*, 128-131.

[33] McCarthy, *Ottoman Turks*, 128.

[34] Donald Quataert, *Ottoman Empire*, 173.

While religion had an impact on the individual's life choices and life
experience it did not lead to formal sectarian segregation. Quataert maintains that
patterns of residential settlement in the Ottoman Empire demonstrate that "overall,
residential exclusivity by community was not the rule in the 1700-1922 era." Instead
other criteria, such as wealth and occupation, were the main factors behind urban
segregation.[35] This observation is borne out in research on the demography of
Ottoman Palestine, particularly on the urban development of Jerusalem, which
indicates that religious communities lived together in mixed neighborhoods and
engaged in everyday social and economic interactions. For example, the Jewish
quarter has seen an uneven and mixed pattern of settlement throughout its history,
with Muslims and Armenian Christians making up a significant part of the population
until the birth of the State of Israel. Moreover, Jewish settlement in the Old City was
not confined to the Jewish quarter before the mandate period, a fact emphasized by the
modern Jewish settler groups who have been moving into the Arab quarter in recent
years.[36] Salim Tamari has decried the tendency of historians to see Jerusalem through
present day realities, the impulse to use current divisions to retroactively "define the
contours of the city before the ruptures of war."[37] This point is re-emphasized by
Rochelle Davis, who observes that although there were ethno-religious divisions in

---

[35] Quataert, *Ottoman Empire*, 177-8.

[36] Groups aligned with the far-right Gush Emunim movement, such as Ateret Cohanim, Torat Cohanim, the Young Israel Movement, and Yeshiva Birkat Avraham emerged in the 1980s as advocates of a large-scale Jewish settlement in the Muslim areas of the Old City of Jerusalem. See Michael Dumper, *The Politics of Sacred Space: The Old City of Jerusalem in the Middle East Conflict* (Boulder: Lynn Reiner, 2002), 39-71.

[37] Salim Tamari, "Jerusalem 1948: The Phantom City," *Jerusalem 1948: The Arab Neighborhoods and Their Fate in the War,* ed. Salim Tamari (Jerusalem: Institute of Jerusalem Studies, 1999),

Ottoman Jerusalem, "the current modern appellations and division into quarters (Muslim, Christian, Jewish, and Armenian) did not exist."[38]

We also know from accounts of the Ottoman and Mandate periods by Palestinian writers such as Wasif Jawhariyyeh, Khalil Sakakini, and Hala Sakakini that there was a great deal of social, cultural, and religious interchange between the three communities. Christians attended Muslim religious festivals (particularly Nabi Musa), entered Muslim holy places (it was customary for Christian families to picnic on the grass within the *Haram al-Sharif*), and on occasion even studied the Qur'an.[39] Meanwhile, Muslim folk festivals were celebrated alongside Orthodox holidays (such as the Ceremony of the Holy Fire) and Easter celebrations merged with the festivities of Nabi Musa. This religious interaction also extended to Jewish festivals such as Purim and Pesach that were celebrated by Muslims and Christians in Jewish neighborhoods.[40]

V - The Status Quo

The self-regulation of the *millet* system did not mean that the early modern Ottoman state left religious communities completely to their own devices. Even before the centralizing reforms of the *Tanzimat*, the Ottoman authorities intervened in cases

---

[38] Rochelle Davis, "Ottoman Jerusalem," *Jerusalem 1948: The Arab Neighborhoods and Their Fate in the War*, ed. Salim Tamari (Jerusalem: Institute of Jerusalem Studies, 1999), 13.

[39] See for instance Salim Tamari, "Jerusalem's Ottoman Modernity: The Times and Lives of Wasif Jawhariyyeh," *Jerusalem Quarterly* 9 (2000), Hala Sakakini, *Jerusalem and I: A Personal Record* (Jerusalem: Habesch, 1987), and John H. Melkon Rose, *Armenians of Jerusalem: Memories of Life in Palestine* (London: Radcliffe Press, 1993).

[40] Salim Tamari, "Jerusalem's Ottoman Modernity."

where religious controversy or conflict threatened to upset relations between local communities and potentially undermine public order.

This is shown most clearly in the Ottoman policy of protecting the "status quo" at the country's holy sites. The "status quo" was a retrospective term used by the Palestine government and European Christians for two Ottoman edicts (*firmans*) that established guidelines over the ownership and usage rights of Christian sects to various holy sites in Palestine.[41] The term refers specifically to an 1852 *firman* promulgated by Sultan Abdul Mecid that committed the Ottoman Empire to maintaining the existing rights of the Christian sects, known to later commentators as the "status quo". Those rights had first been laid out in a *firman* promulgated in 1767, in which the Porte had divided the church among its various claimants, a division that recognized the Greek Orthodox as the preeminent sect at the site. The 1852 *firman* was promulgated to reconfirm that earlier decision with the hope that this would definitively fix religious rights at the Church of the Holy Sepulchre and the Church of the Nativity. The motivation behind this was an Ottoman desire to end the fierce competition between Christian sects over their rights of ownership and access at the holy sites of Jerusalem and Bethlehem that raged throughout the eighteenth and early nineteenth centuries.[42] And to make sure that this decree was followed, the Ottoman

---

[41] Michael Dumper offers a succinct account of the Status Quo in *The Politics of Sacred Space*, 20-21. For an account of the Status Quo from a Franciscan point of view see the work of Albert Rock, *The Status Quo in the Holy Places* (Jerusalem: Franciscan Printing Press, 1989).

[42] The past sectarian conflicts and competition over these sites is described in Rock, *The Status Quo*. The British public first became aware of this competition through Robert Curzon's account of the Ceremony of the Holy Fire and other Orthodox celebrations in Robert Curzon, *Visits to the Monasteries in the Levant* (London: Century Publishing, 1983), which was originally published in 1849.

authorities posted troops at the Church of the Holy Sepulchre to keep order between

the various Christian sects.[43]

This meant that while in principle the millets were free to conduct their own

affairs, the Ottoman authorities intervened in cases where public order was threatened,

as was the case when two different millets came into conflict. Not surprisingly, such

moments became more common in the nineteenth century with its influx of European

pilgrims and increase in imperial competition. Albert Hyamson relates one such

incident in 1847, in which the local pasha intervened in a controversial conversion of a

Jewish youth, Myer Maruka, to Christianity.[44] Government intervention was brought

about by the Chief Rabbi of Jerusalem, who challenged the conversion on the grounds

that the youth was underage and was a non-Muslim subject (*ray'a*) of the Ottoman

Empire.[45] The matter was referred to Istanbul and the youth was taken into the

guardianship of the local Ottoman authorities until a response was received.

Eventually after consulting with officials in Istanbul, the governor set Maruka free and

allowed him to choose whichever faith he wanted. The state's involvement in the

conversion of Myer Maruka was atypical; conversion was traditionally a matter of

negotiation between the respective religious communities in which the state was a

virtual nonparticipant. But in this case the argument between the Chief Rabbi and

---

[43] Shepherd, *Zealous Intruders*, 25.

[44] Hyamson's book includes a copy of a letter from the British consul James Finn to Viscount
Palmerston from March 11, 1847, which discusses the incident in detail. See Albert M. Hyamson, *The
British Consulate in Jerusalem: in relation to the Jews of Palestine 1838-1914*, volume 1, (London:
Edward Goldston, 1939), 94.

[45] Conversion of Ottoman citizens, Muslim or otherwise, by missionary groups was illegal.

local Christians necessitated a response. As in the issue of the status quo, the state was prepared to take action if religious issues erupted onto the public stage.[46]

VI - Local Islam under the Ottomans

The central state's relationship with its Muslim population differed from its relationship with non-Muslims, since Islam was the religion of the ruling dynasty. The Muslim community was not a *millet* in the legal or popular sense of the term. In some ways it operated much like one, especially in the premodern period, for Muslim religious authorities provided the same sort of services that the Christian and Jewish authorities offered, such as education, welfare, and facilities for worship. However, the Muslim community was more intimately tied to the Ottoman state, on account of the traditional right in Islam of the civil leader (sultan) to oversee the practice of Islam in his domains. And the Ottoman sultan was not simply any Muslim leader; the sultan also claimed the title of caliph (i.e. the leader of the Muslim *umma*), although this title was not invoked with much frequency before the reign of Abdulhamid II (1876-1909).[47] This meant that the notion of a separate Muslim nation within the Ottoman state was difficult to imagine.

---

[46] It might be tempting to treat this 1847 case as an early example of the state's increased intervention into the lives of its subjects during the *Tanzimat* period (1839-1876). But, it seems more likely that the governor's intervention in this case had to do with traditional concerns for security than a new governmentality, for the modern centralizing reforms of the *Tanzimat* had hardly reached Palestine at this time. Even so, it is interesting that the British consul in Jerusalem at the time reacted with shock to the Porte's break with tradition, suggesting that at least one observer saw the case as a shift in Ottoman policy towards the *millet* system. Hyamson, *British Consulate*, 94.

[47] The Muslim identity of the empire was emphasized by Abdulhamid as a conservative reaction to the pressure of European confrontation. Selim Deringel offers a very useful account of the place of Islam during the Hamidian period in Selim Deringel, *The Well Protected Domains: Ideology and the Legitimation of Power in the Ottoman Empire 1876-1909* (London: I.B. Tauris, 1998). The power of

The Ottoman state's supervision of Islam can be seen most clearly in its oversight of the ulama. As with the treatment of religious minorities, state policies were guided by historical precedent. State control over the position of the qadi had long been part of governance in the Islamic world. As Daniel Brown points out, despite the fact that some prominent early legal theorists, such as Abu Hanifa, rejected state service, "the office of qadi, or judge, was by its very nature tied to the political establishment, and government appointed qadis were handing down legal decisions from the early Umayyad period onward."[48] In the highly bureaucratic Ottoman Empire, the state's control over the ulama was even stronger:

> The *ulama*, schools, and the courts were brought within the state's bureaucracy. Through royal patronage, the empire developed a hierarchy of Islamic institutions: local Quran schools, mosque-universities (*madrasas*), and courts. At the apex of the state's religious bureaucracy was the *shaykh al-Islam*, who like the chief *qadi* (judge), was appointed by the sultan. Thus, Ottoman *ulama* families became a religious aristocracy.[49]

In Palestine the Ottoman government's control over formal Islamic institutions was based mostly upon its control over appointments. As Judith Tucker has explained, "in the Ottoman period in Syria and Palestine, all major cities and towns housed an Islamic court or tribunal (*makhama*) presided over by a qadi appointed by the Ottoman government."[50] Government control over the appointment of the qadi gave the Ottomans the ability to ensure that Islamic law was applied uniformly across the

---

Islam at the end of empire was revealed in the sultan's call for a jihad against the Entente powers during the First World War.

[48] Daniel Brown, *A New Introduction to Islam* (Malden, MA: Blackwell, 2004), 122.

[49] John Esposito, *Islam: The Straight Path*, revised third edition (Oxford: Oxford University Press, 2005), 62.

[50] Judith Tucker, *In the House of Law: Gender and Islamic Law in Ottoman Syria and Palestine* (Berkeley: University of California Press, 1998), 17.

empire, and to promote judges who conformed to their brand of Islam. As a result,

some local qadis, especially those that were deemed strategically important, were

Turkish-speaking Ottoman officials who were appointed from outside to serve in local

courts for a year or two.[51] One such office was the qadiship of Jerusalem, considered

one of the most important judicial positions in the empire, which was a position that

had been filled by Turkish Ottoman officials on a yearly basis since the late

seventeenth century.[52] Even if a qadi was a local figure, the government's control

over his appointment meant that he was beholden to the Ottoman state. Such control

over judicial appointments was especially useful in the "politics of notables", for it

allowed the Ottoman state to trade appointments in the religious hierarchy to local

notable families in return for their loyalty to the state.[53]

However, the state's control over appointment did not automatically mean that

the qadi toed the official line. In must not be forgotten that the Ottoman Empire was

vast and for much of its history was ruled in a decentralized manner. This meant that

qadis in the provinces felt less pressure from the state to apply the law in a particular

way than those that resided in Istanbul. When it came to religion, state intervention

was also checked to some degree by the traditional respect paid to the ulama in

Muslim society. Finally, Haim Gerber has argued that qadis of the eighteenth century

---

[51] Tucker, *House of Law*, 21.

[52] Khalidi, *Palestinian Identity*, 65.

[53] The concept of the "politics of notables" refers to the situation in the Arab provinces of the Ottoman empire, especially in provincial capitals like Damascus, in which leaders of the local notability acted as intermediaries between the Ottoman state and the local population. This relationship was based on a *quid pro quo*. The Ottoman government granted these notables political and religious offices in return for their help in making sure that there was order in their provinces. Albert Hourani, "Ottoman Reform and the Politics of Notables," *The Modern Middle East: A Reader*, eds. Albert Hourani, Philip Khoury, Mary Wilson (Berkeley : University of California Press, 1993), 83-109.

were inherently independent because Islamic law was not codified. In other words,

even if there was an official policy that the Ottoman state wanted qadis to adopt (and

there is little indication that this was the case), it wasn't one that could be followed as a

set of instructions.

> What Weber meant by "kadi-justice" was a legal system where there are few
> strict rational rules on the basis of which the judge operates, but rather, he
> acts according to intuition. As can be appreciated only through reading *kadi*-
> protocols of the Ottoman Empire, this description is surprisingly precise. The
> Ottoman Kadi had no written code of laws to guide him. He had of course
> the orthodox manuals, some of which are considered superb. But there was
> also state law (*kanun*) to be taken into consideration as well as local custom.
> What he would decide in any specific case was entirely up to him. He had to
> explain his decision to no one, and most legal decisions in the Ottoman court
> protocols are not justified.[54]

Muftis have traditionally been even less closely tied to the state than qadis in

Islamic history. Unlike the qadi, who works within a court system that the state

oversees, the mufti does not have to be attached to a particular institution. This was

generally the case in Ottoman Islam, but this did not mean that mufti operated freely

within the empire. The state actively tried to control the issuance of legal opinions

(*fatwa*s in Arabic, *fetva*s in Ottoman Turkish) by elevating a single mufti in Istanbul to

the position of *shaykh al-Islam* (*şeyhülislam* in Ottoman Turkish), "the ultimate source

of authority in matters relating to the shari'a."[55] The office was created during the

reign of Murad II (1421-1451) and was further bureaucratized under Sultan Suleyman

the Magnificent (1520-1566) when the *shaykh al-Islam* became part of a bureaucratic

---

[54] Haim Gerber, "A New Look at the Tanzimat: The Case of the Province of Jerusalem," *Palestine in the Late Ottoman Period: Political, Social, and Economic Transformation*, ed. David Kushner (Jerusalem: Yad Izhak Ben-Zvi Press, 1986), 38.

[55] Muhammad Khalid Masud, "Muftis, Fatwas, and Islamic Legal Interpretation," *Islamic Legal Interpretation: Muftis and Their Fatwas*, eds. M. K. Masud, B. Messick and D. S. Powers (Cambridge, MA: Harvard University Press, 1996), 11.

hierarchy of jurists scattered throughout the empire. And eventually an official department for issuing fatwas was founded by the in Istanbul with a professional staff headed by a fatwa supervisor.[56]

By the eighteenth century, muftis of the core regions (i.e. in the European provinces and Anatolia) were government officials who "tended to issue fatwas that supported official Ottoman edicts and standardized certain points of law at the expense of the qadis' discretionary leeway."[57] Judith Tucker describes these muftis as "an interface between the state and the courts, so as to ensure that court decisions were compatible with official interpretations of the law."[58] But in the Arab provinces, the mufti's relationship to the state was quite different. Muftis in Syria and Palestine during the seventeenth and eighteenth centuries were local men who were not part of Ottoman officialdom. Their role within the legal system was also different, for rather than being integral to court proceedings their *fatwas* were often unconnected to court cases and were simply "responses to individual requests for a legal opinion, or even reflections on specific local situations they came to know of."[59]

What this meant is that whereas fatwas in the central Ottoman lands could be considered something akin to imperial legal opinions, in Palestine and Syria the "work of a particular mufti often seem[ed] to bear the stamp of the town in which he operated."[60] This localism was reinforced by the fact that the Ottoman government

---

[56] Masud, "Muftis, Fatwas, and Interpretation," 12.

[57] Tucker, *House of Law*, 20.

[58] Ibid.

[59] Tucker, *House of Law*, 21.

[60] Tucker, *House of Law*, 30.

did not send its own muftis to work in the Syrian provinces.[61] This type of religious localism has largely been lost in the modern world of the centralized state and printing press but was a dominant feature of Islam in Palestine in the pre-modern period.

Another factor that made the practice of Islam less centralized in Palestine and other provinces was the fact that local notable families controlled the waqf system until the nineteenth century. While the largest waqfs in Palestine (the Dome of the Rock and the Hebron sanctuary) were controlled by the Ottoman government, the majority were run by local agents, including great public waqfs.[62] Like the positions of qadi and mufti, the position of the *mutawalli* (caretaker of a waqf) was used by notable families such as the al-Husaynis and al-Khalidis in Jerusalem) or the 'Abd al-Hadis in Nablus to consolidate their position as religious and political powerbrokers.

VII - Modernization and the Tanzimat

The state of religion under Ottoman rule that has been discussed applies to the period from the sixteenth century until the early nineteenth century. Before the nineteenth century the Ottoman state had been a pre-modern empire whose rule was uneven, diffuse, and decentralized.[63] In the Ottoman heartlands, sub-state actors, such as the

---

[61] Uri Kupferschmidt, "A Note on the Muslim Religious Hierarchy Towards the End of the Ottoman Period," *Palestine in the Late Ottoman Period: Political, Social, and Economic Transformation*, ed. David Kushner (Jerusalem: Yad Izhak Ben-Zvi Press, 1986), 127.

[62] Gabriel Baer, "Jerusalem's Families of Notables and the Wakf in the Early 19th Century," *Palestine in the Late Ottoman Period: Political, Social, and Economic Transformation*, ed. David Kushner (Jerusalem: Yad Izhak Ben-Zvi Press, 1986), 112.

[63] Eighteenth century Ottoman rule was built around a partnership between the state and its provincial notables who were granted lifetime tax farms (*malikanes*) in exchange for their military and security assistance to the state. As has been mentioned, this also meant that religious groups played a great role in society, for they provided educational, religious, and welfare services that the distant Ottoman

Janissaries, guilds, tribes, and the ulama, enjoyed a great deal of power alongside the central state. As we have seen, the power of the state in the provinces was even weaker, with local warlords holding military power and local notable families and religious authorities providing administration and public services. Nineteenth century Ottoman reforms, particular those of the *tanzimat* period (1839-1871), profoundly changed the state's relationship with these sub-state actors, as the Ottomans pursued a policy of centralization aimed at making the empire competitive with its European rivals and the Egypt of Mehmet 'Ali. It also changed the way in which religion was treated by the Ottoman state.

The elimination of the Janissaries in 1826; the abolition of tax farming, the call for conscription, and promises of equality of citizenship in the Hatt-ı Şerif of Gülhane of 1839; the Hatt-ı Humayun's guarantee of equal access to state schools and state employment in 1856 were reforms aimed at creating a new Ottoman citizenry that would be less divided by religious, territorial, professional, or class loyalties. The new citizen's primary relationship would be with the state. To achieve this, the Ottoman government expanded its role in society, thereby marginalizing or eliminating the role of those sub-state actors. As Donald Quataert has pointed out, not only did the number of Ottoman civil servants rise from 2,000 to 35,000 over the course of the nineteenth century but the state "embraced spheres of activity previously considered

government did not provide. This reliance on provincial governors has typically been seen as a sign of the weakness and decline of the Ottoman Empire, but some scholars, such as Ariel Salzmann have argued that it was viable strategy of adaptation that enabled the Ottoman Empire state to keep its power in a changing economic and political situation. See Ariel Salzmann, "An Ancien Regime Revisited: 'Privatization' and Political Economy in the Eighteenth-Century Ottoman Empire," *Politics & Society* 21, no. 4 (1993).

outside the purview of the state." This had an important effect on religious groups because, whereas "state functionaries once performed a limited range of tasks, mainly war making and the collection of taxes, leaving much of the rest for the state's subjects and their religious leaders to address," by the beginning of the twentieth century the Ottoman state had created "separate and parallel state educational and charitable institutions.[64]

This expansion of the Ottoman state mimicked the enlargement of the central state in the countries of eighteenth and nineteenth century Europe and was tied to the same processes of state-building nationalism and economic modernization. The result was that the state emerged as a far more important factor in peoples' lives than it had been in the past, as it demanded more of its citizens.

The first modern reforms that were enacted in Palestine actually came from Cairo rather than Istanbul. It was during the brief period of Egyptian control (1831-1841) that "the first attempt was made to institute a regular system of civil administration, together with military conscription, partial secularization of the law courts and the concession of equal political status to Christian and Jewish subjects."[65] Ottoman reforms didn't really take off until the 1860s, despite the Ottoman

---

[64] Quataert, *Ottoman Empire*, 62. This shift from a pre-modern to a modern form of state rule can be seen in the creation of ministries of trade and commerce, health, education, and public works within Ottoman government, and in the use of modern techniques of state surveillance and control: direct taxation, conscription, census taking, and domestic spying.

[65] Carter V. Findley, "The Evolution of the System of Provincial Administration as Viewed from the Center," *Palestine in the Late Ottoman Period: Political, Social, and Economic Transformation*, ed. David Kushner (Jerusalem: Yad Izhak Ben-Zvi Press, 1986), 4.

reoccupation of the country in 1841, a sign of the slow pace in which *Tanzimat* reforms were brought to the Arab provinces.

The elevation of the sanjak of Jerusalem to an independent sanjak (*mutasarrifiyyah*) in 1874 was the clearest sign of the new Ottoman interest in Palestine. The change meant that the district (which included the two major population centers of Jerusalem and Jaffa) was linked directly with Istanbul rather than being under the control of the *vilayet* of Syria, as it had been traditionally. This move was atypical but not without precedent, for the *mutasarrifiyyah* of Mount Lebanon had been established thirteen years earlier. As in the Lebanese case the decision to tie Jerusalem directly to Istanbul was an attempt by the Porte to assert its authority over a part of the empire that was subject to European interest and competition.

The elevation of Jerusalem was complemented by a wider project of Ottoman financial and security investment in Palestine, which helped to fuel the financial and demographic growth of cities such as Jerusalem, Haifa, and Jaffa.[66] This investment was shown in the inauguration of public works projects that were intended to modernize the country, such as the improvement of the port of Jaffa, the construction of new urban and inter-urban roads, the installation of telegraph lines, and the

---

[66] As Ruth Kark has observed the two cities were transformed in the latter-half of the nineteenth century from small, almost forgotten towns, to the main urban centers of the country, with Jaffa enjoying a 15-fold expansion and Jerusalem an almost six-fold increase in size from 1840 to 1917. See Ruth Kark, "The Contribution of the Ottoman Regime to the Development of Jerusalem and Jaffa, 1840-1917," *Palestine in the Late Ottoman Period: Political, Social, and Economic Transformation*, ed. David Kushner (Jerusalem: Yad Izhak Ben-Zvi Press, 1986), 46.

establishment of local branches of the Ottoman postal service.[67] It should be noted that the secular nature of government work projects in the late-nineteenth century was in great contrast to the religious construction at the beginning of the Ottoman rule, reflecting the different priorities of the modernizing state. This secularism was reflected in the urban architecture of Jerusalem, for the city saw the construction not of religious sites but modern buildings such as a municipal hospital (1890), a municipal park (1891), a museum of antiquities (1901), a theater (1901), and public toilets in Jerusalem's "new city".[68]

These projects were made possible because of the Ottoman state's reassertion of control in and around Jerusalem, which had eliminated the threat of Bedouin tribal raids. This would prove crucial for the future growth of the city, for it allowed for the construction of new neighborhoods outside the walls of Jerusalem. New laws of provincial administration promulgated in 1864 and 1871 led to the creation of an administrative council, staffed by Ottoman Turkish functionaries and urban notables. This regularized provincial administration and allowed the government to take a more direct role in provincial governance than it had in the past.[69] Local municipal councils, such as the *majlis baladi* established in Jerusalem in 1863, were also tools

---

[67] Kark, "Development of Jerusalem and Jaffa," 53.

[68] These developments are discussed in Yehoshua Ben-Arieh, *Jerusalem in the 19th Century: Emergence of the New City* (Jerusalem: Yad Izhak Ben-Zvi, 1986), 349-360; Davis, "Ottoman Jerusalem,"; and Ruth Kark and Michael Oren-Norheim, *Jerusalem and its Environs: Quarters, Neighborhoods, Villages 1800-1948* (Jerusalem: Hebrew University, 2001). Salim Tamari's article on the diaries of Wasif Jawhariyyeh, gives a taste of the bourgeois excitement of the New City before the British arrival. See Salim Tamari, "Jerusalem's Ottoman Modernity: The Times and Lives of Wasif Jawhariyyeh," *Jerusalem Quarterly* 9 (Winter 2000).

[69] It is important to note however that since these councils also consisted of local representatives, the traditional notability was able to retain much of its power by making sure its members were elected to the council. Findley, "Evolution of Provincial Administration," 12.

for Ottoman modernization, for these councils worked under the Ottoman authorities to provide public services, such as education, welfare, health services, and urban planning.[70]

At the same time the government's reach into society was strengthened through its registration of the population from the 1860s onwards and the imposition of new forms of taxation, such as the *werko* land tax.[71] As might be expected, these kinds of centralizing reforms did not have the same success or impact in the vast Ottoman empire as related reforms had in the smaller nations of Western Europe, but the application of these methods was a sign of the government's determination to create a new society through modern rule. Thus, according to Donna Robinson Divine, despite the fact that the Ottoman Empire was "not a highly centralized polity," compared to European countries of the period, "by the end of the century, a more

---

[70] Rochelle Davis notes that the municipality was responsible before the turn of the nineteenth century for building a sewage system, establishing a regular garbage service, installing kerosene street lamps, and creating a city park. The municipality also created the city's first police force in 1886, a professional fire department in the mid-1890s, and a municipal hospital in 1891. The municipality also directed urban planning through the issuance of building permits. Davis, "Ottoman Jerusalem," 12.

[71] Justin McCarthy has noted that the use of the term census in the Ottoman context is misleading as the population studies that the Ottomans undertook do not conform to modern notions of census taking, nevertheless he does point out that "Ottoman population records were extensive and consistent. They were part of a regular system of population registration that intended to provide the central government with an accurate picture of the Empire's population, are valuable demographic resources." Not surprisingly he notes that population registration was intimately tied to the power of the government in the region: registration began after the Ottoman conquest of 1516 for tax purposes, disappeared after the 16th century due to the decline of Ottoman power in the provinces, and reappeared as part of the nineteenth century effort at centralization. Moreover, he points out that during the nineteenth century the authorities came to realize that population statistics could be used for more than tax or conscription information, so that by the time of Abdul Hamid II, "data on population characteristics were recorded and published without any immediate governmental justification beyond advancing knowledge of the Empire." Justin McCarthy, *The Population of Palestine: Population History and Statistics of the Late Ottoman Period and the Mandate* (New York: Columbia Press, 1990), 2-5.

This desire to know the Ottoman population was undoubtedly influenced by a European nationalist mania for statistics during the nineteenth century. For a discussion of this phenomenon see Silvana Patriarca, *Numbers and Nationhood: Writing Statistics in Nineteenth Century Italy* (Cambridge: Cambridge University Press, 1996).

complex legal system and a larger bureaucracy had rendered government both less remote and more relevant: Government increasingly made a difference in the lives of the ordinary people."[72]

VIII - Transformations in education, the law, and the concept of personhood

Educational reform was deemed particularly important by Ottoman reformers, who viewed knowledge of the modern arts and sciences to be crucial in their efforts to compete with Europe. Since the Ottoman bureaucrats and their European advisors saw the traditional Muslim school (*kuttab*) as hopelessly backward, a network of state-run public schools was established in order to teach modern secular subjects. For example, the government established a secondary school in Jerusalem in 1891, where students "regardless of religion could attend classes in Arabic, Turkish, French, and the basic sciences," a sign of the Ottoman state's interest in producing students with a knowledge of modern subjects.[73] Such schools "were modeled in some ways on the foreign missionary institutions whose attractiveness to Arab students was feared by Ottoman reformers. Unlike these foreign schools, however, the state public schools taught most subjects in Turkish, and laid stress on Ottoman patriotism."[74] With their emphasis on secular subjects and Western-style of pedagogy, such schools produced a

---

[72] Donna Robinson Divine, *Politics and Society in Ottoman Palestine: The Arab Struggle for Survival and Power* (London: Lynne Rienner, 1994), 3.

[73] Davis, "Ottoman Jerusalem," 14.

[74] Khalidi, *Palestinian Identity*,

new type of student who was more familiar with European intellectual traditions than with traditional religious knowledge.[75]

Another area in which the state took action was in legal reform, which according to William Cleveland worked to "break down the religious and cultural autonomy of the *millets*," by giving the Ottoman state a greater role in determining the law and the legal status of its subjects.[76] The *tanzimat* period was marked by the adoption of European-style legal codes, which standardized legal practice across the empire and turned law into a tool of statecraft. Two developments were particularly important in regards to religion. The first was the gradual introduction of a system of secular courts in the Ottoman empire. This began with the creation of mixed commercial courts in the 1840s, which were successful enough that they were reorganized and expanded after the Reform Edict of 1856. They were followed by the creation of a secular *Nizamiye* court system in 1869. Secular courts had existed in the Ottoman Empire for centuries, such as the Sultan's *kanun* courts, which dealt with matters outside the *shari'a*s purview, such as ceremonial, administrative, and police law, but these new courts were a new kind of court, since they dealt with matters that

---

[75] Brinkley Messick and Timothy Mitchell have both pointed out that the arrival of the modern school system to the Middle East standardized the content and transmission of knowledge. Traditional instruction relied on a kind of apprenticeship at the foot of the religious expert, leading to a localism and diversity in education that was unacceptable to the modern system of pedagogy that was based around the textbook, the curriculum, and the examination. See Timothy Mitchell, *Colonising Egypt* and Brinkley Messick, *The Calligraphic State: Textual Domination and History in a Muslim Society* (Berkeley: University of California Press, 1993).

[76] William Cleveland, *A History of the Modern Middle East,* third edition (Boulder: Westview, 2004), 83.

had been under the jurisdiction of the shari'a, such as criminal and commercial law.[77]

This led to a reduction in the jurisdiction of Islamic courts, which became limited to

matters of personal status and *waqf.*

A second and related change was the adoption of the Ottoman Civil Code (Ar.

Majalla, Tr. *Mecelle*) in 1876, which involved a substantial codification of Islamic law

based upon French civil codes. This transformed Islamic law from a system of legal

interpretation based upon specific religious sources (the Qur'an, hadith, and other

precedents) to a body of codified law that could be applied precisely by the judge. As

Wael Hallaq has argued, "Codification is not an inherently neutral form of law, nor is

it an innocent tool of legal practice, devoid of political or other goals. It is a deliberate

choice in the exercise of political and legal power, a means by which a conscious

restriction is placed on the interpretive freedoms of jurists, judges, and lawyers."[78]

Along these lines, Selim Deringel has argued that the creation of the *Majalla* was an

"Ottomanization of the Şeriat," i.e. an attempt to make Islamic law conform to the

dictates of Ottoman governmentality.[79] As such the *Majalla* was an attempt by the

state to boldly assert its right to determine all law, an act, which as Hallaq has pointed

out, "assigned it a place above the law."[80]

---

[77] Dora Glidewell Nadolski, "Ottoman and Secular Civil Law," *International Journal of Middle East Studies,* Vol. 8, No. 4, (Oct, 1977), 520.

[78] Wael Hallaq, "Can the Shari'a be Restored?" *Islamic Law and the Challenges of Modernity,* ed. Yvonne Haddad and Barbara Stowassar (Walnut Creek: Altimara Press, 2004). <http://www.globalwebpost.com/farooqm/study_res/islam/fiqh/hallaq_shariah.html>

[79] Deringel, *Well Protected Domains,* 50.

[80] Ibid.

The creation of the *Majella* and civilian courts was part of a major shift in the government's relationship to law. Over the course of the nineteenth century, the ruler's traditional deference to religious law (which was admittedly tempered by his issuance of *qānūn* rulings) was replaced by the modern state's control over, and indeed superiority over, all types of law. A central tool in this transformation was codification, which replaced the traditional legal pluralism of Muslim law—and the localism that went along with it—with a rigid code by which law became an extension of state control.[81] As Brinkley Messick has succinctly put it, codification involved the closure of what had been the shari'a's open-ended nature.[82] Greater state control over Islam was also achieved through the creation of the Ministry of Imperial Pious Endowments in 1826 during the reign of the modernizing Ottoman sultan Mahmud II. This brought the major *waqf*s of the empire under the control of the Porte, thereby removing a major source of financial power from the hands of the religious elite.[83]

A final change connected to these legal reforms was a movement towards making Ottoman identity the primary identification for subjects throughout the empire. The Hatt-ı Sharif of Gulhane of 1839 announced that all subjects of the empire, regardless of religious background, would enjoy the same rights of security of person and property, a commitment that was reinforced in the Hatt-ı Hümayun of 1856. This helped to lessen the significance of religion as a marker of difference within society, especially when coupled with legislation that sought to eliminate differences in

---

[81] Pluralism was intrinsic to traditional Muslim law since the system depended heavily upon the legal interpretations of individual muftis and qadis.

[82] Messick, *Calligraphic State*, 56-59.

[83] Hallaq, "Shari'a."

communal and occupational dress. In place of religious or social differences, this legislation promoted Ottoman identity, *osmanlilik*, which, in the words of James Gelvin "was analogous to what in a later period would be known as a civic form of nationalism—a community of equal citizens bound together by their residence in a common territory and their commitment to a common set of legal norms," or alternatively to a particular dynasty or state.[84] Ottoman identity was further emphasized in the Nationality Law of 1869, which proclaimed that individuals in the empire shared a common Ottoman citizenship regardless of religion. Indeed, in the Ottoman Constitution of 1876 in which equality under Ottomanism was emphasized, the *millet*s were not mentioned at all.[85]

This move by the Porte to develop an Ottoman identity must be seen as an example of the sort of 'official nationalism' promoted by dynastic regimes in the nineteenth century as discussed in Benedict Anderson's *Imagined Communities*.[86] Searching for new bases of legitimacy in a world in which the nation-state was becoming the economically and politically dominant type of polity (at least in Europe) and nationalism was on the rise within the empire itself, the Ottoman authorities invented their own brand of civic identity. It seems likely that the development of Ottomanism was a defensive move aimed at adapting modern European ideas to the Ottoman context, an approach to governance that has aptly been termed 'defensive

---

[84] James L. Gelvin, "Secularism and Religion in the Arab Middle East: Reinventing Islam in a World of Nation-States," *The Invention of Religion: Rethinking Belief in Politics and History*, eds. Derek R. Peterson and Darren R. Walhof, (New Brunswick: Rutgers, 2002), 120.

[85] Cleveland, *History of Modern Middle East*, 86.

[86] See chapter 6, "Official Nationalism and Imperialism," of Anderson, *Imagined Communities*, 83-112.

developmentalism' by Gelvin.[87] To be sure, other identifications were emphasized by the Ottoman state during the nineteenth and early twentieth centuries. Islamic identity was also promoted during the Hamidian period and Turkishness emphasized by the Committee of Union and Progress. However these other identifications were always intended to complement Ottomanism, which was promoted throughout the nineteenth century.

IX - The Changing Role of Religion in Palestine

With the state expanding its role into areas that had previously been seen as core competencies of the religious communities—such as in the provision of education and the adjudication of law—the influence of religious institutions in the social and political life of Ottoman Palestine became less pronounced. At the same time the promotion of alternative identifications to communal identity—such as in the promotion of Ottoman identity by the Ottoman state or Arabism by Arab intellectuals in Syria and Lebanon—meant that religious identity competed against other loyalties that made similar claims to universality.

The opening of schools, both by the government and to a lesser extent by Christian missionary groups, ended the virtual monopoly that the traditional religious authorities had over the provision of education. And, with the creation of jobs dependent upon modern secular training, particularly within the Ottoman administration, western-style education became an alternative and increasingly

---

[87] See chapter 5, "Defensive Developmentalism," in James Gelvin, *The Middle East: A History* (Oxford: Oxford University Press, 2005), 73-88.

preferred route to financial success and social advancement in Palestine, although this did not mean that religious education ceased to be important.

The shift towards secular education is reflected in Rashid Khalidi's account of the changing educational and career paths of his family in the nineteenth century. He presents al-Sayyid Muhammad 'Ali al-Khalidi (1781-1865) as a traditional member of the notable elite who had had a traditional religious education and had been subsequently appointed to a position in the religious elite as *rais al-kuttab wa na'ib* (chief secretary and deputy) to the qadi of the shari'a court in Jerusalem. On the other hand, his third son Yusuf Diya' al-Din Pasha al-Khalidi (1842-1906) represented a different generation that grew up during the *tanzimat* period, attended secular institutions and enjoyed an entirely different career path as educators, politicians, and diplomats. [88] Such a shift was evidenced in other notable families as well, such as the al-Husayni family, as the Arab notability increasingly found advancement in their position as administrators and employees of the Ottoman government.

This shift towards secular careers was also helped by a diminution in the power of religious appointment due to the codification of religious law and the limitation of shari'a law to personal status issues. The codification of Islamic law in modern times,

---

[88] The career of al-Sayyid Muhammad 'Ali al-Khalidi (1781-1865) represents that of the traditionally trained religious official. Installed as the *ra'is al-kuttab wa na'ib* (chief secretary and deputy) to the qadi of the shari'a court in Jerusalem in 1805, Muhammad 'Ali al-Khalidi continued his family's long tradition of religious appointment in Palestine (the position of chief secretary had been in the family since the late 19th century). Although some of his sons were trained as *ulama*, his third son Yusuf Diya' al-Din Pasha al-Khalidi, took a largely secular educational path, which took him to the Malta Protestant College and to the Imperial Medical College and Robert College in Istanbul. After this training Yusuf Diya' entered the life of politics, serving in the first Ottoman parliament, becoming a three-time mayor of Jerusalem, and working as an Ottoman diplomat, before settling down to an academic career. Khalidi, *Palestinian Identity*, 65-68.

beginning with the promulgation of the *Majalla*, meant that "a key dimension of interpretive authority passed from the hands of individual jurists, including muftis, to the collective bodies of national legislatures."[89] For qadis and muftis these reforms meant a loss in the scope of their power as their competency became limited almost exclusively to personal status matters, which the state still regarded as untouchable.

A final change came in the fact that the preeminent position of the Muslim community was challenged by changes in the religious life of Jerusalem and by Ottoman reforms that granted non-Muslims greater civil rights. The Islamic Arab character of Jerusalem was affected first of all by the arrival of greater numbers of Christian and Jewish pilgrims and settlers during the nineteenth century. This led to the construction of various new churches and hostels in and around Jerusalem with the consent of the Ottoman authorities, such as the massive Russian compound (Moscovia) outside the Old City. At the same time, the Ottomans relaxed their control over religious sites in and around Jerusalem. Admission to the Church of the Holy Sepulchre, for example, was made more accessible in the late nineteenth century by the removal of a large stone barrier at its entrance, which had been used to control access to the site.[90] The visit of European Christians to the Haram al-Sharif was also permitted for the first time. The nineteenth century also saw greater Ottoman recognition of the Jewish presence in and around Jerusalem. In 1842, the local Sephardic community was recognized when Rabbi Abraham Hayyim Gagin received an *irade* (a Sultanic decree) acknowledging him as the first *hakham bashi* (Chief

---

[89] Masud, "Muftis, Fatwas, and Interpretation," 27.

[90] Shepherd, *Zealous Intruders*, 122.

Rabbi) of Palestine.[91] Jewish immigration was also permitted (with some

reservations) to Palestine during the late-Ottoman period.[92]

These changes were also influenced by religious reforms that granted non-

Muslim communities greater rights. Reforms such as the Hatt-i Sharif (Hatt-ı Şerif) of

Gülhane and the Hatt-ı Hümayun granted the millet's religious equality and promised

freedom of religion throughout the empire. Jews and Christians were also given more

opportunities to serve in Ottoman government. This translated into changes on the

local level. For instance, in Jerusalem from the 1850s onwards, Muslims were forced

to make public redress for insulting Jews.[93] These policies were certainly a response

to European calls for Ottoman reform but must also be seen as part of a transformation

in the way in which the empire approached religious matters. Over the course of the

nineteenth century sub-state identities, such as religious identity, became less

important as an Ottoman identity was promoted as part of the state's centralizing

reforms.

X- Conclusion

It is important that we do not overstate this transformation in the role of religion.

While the modernizing and centralizing reforms of the nineteenth century tended to

---

[91] Richard Goethil et al., "Jerusalem," *Jewish Encyclopedia,* eds. Isidore Singer, Cyrus Adler, et al. (New York: Funk and Wagnells, 1906) <http://www.jewishencyclopedia.com/view.jsp?artid=242&letter=J>

[92] The first Aliyah is conventionally dated from 1882 to 1903 and mostly involved the immigration of members of the Bilu and Lovers of Zion movements from Russia. The second Aliyah occurred from 1904-1914 and was in part a reaction to pogroms and anti-Semitism in the Russian empire. During this time around 75,000 Jews immigrated to Palestine.

[93] Shepherd, *Zealous Intruders,* 121.

secularize the Ottoman empire, they did not turn the empire into a secular polity, nor were they intended to. Compared to British India—where Anglo-Mohammedan law replaced the shari'a—or the secular Turkish state of Ataturk—which would aggressively turn its back on the Ottoman Islamic heritage—the reformers of the Ottoman state did not aim to remove the power of the ulama and the shari'a from society. Though inspired by European ideas, Ottoman reforms were not intended to westernize the empire but protect it.

This meant that religious office retained some of its importance despite the emergence of new secular positions of authority in society. The aforementioned Yusuf al-Din al-Khalidi may have broken away from the family tradition of religious service but his brothers still trained and served as ulama. It would be wrong therefore to view the notability's embrace of secular service as some kind of rejection of their traditional role as members of the religious elite. Instead we might see this shift as a diversification of the "politics of notables," by an educated elite that was adjusting to the new demands of the Ottoman state. Moreover, religious and secular training could be combined in a single career. This was shown by the education of Muhammad Amin al-Husayni, better known as Hajj Amin al-Husayni, the mufti of Jerusalem for much of the British period, who attended both the venerable Muslim institution of al-Azhar University and the modern Military Academy in Istanbul.[94]

What this chapter has argued is that the role of religion in society had changed because of the growth of the Ottoman state. In discussing the emergence of

---

[94] Mattar, *Mufti of Jerusalem*, 8-10.

Palestinian nationalism as the dominant identification among Palestinian Arabs in mandatory Palestine Rashid Khalidi points to the waning influence of other identifications. "The Ottoman Empire had disappeared, the importance of religion in public life *had declined somewhat*, Arab nationalism and its association with Syria has suffered defeats at the hands of the French…All these changes intensified and transformed the preexisting identification with Palestine."[95] Khalidi offers little evidence to back up his statement that religion's role in public life had declined, but his statement is accurate in describing the impact of the reforms of the late-Ottoman period. In short, when the British arrived they found a situation in which religion's institutional power and influence in wider society had been deemphasized by the government's modernization of society.

But what did the British understand of the place of Islam in Palestine? The proliferation of reports about local traditions indicates that the British were interested in understanding the local situation directly. It is perhaps telling however that the most important text that British officials used to understand the Ottoman past was George Young's *Corps de Droits Ottomans*, a compendium of select regulations from the Ottoman law code that was published in 1905. The book's utility for colonial administration was recognized in by D. G. Hogarth, the archaeologist and Oxford Don who headed the famous Arab Bureau in Cairo during WWI, who argued in a book review that "To discover the actual state of Ottoman law on points vitally affecting themselves has long been the despair of men of affairs in Turkey, and to trace the

---

[95] Khalidi, *Palestinian Identity*, 19. Emphasis added.

genesis of existing Ottoman usage has been no easier for historical students. Mr. Young's book will be of inestimable service to both."[96]

It is likely that the book traveled to Palestine with officials who served in Egypt, such as Ronald Storrs, Gilbert Clayton, and G. S. Symes (who served under Hogarth at the Arab Bureau). We know for certain that some "additional" 20 copies were sent from the Colonial Office to Palestine in 1922 at the urging of Hogarth, where it was soon used by the British high commissioner to resolve religious questions pertaining to conversion and the affairs of the Armenian Patriarchate in Jerusalem.[97] The value of Young's work for British administrators came in its presentation of Ottoman law as a concrete set of precedents and principles, which could be picked up, examined, and used by colonial legislators. But while Young's text cut through the messiness and complexity of Ottoman law it failed to account for the gap between the promulgation and application of law which led to local differences in the practice of Ottoman law across the empire.

Young's text and by extension the British understanding of Ottoman law was also out of date. As this chapter has pointed out that the place of religion was shifting under the modernizing and secularizing reforms of the Ottoman state. This project to secularize Ottoman law was shown most clearly in the revolutionary Ottoman Law of Family Rights, which was promulgated by the CUP in 1917. This law codified two

---

[96] D. G. Hogarth, "*Corps de Droits Ottomans* par George Young," *The English Historical Review*, Vol. 21, No. 81 (Jan., 1906), 186.

[97] See High Commissioner to Churchill, April 12, 1922, ISA, High Commisioner's Files, Record Group 1, 573/6/231. Herbert Samuel made reference to "Young" in order to understand how the Armenian Patriarchate was treated in Ottoman law and how the Ottomans handled religious conversion. See PRO CO 733/5/CO44266 and CO 733/63.

major areas of personal status—marriage and divorce—and was designed to make the last area of independent *shari'a* authority subject to government oversight. The legislation would have also ended the autonomy of the millet system by making the *shari'a* courts national courts of personal status.[98] As Robert Eisenman has pointed out the law effectively made *shari'a* courts throughout the empire an extension of the Ottoman state structure.[99] As such the law followed the direction of tanzimat reform, which as Michael Dumper has put it, "converted the waqf system from a collection of independent and overlapping charitable institutions into an embryonic social welfare arm of a government bureaucracy."[100] Though this reform may not yet been applied in Palestine before the British arrival—no doubt due to the difficulty of quickly instituting bureaucratic changes across a vast empire—it indicated the direction in which Ottoman law was trending in the country.

What did the British conquest of Palestine mean for a religious system that was predicated upon Ottoman control? Would the British continue Ottoman reforms that worked to extend the reach of the central state and circumscribe the powers of non-state actors, such as Muslim authorities? Would British rule bring about a full-scale secularization of law and politics as part of a civilizing mission? Another possibility lay in the amalgamation of local practice and British legal traditions as in the Anglo-Muhammadan law of India. Or would the British simply preserve what they saw as

---

[98] Robert Eisenman, "The Young Turk Legislation, 1913-17 and Its Application in Palestine/Israel," *Palestine in the Late Ottoman Period: Political, Social, and Economic Transformation*, ed. David Kushner (Jerusalem: Yad Izhak Ben-Zvi Press, 1986).

[99] Eisenman, "Young Turk Legislation," 64.

[100] Michael Dumper, *Islam and Israel: Muslim Religious Endowments and the Jewish State* (Washington DC.: Institute of Palestine Studies, 1994), 8.

Ottoman "traditions"? British officials, using Young's 1905 account of Ottoman law, chose the last option, by emphasizing the significance of "traditional" religious precedents, such as the millet system and the status quo. As a consequence British officials preserved an Ottoman system that was already out of date when they arrived.

As the next chapter reveals specific values and fears within the British colonial administration made further secularization of Palestinian society undesirable, leaving the Palestine government to pursue an approach that aimed at returning to what they saw as being the fundamentals of the Ottoman system (e.g. the millet system and the Ottoman concept of the status quo). This conservative approach meant that British Palestine would end up being more "traditional" than most of the other states that emerged out of the Ottoman empire. But, as we shall see in the next chapter, the preservation of these traditions created a new form of Islam that carried a strong British imprint.

Chapter Three

Building a System

I - Introduction

On December 11th 1917 General Edmund Allenby delivered the first official speech of

the British occupation. Laying out the terms of martial law, Allenby assured the

assembled crowd that Britain would respect local religious customs:

> To the inhabitants of Jerusalem the Blessed and the people
> dwelling in the vicinity. The defeat inflicted upon the Turks by the
> troops under my command has resulted in the occupation of your city
> by my forces. I therefore here and now proclaim it to be under martial
> law, under which form of administration it will remain so long as
> military considerations make it necessary. However, lest anyone of
> you be alarmed by reason of your experience at the hands of the enemy
> who has retired, I hereby inform you that it is my desire that every
> person should pursue his lawful business without fear of interruption.
> Furthermore, since your City is regarded with affection by the
> adherents of three of the great religions of mankind, and its soil has
> been consecrated by the prayers and pilgrimages of multitudes of
> devout people of these three religions for many centuries, therefore do I
> make know to you that every sacred building, monument, holy spot,
> shrine, traditional site, endowment, pious bequest, or customary place
> of prayer, of whatsoever form of the three religions, will be maintained
> and protected according to the existing customs and beliefs of those to
> whose faiths they are sacred.[1]

The reaction of Jerusalem's inhabitants to the British conquest was generally

positive. Wasif Jawhariyya, a Christian Arab musician whose memoirs cover the

Ottoman and mandatory periods in Jerusalem, recalled that the Arab population

---

[1] See Henry Kendall, *Jerusalem, the City Plan: Preservation and Development during the British Mandate 1918-1948* (London: His Majesty's Stationary Office, 1948), 4. The official name of the proclamation was the "Proclamation of Martial Law in Jerusalem," which was first promulgated on December 9, 1918. See Great Britain, *Proclamations, Ordinances, and Notices Issued by O.E.T.A. (South) to August 1919* (Cairo: Printed by Oriental Advertising Company, 1920), 35.

143

joyfully danced in the streets, Jews greeted the arrival of British troops with hugs, and Christians rang church bells across the city in appreciation.[2] With a population suffering under the effects of starvation, a typhus outbreak, an unemployment rate as high as 90%, and an influx of refugees, it was no surprise that the arrival of the British soldiers, nurses, and grain supplies from Egypt was met with joy.[3] Of course this positive response, at least on the part of the majority Arab population, was also helped by their ignorance of Britain's commitment to the Jewish national home.[4]

In contrast, Allenby's speech got a mixed reception. The city's Protestant population was naturally excited by the arrival of their coreligionists. Bertie Spafford Vester, an American Evangelical Protestant, wrote an ecstatic account of Allenby's arrival in Jerusalem, describing it as "one of the great events of history."[5] For Vester, Allenby was the conquering Christian general who had finally returned the holy city to its rightful Christian owners.[6] For other groups the British conquest was unsettling. Allenby's carefully choreographed entrance on foot "as a pilgrim" (as Vester put it in her memoirs) played well with his Western audience, but his entrance was seen in a

---

[2] Jawhariyya describes how the population of Jerusalem greeted the arrival of the British as a blessing after the difficulties of the war, pointing out that both Christian and Muslim Arabs were happy with the British arrival. He explains to the reader that he and his friends danced in the streets and drank to the occupation, oblivious to the future cost of occupation for the Arab community. He witnessed Jewish women greeting the conquering British troops with real passion (*yastukblnahu bi-haraarat za'idat*) and hearing church bells ringing out across the city in appreciation. Jawhariyya, *Muthakirat*, 276.

[3] Bayan Nuwayhed al-Hout, *Al-Qiyadat wa al-Mou'assassat al-Siasiyyah fi Filastin 1917-1948* [The Leadership and the Political Organizations in Palestine 1917-1948], (Beirut: Institute for Palestine Studies, 1981), 78.

[4] Jawhariyya, *Muthakirat*, 276.

[5] Bertie Spafford Vester, *Our Jerusalem: An American Family in the Holy Land 1881-1949* (Jerusalem: Ariel Publishing House/American Colony: 1988), 280.

[6] Vester was a member of the American Colony, a neighborhood north of the Old City of Jerusalem, which was settled in the late-1800s by a group of pious Protestants from the United States and Sweden.

different light by local Muslims.[7] While Jawhariyya described Arabs as dancing in the streets, he also noted that this euphoria was quickly tempered by apprehension about the impact of Christian rule. As we might expect the crusader language did not play well with this audience. According to Jawhariyya some of Jerusalem's Muslim leaders left angrily during Allenby's speech when the Major-General referred to the conquest as the end of the crusades.[8]

Even more serious were criticisms of the British occupation that came from foreign groups. The Foreign Office received from Christian, Muslim, and Jewish groups from around the world searching for reassurance about Britain's intentions in Palestine. These were an immediate irritation for British policymakers who had hoped to quickly integrate Palestine into the empire but instead found themselves worrying that European religious competition over Jerusalem would persist under British rule. They also worried about the opposition of Muslim groups to the British takeover, particularly Indian Muslim groups, which British officials feared could be used to unsettle the Muslim subjects of the British empire.

---

[7] Allenby entered Jerusalem through Jaffa Gate on foot, in deliberate contrast to the ostentatious entrance of Kaiser Wilhelm II on horseback in 1898, which had necessitated the opening up of a gap in the city walls. For Vester, Wilhelm's entrance was artificial, "The Emperor was not only an artist in his choice of his costume to impress his oriental audience, but also actor", whereas Allenby's entrance was authentic because it was the entrance of the pilgrim. This favorable comparison of Allenby's entrance was often made in British press reports and completely ignores the fact that the British procession into the city was also highly choreographed. Vester, *Our Jerusalem*, 279.

[8] It is difficult to make sense of the contradiction between Allenby's reference to the crusades and the overall purpose of his speech, which was to reassure the local population that the conquest had nothing to do with religion. It is possible that Allenby mentioned this point in order to indicate that the enmity between the two religions was over. It should also be noted that Jawayariyya's account is not completely straightforward as it refers to the speech "as alluding to" or "pointing to" (*ishaaru*) the end of the crusades. This raises the possibility that it wasn't the words of the speech but the spectacle of a Christian giving a conqueror's speech that raised the connection to the crusades. Jawhariyya, *Muthakiraat*, 280.

In response to these criticisms, the British forces realized that they had to develop a policy towards religion that would both reassure the local population and ensure that religious matters were handled locally. This approach involved transforming Allenby's vague commitment to "protecting" religious rights in Palestine into a distinct policy of the colonial government. This chapter discusses the three elements that made up this approach; 1) the creation of the notion of a "status quo ante" that had to be protected; 2) the postponement of religious questions (such as communal rights at shared holy sites) that undermined the notion of the status quo; and 3) the recognition of local religious bodies to run traditional religious institutions. This approach was not developed out of a single well-defined policy but was an *ad hoc* set of responses to local and international pressures. Nevertheless, this approach produced the religious structures that would determine the Palestine Government's relationship with local religion for the remainder of the British mandate.

II - The Nature of Imperial Rule in Palestine

When describing British rule in Palestine it is important to place the colony within the context of empire. Palestine was not a major prize in the British empire. Economically it offered Britain little of value; lacking significant natural resources or major commercial markets, the country would never play a significant role on the imperial balance sheet. And even though Palestine was important to the defense of the Suez Canal—the country ended up being of secondary importance to British post-war strategy. The base of British power in the Middle East until the dissolution of empire

146

was Egypt, and other places like Aden, Iraq, and Cyprus had more strategic importance than Palestine.

It was for these reasons that, while it could be said that the "east was a career," service in Palestine represented a rather minor posting for the colonial servant. The economic austerity of the British empire in the wake of the First World War also meant that the new colony did not receive much financial help from the British government. As the geographer Gideon Biger has put it, after the First World War the British employed the "Cromer system," which "emphasized the importance of low taxation, efficient fiscal administration, careful expenditure on remunerative public work, and a minimal interference in the internal and external traffic of goods."[9] Furthermore the "traditionally parsimonious attitudes of the British metropolis toward colonial finances were, when not influenced by international legal considerations, further reinforced," according to Barbara Smith, "by the argument that the ill-tempered British taxpayer could not be expected to bear the burden of supporting the emergent Jewish National Home in Palestine."[10] Indeed, the government of Palestine was expected throughout the mandate to produce a budget that made sure that the country would not be a drain on the imperial coffers and led the first high commissioner to reassure the British population that Palestine was self-supporting.[11]

---

[9] Gideon Biger *An Empire in the Holy Land: Historical Geography of the British Administration in Palestine: 1917-1929* (New York: St. Martin's Press, 1994), 20.

[10] Barbara Smith, *Roots of Separatism*, 6.

[11] It is for this reason that High Commissioner Herbert Samuel assured the British taxpayer in 1924 that "all that has been accomplished by the Government of Palestine has been done with its own resources. Great Britain has paid nothing towards the cost of civil administration." The quote came from the high commissioner's introduction to a handbook that accompanied Palestine's display at the British Empire

This parsimony led to a lack of investment in the local economy, the

educational system, and Palestine's infrastructure that is a familiar theme in accounts

of the mandate period.[12] It also contributed to an emphasis on tradition over

modernization. In education this was shown in the privileging of agricultural training

over western-style learning in government schools that trained Arabs.[13] In urban

planning this led to the adoption of policies that preserved the historical aspects of the

Old City, often by stripping away modern development.[14] And in politics it led British

officials to partner with the older generation of the notability as opposed to the

western-educated and nationalistic younger generation. In short, despite the duty of

the mandatory to help the occupied country to modernize and British claims to be

bringing development to Palestine, British rule was not driven by a civilizing mission.

The "defense of the past" was a far more potent consideration in colonial rule.

Exhibition of 1924. See Palestine Pavilion Organizing Committee, *Palestine Pavilion Handbook and Tourist Guide* (London: Fleetway Press, 1924), 21.

For more information about the Palestine pavilion at the exhibition see Nicholas E. Roberts, "Palestine on Display: the Palestine Pavilion at the British Empire Exhibition of 1924," *Arab Studies Journal*, Vol. 15, No. 1 (Spring 2007): 70-99.

[12] Besides Smith's and Biger's accounts of Palestine's economic development the reader is directed to Ylana Miller, *Government and Society in Rural Palestine 1920-1948* (Austin: University of Texas, 1985) and Warwick Tyler, *State Lands and Rural Development in Mandatory Palestine, 1920-1948* (Brighton: Sussex Academic Press, 2001).

[13] This emphasis on agricultural or vocational training was not unique to Palestine and was also seen in British Egypt and India.

[14] For instance, a major project of the Pro-Jerusalem Society, a semi-private British-run preservation and urban planning society, was the preservation of the walls of the Old City and the creation of a "Rampart Walk" along the top of the wall (much of which exists today). In a number of places this involved the stripping away of local businesses and structures that abutted the wall. Another project involved the removal of local markets from the Old City because commerce was not seen to be appropriate to the Old City. See *Jerusalem 1918-1920: Being the Records of the Pro-Jerusalem Council.*

III - Outside Pressures

It is often forgotten that the conquest of Palestine was not originally intended to lead to British rule. In the Sykes-Picot Agreement of 1916, most of the territory that became mandatory Palestine was designated to be ruled as an allied condominium under British, French, and Russian rule.[15] With Russia's withdrawal from the war, the terms of the agreement were made obsolete, but France still retained an interest in Palestine. This was not completely forgotten by the conquering British forces, which recognized the contributions that France (and Italy to a lesser extent) played in the Middle East campaigns by having representatives of the French and Italian military flank Allenby at the opening ceremony of occupation.

Nevertheless, the British conquest of the country and the introduction of the Egyptian pound as the currency of Palestine soon aroused French suspicions about Britain's long-term intentions. In response the Quai d'Orsay, as Margaret MacMillan mentions in her excellent account of the Paris peace negotiations, warned that the French could not accept that "France be deprived of benefits which were rightfully hers by those who diverted their troops at the crucial moment."[16] François Georges-Picot (he of the Sykes-Picot agreement) was also quickly dispatched to Palestine to assert France's role as protector of the country's Roman Catholic population. He did this by presenting himself as the legitimate representative of the Holy See at the local

---

[15] This arrangement was intended to respect the competing religious claims of the three major allied powers in Palestine and most specifically in Jerusalem. The only area of the country that was separated from this agreement was the region around Haifa and Acre, which was intended to have been under complete British control.

[16] Margaret MacMillan, *Paris 1919: Six Months that Changed the World* (New York: Random House, 2003), 385.

Lent and Easter ceremonies, and by pushing for the right of French troops to guard

local Catholic sites, much to the consternation of other Catholic groups and to the

annoyance of British officials.[17]

The French were right to suspect British intentions. Even before the war ended

British policymakers drew up plans to limit French ambitions in the Arab provinces of

the Ottoman empire.[18] And immediately after the war, The Eastern Committee of the

War Cabinet under Lord Curzon, set about burying the Sykes-Picot agreement so that

Palestine would remain in British hands and the Suez Canal remain protected.[19]

British officers in Palestine looked upon Picot's actions with a mixture of

amusement and irritation. The Reverend P. N. Waggett, a clergyman and major in the

British army who was an expert on local Christianity, saw Picot's assertion of French

rights as a simple continuation of the nineteenth- century European competition in

Jerusalem.[20] But others saw Picot's presence in the country as a dangerous challenge

to Britain's position. The British presence in Palestine had opened up the possibility

---

[17] See French Ambassador to FO, March 1918, FO 371/3389/56069 and French Ambassador to FO, March 28, 1918 FO 371/3389/56084.

[18] MacMillan notes of a colleague of Sykes who drew up a plan to "clear out" the French from the entire Arab region except the Lebanon, in exchange for control over Kurdish and Armenian territories. Macmillan, *Paris 1919*, 384.

[19] The primary motivation here was the defense of the Suez Canal. It is important to note however that not all officials regarded this approach as necessary. MacMillan quotes Balfour, who argued that "Everytime I come to a discussion—at intervals of, say, five years—I find there is a new sphere of which we have got to guard, which is supposed to protect the gateways of India. Those gateways are getting further and further from India, and I do not know how far west they are going to be brought by the General Staff." MacMillan, *Paris 1919*, 385.

[20] See FO 371/4164/89849, FO 371/4164/67183, and FO 371/4164/101480. Waggett would become the first British official to suggest that an international religious commission should be set up to deal with unresolved religious questions. He also was a defender of the British approach to religion in the army produced paper, *The Palestine News*. See *Palestine News*, March 6, 1919.

for Europeans to rewrite the rules of the game, and it appeared that France was eager

to play a part in this rewriting.

The Zionist Organization was also interested in taking advantage of the

moment and within months of the occupation tried to secure ownership of the Western

Wall, the holiest religious site in Judaism. In May 1918, its president Chaim

Weizmann wrote a letter to Balfour advocating that the wall and its surrounding

neighborhood be taken over by the Jewish community:

> We Jews have many holy places in Palestine, but the Wailing Wall—
> believed to be a part of the old Temple Wall—is the only one which is
> in some sense left to us. All the others are in the hands of Christians or
> Moslems, and even the Wailing Wall is not really ours. It is
> surrounded by a group of miserable, dirty cottages and derelict
> buildings, which makes the whole place from the hygienic point of
> view a source of constant humiliation to the Jews of the world. Our
> most sacred monument, in our most sacred city, is in the hands of some
> doubtful Moghreb religious community, which keeps these cottages as
> a source of income. We are willing to compensate this community very
> liberally, but we should like the place to be cleaned up; we should like
> to give it a dignified and respectable appearance.[21]

Attempts to purchase the wall had been made by Jews before the First World War but

Weizmann's attempt was far more significant because of the Balfour Declaration.[22]

By arguing that "our most sacred monument" needed to be purchased so that it could

---

[21] Weizmann to Balfour, May 30, 1918. CZA L3/310.

The Zionist argument was based upon the notion that the Wall was a Jewish site that had been and was still being encroached upon by local (Muslim) development, a concept that would lead ultimately to the erasure of the Maghrebi neighborhood in 1967. Rabbi Kook, the Chief Rabbi, for instance, argued that the Temple Mount was "bound in the end to revert to us" and called upon the Government to entrust the Wall to the protection of the Jewish community. See the Palin Report (the unpublished British account of the April 1920 riots) in PRO WO 32/9614.

[22] Yehoshua Porath states that Nissim Bechar and Baron Edmond de Rothschild had attempted to purchase the wall before the First World War. Porath, *Emergence*, 258, 259.

be preserved, he appealed both to Allenby's speech which pledged that the British

forces would preserve and maintain religious sites and the declaration's commitment

to the Jewish national home. In doing so, Weizmann's argument that the Jews were

owed the site was quite different from the deferential approach of Edmund de

Rothschild, who had tried to purchase the wall from the Ottoman authorities. Like the

French, Zionist leaders like Chaim Weizmann believed strongly that "to the victor

belong the spoils."

Other outside groups sent letters to the British government requesting

confirmation that their religious rights would be protected under British rule. The

Vatican sent letters to the Foreign Office asking that Catholic rights be protected under

the new Protestant government.[23] Its chief concern was that British rule would lead to

a revision of the religious hierarchy that had operated under the Ottomans, which was

understandable given the British government's strong working relationship with the

local Protestant church during the mid-nineteenth century (discussed in chapter two).

The Muslim position also had a champion in the form of the All India Muslim League

whose petitions on behalf of Islamic rights in Palestine were forwarded to the Foreign

Office by the Indian Viceroy.[24] Like the Vatican, the All India Muslim League

viewed the British takeover with suspicion and called for the imperial power to respect

past religious precedent. At the same time, diasporic groups of Palestinians and

---

[23] The Vatican was especially concerned about the proposal in the early 1920s for an international commission on holy places (discussed later in this chapter), which led to a series of critical letters on the British proposal to open a religious Pandora's box. Even before this proposal the Vatican was concerned about what British rule meant for Catholic rights, which led Herbert Samuel to reassure the Pope about British intentions in his meeting with the Pope. See

[24] FO 371/4164/20404 and FO 371/4164/23796.

Syrians—with names such as "Union Sirio de Torreon, Coah, Mexico," and the "Colonia Palestina Residente en la Republica de El Salvador"—expressed their opposition to the creation of the Jewish National Home and called for Palestine to be joined to Arab-ruled Syria.[25]

IV – Facing Criticism

The British response to these foreign groups was to deal with them individually. Petitions from Palestinian groups outside the country were ignored because these groups lacked political power, but other petitions were handled with some care given the political influence of the petitioners.

A particular concern early on was with the Catholic powers. The Pope's fears about British rule were taken seriously by the Palestine Government, not because of the Vatican's direct influence in Palestine but because of his influence on Catholic world opinion. In response to the Pope's concerns, Herbert Samuel made a special visit to the Vatican a week before his appointment as high commissioner. It was hoped that Samuel's mission would persuade the Pope to give his blessing to the

---

[25] Petitions and letters from Palestinian communities in the West (mostly from South America) are found in the records of the Foreign Office, evidence of the strong interest that Palestinians abroad retained in their homeland. These groups have not been studied by scholars, but it would appear that they represented small Palestinian social clubs and political societies formed in some of the major cities of the Western Hemisphere. See PRO FO 570/10/114 and *Watha'iq al-harakah al-wataniyah al-Filastiniyah 1918-1939: min awraq Akram Za'itar* [Documents of the Palestinian Nationalist Movement 1918-1939 from the Papers of Akram Za'itar], ed.Bayan Nawhid al-Hut (Beirut: Mua'ssasat Ad-Dirasat Al-Filistiniyah, 1979), 8-11.

British occupation, and while he failed to achieve this objective, Samuel visit seemed to have reassured the Pope about Britain's intentions.[26]

French claims had to be handled more delicately because of the 1916 Sykes-Picot agreement. The French had expected to play a large role in the administration of the country because of this agreement and their traditional role as protectors of the Catholic community. This expectation was strengthened when French troops were permitted to work alongside their British counterparts in guarding holy sites in the early days of the occupation.[27] But British officials and politicians had no intention of sharing the country with any other power. As early as April 1917, Prime Minister David Lloyd George had argued that Britain alone had a historic role to play in Palestine because Britain was "of no particular faith and the only Power fit to rule Mohammedans, Jews, Roman Catholics and all religions."[28] After the war he was even more convinced that Britain alone should rule Palestine, as he crudely explained in an angry exchange during the Paris Peace Conference of 1919:

> Except for Great Britain no one had contributed anything more than a handful of black troops to the expedition in Palestine…The British had captured three or four Turkish armies and had incurred hundreds of thousands of casualties in the war with Turkey. The other

---

[26] This meeting is recounted in Samuel to Curzon, June 26, 1920, ISA, Record Group 100, 649/6. Later correspondence reveals that the Vatican remained suspicious of British intentions towards religion into the 1920s (especially a plan for setting up an international commission on religious affairs), necessitating further diplomatic meetings between British and Vatican representatives. See PRO CO 733/33/47428, CO 733/33/48659, CO 733/33/49851, CO 733/33/55907, CO 733/55/2168, FO 371/6389/E5879, and FO 371/6389/E7124.

[27] Indeed the British requested French help in keeping the peace between the various Christian sects. Lord Hardinge to Lord Balfour, January 29, 1918, PRO FO 371/3388/18170.

[28] See Wasserstein, *British in Palestine*, 9. The quote originally comes from the Diary of Lord Bertie of Thame, who was the British Ambassador in Paris to which Lloyd George made the comment, and was first published in Leonard Stein, *The Balfour Declaration* (London: 1961), 335 and 628.

Governments had only put in a few nigger policemen to see that we did
not steal the Holy Sepulchre![29]

London's determination to keep Palestine led officials to quickly undermine the

French position in the country. While French troops were permitted at first to guard

religious sites, they were only allowed to guard Catholic sites and were expressly

prohibited from guarding the *Haram al-Sharif*, the most prominent of Palestine's

religious sites.[30] And while French and other Catholic allied troops were allowed to

celebrate mass in Palestine's churches, Picot was denied the right to represent the

Catholic community at local religious celebrations and was deliberately kept at arms'

length by the British authorities, much to his consternation.[31]

British officials were more receptive to Weizmann's attempt to gain control

over the Western Wall and briefly considered his plan as will be discussed in greater

detail in chapter six. But Weizmann's plan met with strong protest from the local

Arab population, who accurately saw it as a crude attempt to drive out the local Arab

population and (with less evidence) claimed the purchase was the first step in a Jewish

takeover of the *Haram al-Sharif*. The strength of this response led British officials to

back away from their initial support and remind Weizmann of Allenby's pledge to

support existing rights in the holy city. This was an early sign that when it came to

---

[29] As quoted in MacMillan, *Paris 1919*, 374.

[30] The British argued that it was only fair to keep the French out, since the Italians were also not given a role. Italian troops were not considered acceptable as guards for the *Haram al-Sharif* since they did not have any Muslim soldiers. The British used Indian Muslims to guard the site. The guarding of Palestine's holy sites is discussed further in chapter six.

[31] Correspondence between London and Jerusalem indicates that the presence of French and Italian troops was problematic for officials that were not in the habit of sharing political power with rival countries. PRO FO 371/3389/62090, FO 371/3389/82166, FO 371/3389/52712, FO 371/3389/62090.

religious and cultural matters, a "protection of religious tradition" approach would be adopted.

V – Responding to Muslims

While the petitions of foreign Palestinian clubs were brushed aside by British officials, those of The All India Muslim League were taken seriously. This was due to the fact that officials in London and India worried that the Palestine question could be used by Indian Muslims to create nationalist trouble in India. This would be a persistent fear in the early years of the mandate period, leading in 1920 to the creation of a joint intelligence operation between the intelligence departments of the Indian and Palestine governments to monitor contacts between Indian and Palestinian Muslim officials.[32]

Another factor in British concern about Muslim opinion was their fear of what was called the "Pan-Islamic Movement," an amorphous term that was used to refer to various groups that seemed to use Islam in politics. In January 1919, the Foreign Office produced a pamphlet for British planners that offered a history of the "movement" from Jamal al-Din al-Afghani through Muhammad Abduh to the caliphal pretensions of the Ottoman Sultan.[33] At the same time the pamphlet provided examples of Pan-Islamist propaganda from across the world. The objective was to

---

[32] This joint effort was suggested by the Director of Public Security P. Bramley in September 1920 in reaction to what he saw as "steadily increasing liaison between Syrian-Turkish and Indian Pan-Islamic propaganda," which was starting to affect Palestine. He argued that one British officer and one Indian officer be deputized to the Palestine Civil Intelligence Department. In November of that year the Viceroy in India consented to send over Captain Abdul Samad Shah. See Bramley to Deedes, September 16, 1920, Deedes to Curzon, October 6, 1920, and Viceroy to Deedes, November 1920 all in ISA Record Group 2, 5/163/78/CID/S.

[33] This handbook was made up of two parts, the first entitled "The Rise of Islam and the Caliphate," and the second part, "The Pan-Islamic Movement." See PRO FO 373/5/6.

indicate how Muslim politics, particularly the Salafism of al-Afghani, Abduh, and Rashid Rida, could work against British interests, particularly when combined with Muslim state policy, such as in the late-Ottoman empire.

This interest in pan-Islamism continued into the early 1920s. Both the military and civilian authorities in Palestine were sent infrequent reports about Muslim political movements from as far afield as Afghanistan and the Dutch Indies.[34] These reports investigated the spread across the Muslim world of what one correspondent called a "political contagion," and served as a warning for what might occur in Palestine.[35] It is important to note that "Pan-Islam" was not conceived by British officials as the use of Islam as a political ideology, what scholars refer to today as Islamism, but was seen as the use of Islamic language to further the preexisting political agendas of those who opposed Britain, such as the French, the Sharifians, and the Turkish Caliph. This view played upon a stereotype that uneducated Muslims were prone to fanaticism and could easily be incited by cynical preachers or *agents provocateur* to support various movements, so long as they felt that Islam was under attack. As such, it would probably have been more appropriate to label Pan-Islam a

---

[34] These materials were collected in a file entitled "Councils, Committees, Societies, etc. Pan-Islamic Movement," which was part of the records of the Civil Secretary (later called the Chief Secretary). See ISA, Record Group 2, 5/163. This file also contains information about the potential for the Pan-Islamic movement to succeed in Palestine, which was discounted by local observers. One of the reasons that information about foreign Pan-Islamic movements were sent to Palestine was the fact that some of these groups mentioned the Balfour Declaration and the supposed threat of British rule to the *Haram al-Sharif* in their propaganda.

[35] The description comes from a secret report on the activities of the Sharikat Islam movement in Indonesia that was sent to Palestine by the Foreign Office along with other materials on Pan-Islam around the world. See ISA, Record Group 2, 5/163/ E6024/1942/44.

phenomenon rather than a movement, which implied a level of coordination of action and ideology that simply didn't exist between these different groups.

British concern with Pan-Islamism in Palestine was strong at certain moments—after the riots of the Nabi Musa festival of 1920, during the khutba scare of the same year, and during the mufti of Jerusalem's appeal to the Muslim world in the mid-1920s for financial and moral support—but for the most part Pan-Islam wasn't regarded as much of a threat. In 1923, Gilbert Clayton, the civil secretary of Palestine, argued to his superiors in London that British intelligence reports gave

> rather undue emphasis to the extent and intensity both of pro-Turkish
> and Pan Islamic propaganda in Palestine and are inclined to treat these
> influences as the driving power of the situation here. In my opinion it
> is the local political issue which really appeals to the people of
> Palestine but Pan Islamic and pro-Turkish agents are doubtless quick to
> seize any opportunity of turning any local agitation or discontent to
> their own purposes.[36]

R. V. Vernon in the Foreign Office agreed with Clayton and observed that "the "pan-Islamic peril" seems to me as much liable to exaggeration as the "Soviet menace", which is the favourite bogey over here."[37] Even the 1919 Foreign Office pamphlet, which had sounded the warning about the Pan-Islamic movement, downplayed its cohesiveness and effectiveness, though this had not stopped some officials from warning about Pan-Islam's power.[38]

---

[36] Gilbert Clayton to H. W. Young, October 5, 1923, PRO CO 537/859.

[37] Minute from Vernon, Ibid.

[38] The handbook cites the argument of one unnamed 'Oriental writer' that Pan-Islam was "a phantasm abstracted from the Moslem profession of religious fraternity magnified by the European imagination," and the view of another unnamed authority that, "the notion of a Pan-Islamic movement was an invention of European politicians, whose purpose was to excite animosity against the Muslims and so

But even if the movement was more apparent than real the latter part of Clayton's statement was worrying for British officials. The fact that religious issues could be picked up by local groups and used against the British meant that religious petitions could not simply be disregarded. This was especially the case when religious arguments were made by well organized nationalist groups such as the All India Muslim League, which used the issue of Britain's takeover of Jerusalem to criticize the empire's policy towards Muslims. As a result the All India Muslim League was reassured by the Palestine government that existing Muslim rights would be respected. This assurance was also given to Palestinian Muslim leaders who, while they were not organized or nationalistic at this time, could disrupt the British attempt to rebuild Palestine.

VI – Defending Religious Tradition

The different responses were all stop-gap measures that were used to blunt criticism about British policy and buy some time for the military authorities to establish their administration. In order to head off future criticism a more coherent policy had to be adopted. Building on Allenby's pledge to protect existing rights officials, officials came to reemphasize the idea that British rule was justified by its "defense of religious tradition." This was encapsulated in the concept of upholding the "status quo ante

---

justify fresh attempts against such independence as any of them still possessed." "The Pan-Islamic Movement," FO 373/5/6, pg. 64.

The authors of the handbook do not endorse these arguments but include them to suggest that some of the specter of Pan-Islamism had been exaggerated in Europe. This fit with their overall thesis that the Pan-Islamic movement had not enjoyed much success before the First World War and was unlikely to be a significant unifying force in the Muslim world given the division between Turks and Arabs.

bellum," or more simply the "status quo." What this meant was that the religious

conditions before the war became the model for how religion should function under

British rule. This had the advantage of forestalling any attempts by any local or

foreign groups to push for a major revision in the balance of power between the

various religions or for the alteration of ownership rights at the holy sites.

The elevation of the protection of the status quo to a central policy in the

British treatment of religion in Palestine was not accidental, but neither was it

inevitable. We have already seen that the idea of defending religious tradition was

part of what I identified as the "Balfour mentality" in chapter one. That is to say,

British planners entered Palestine with the expectation that the civilizing mission

would be entrusted to modern Europeans—British officials and Zionist settlers—while

protecting the religious and civil rights of the "backward" Arab population. The idea

of protecting the status quo also flowed from the regulations that governed military

occupation during war. Allenby's commitment to existing religious rights conformed

to Article 46 of the Hague Convention of 1907, which mandated that for occupying

powers "family honour and rights, individual life, and private property, as well as

religious conviction and worship, must be respected."[39] The Hague Convention also

called for the occupying power to continue to financially support and protect local

religious clergy unless they organized opposition against the military forces.[40]

---

[39] The article comes from the "Regulations Respecting the Laws and Customs of War on Land," which was part of the Hague Convention of 1907. The article was incorporated into the regulations that were used by the British during the war. See Great Britain, War Office, *Manual of Military Law* (London: His Majesty's Stationary Office, 1914), 343.

[40] Clause 378 of the *Manual of Military Law* stated that, "If the salaries of the clergy are paid by the State they must be continued," as per Article 48 of the Hague Convention, but that in return, "The

Moreover, the decision not to intervene in religious matters fit with the conservative

nature of military administrators who had genuine misgivings about the impact of the

Balfour Declaration on their ability to govern the country.[41]

Even so, some Britons hoped that the British occupation would lead to the

strengthening of the Christian position in Palestine, even perhaps to the reversal of the

situation of the Ottoman period when Islam was the preeminent faith in the region.

This perspective flowed from the widespread view (touched upon in the chapter one)

that Allenby's campaign was a modern crusade. A major proponent of strengthening

the Christian position was the Protestant Bishop of Jerusalem Rennie MacInnes, who

argued from his wartime residence in Cairo that the conquest of Palestine should result

in a redistribution of holy sites to the benefit of the Christian faith.[42] In a recent

---

clergy must refrain from reference to politics, and if they use their position to incite the population to
resistance or revolt they may be dealt with as war criminals." Ibid, 291.

      The military authorities adherence to the terms of the convention is indicated by Allenby's
"Scheme for civil administration of occupied territory, which he submitted to the War Office on March
2, 1918. According to the fourth paragraph of that document,

> The general principles upon which the Government of the country should be
> conducted had been carefully considered before the provisional arrangements detailed
> in paragraph three had been made. It had been realised that the requirements of
> International Law must be fully observed; that these are well summarised in Sections
> VIII and IX of "The Laws and Usages of War" (Chapter XIV of "The Manual of
> Military Law"); and that all administrative action should be based upon the principles
> there enunciated.

See Allenby to Secretary War Office, March 2, 1918, PRO T/17511.

[41] The Balfour Declaration was generally seen as an obstacle to sound governance in Palestine by
officials in the O.E.T.A. administration. This was shown by the complaints by Major General Bols and
Major General Watson that the Balfour Declaration was unworkable and should be rescinded. The
declaration was even criticized at one point by Wyndham Deedes, an administrator who was otherwise
very sympathetic to Zionism.

[42] Bishop MacInnes was the Bishop of Jerusalem, but on account of the war was living in Cairo. In
fact, since MacInnes was appointed to his position during the war, he would set foot in Jerusalem for
the first time in 1918. As pointed out in the last chapter, the bishopric of Jerusalem had been
established in 1841 as a joint British and Prussian project. In 1887 the bishopric became the Anglican
Episcopate as a result of a Prussian withdrawal from the joint arrangement in 1882.

dissertation Abigail Jacobson has discussed MacInnes' strong advocacy of a Christian

takeover of the country and the unease that his unorthodox views caused among

British officials.[43] As early as May 1917 MacInnes argued to Gilbert Clayton that the

Palestine administration should adopt a policy whereby "in all lands of which we

become possessed, every building originally erected as a Christian church which is

now used as a mosque or held by Muslim hands, be officially taken back into

Christian possession." Anticipating a negative response to his sectarianism, he

cautioned against taking a soft approach to the Muslim world:

> It is my strong conviction that the British government, in its desire to
> placate the Mohammedan races, is sometimes advised to adopt
> measures which have the very opposite effect. The measure designed
> by the Western mind to show magnanimity and tolerance is regarded by
> the Eastern as a sign of weakness and fear. Where it is designed to
> allay feeling, the deepest suspicion is raised.[44]

MacInnes' arguments were consistently rejected by British planners who came

to regard him as a loose cannon. Wyndham Deedes, the intelligence officer of the

Egyptian Expeditionary Force (and later Civil Secretary in Palestine), argued that the

bishop's proposals, besides being impracticable, were likely to cause anti-British

sentiment to rise in the Muslim world and exacerbate Muslim-Christian tensions

within Palestine.[45] Captain Philip Graves, an official with the Arab Bureau in Cairo,

---

[43] Abigail Jacobson, "From Empire to Empire: Jerusalem in the Transition between Ottoman and British Rule, 1912-1920," Ph.D Thesis, Chicago: University of Chicago, 2006.

[44] The letter is quoted in Jacobson, "From Empire to Empire," 202. The original reference is MacInnes to High Commissioner Egypt, May 2, 1917, National Archives: PRO FO 882/14, PA/17/7, pp. 304-306.

[45] Jacobson, "From Empire to Empire," 203.

As Bernard Wasserstein has pointed out Deedes was an evangelical Christian and deeply committed Zionist. Indeed the Zionist Organization had supported Deedes appointment to the civilian

agreed, pointing out that the bishop's position amounted to an endorsement of the view that the British conquest was a Christian crusade. He granted that such a position might be natural for a Christian bishop but warned that MacInnes' view "does not take into account questions of military and political expediency."[46]

MacInnes' proposals were unorthodox but not altogether outlandish. It wasn't unprecedented for British imperialism to reshape local religious life. In parts of Africa Protestant missionaries had been encouraged by imperial officials to undermine and reshape African religious traditions and/or to inculcate Africans with European Christian values.[47] Missionaries had been less successful in India, but the Raj's religious policies—its favoritism toward the Muslim minority and its introduction of an Anglo-Muhammadan law system—profoundly affected the religious life of the country. Admittedly in 1917 British options towards Islam were more limited. As Uri Kupferschmidt has argued, by the time the British arrived in Palestine, a "century-and-a-half of 'Muslim policies' devised by colonial powers considerably narrowed the options of interference, change and reform," in regards to the administration of Islam or other local religions.[48]

Military officials were convinced that any alteration in the religious landscape, especially one that resulted from British actions, was likely to have a negative impact

---

administration. See Bernard Wasserstein, "Wyndham Deedes in Palestine," Pamphlet No. 40 (London: Anglo-Israel Association, 1973).

[46] Graves to Deedes, October 15, 1917 PRO FO 882/14, PA/17/12. Quoted in Jacobson, "From Empire to Empire," 204.

[47] See John Comaroff, "Images of Empire, Contests of Conscience: Models of Political Domination in South Africa," *Tensions of Empire: Colonial Cultures in a Bourgeois World*, ed. Frederick Cooper and Ann Laura Stoler (Berkeley: University of California Press: 1997), 163-197 and Philip Curtain's chapter on missionaries in Buganda in *The World and the West*.

[48] Kupferschmidt, *Supreme Muslim Council*, 6.

on Britain's ability to rule effectively in Palestine. It was decided that the occupying

forces would maintain a low profile when it came to religion. This was put into effect

on the ground by the decision to limit the visit of British troops to holy sites, and to

establish guidelines stating that British personnel could only visit religious services in

an unofficial capacity as private individuals. The exclusive use of Muslim troops from

the Sudan to guard Muslim holy sites in the opening weeks of the occupation was also

used to ensure that the British presence at religious sites was as inconspicuous as

possible. Perhaps most obviously this policy of non-intervention was enforced by the

reluctance of the military authorities and the civilian authorities that followed to

support Christian mission in the country, a position that was in stark contrast to the

British consulate's strong advocacy of Protestantism during the Ottoman period. As

for MacInnes, his voice was quietly silenced and he was politely asked to stay away

from the ceremony of occupation.

VII - (Re)Inventing the Status Quo

One of the first religious problems that the military authorities faced was a clash

between Greek Orthodox and Armenian Orthodox Christians in Bethlehem on January

19, 1918. The reasons for the clash are obscure, for colonial records simply report that

the clash was a "recurrence of the annual conflict between the Greek Ephiphany and

Armenian Christians."[49] Whatever the cause, the commander-in-chief of the

occupying forces, General Allenby, argued that this sort of activity would not be

---

[49] G.C.O. Egypt to C.I.G.S., January 25, 1918, FO 371/3388/489.

permitted and sent out notice "to inform all heads of religious communities that the 'Status Quo Ante Bellum' will be strongly maintained during the period of military administration and that a Christian administration will not tolerate unseemly incidents in the Holy Shrine."[50] Allenby's letter of January 25, 1918 is the earliest direct reference to the concept of the status quo in the British records. Four days later Under-secretary for Foreign Affairs Lord Hardinge wrote to Foreign Secretary Arthur Balfour that the French (in an agreement between Major-General Gilbert Clayton and Francois Georges-Picot) had agreed to uphold the status quo in religious matters in Palestine.[51] Although this agreement initially caused the British administration some problems when the French insisted that they should share the "burden" of protecting the status quo, it was ultimately successful in forestalling any attempt the French might have taken to unilaterally take on the role of the protectors of the Roman Catholic community.

Chaim Weizmann on the other hand was not supportive of this new policy and soon reacted with great frustration to the limits that it imposed upon his plan to purchase the Western Wall and on future Zionist projects:

> The British Administration here is guided by one fundamental principle
> laid down in the Hague convention, that in Occupied Enemy Territory
> the status quo has to be preserved. It is not for me to express an
> opinion on the advisability of applying to Palestine rigidly a formula
> which has been violated by every belligerent Power during this war,
> and has lost all relation to reality. We have only to accept the fact and
> to see what we can achieve within the limits set by the status quo.[52]

---

[50] Ibid.

[51] FO 371/3388/18170.

[52] Weizmann to Balfour, May 30, 1918. CZA L3/310.

Much like Bishop MacInnes, Weizmann saw British policy as establishing

unnecessary barriers to colonial intervention. In colonial correspondence the decision

to preserve the status quo was presented as an obligation that the military authorities

and their civilian successors had no choice but to fulfill. But Weizmann's perspective

was more accurate; the British decision to protect the status quo was as much a choice

as an obligation. In the post-war period the allied powers had a real opportunity to

remake the Middle East as they saw fit, particularly after the return of the United

States to a position of isolationism. The British decision to uphold the status quo was

made because it appeared to help Britain's administration of Palestine.

Moreover, while the concept of protecting the status quo was based upon rules

laid down in the Hague Convention of 1907, those rules only specified that rights of

worship be protected and that religious institutions continued to be supported

financially by the occupying power. Nothing was mandated about maintaining the

traditional religious precedence among local Christian sects, restricting the work of

Protestant missionaries, allowing religious communities to maintain religious courts,

or giving the Muslim religious authorities supervision over Muslim pious

endowments, all policies that the British authorities would soon justify under the

rubric of protecting the status quo. Nor were those actions implied by the Balfour

Declaration's pledge that the "civil and religious rights of the non-Jewish population"

would not be prejudiced, for that clause was understood to apply only to British

actions that were geared towards the establishment of a national home for Jews.

The most obvious precedent for this policy was the concept of the status quo that operated during the Ottoman period. As mentioned above, this was the agreement set out in an 1852 *firman* that committed the Ottoman government to upholding the rights of access and ownership of the various Christian sects towards Christian holy sites that existed at that time. Michael Dumper has argued that the British concept of the status quo was based on a widening of the Ottoman concept through the addition of Muslim and Jewish sites to the list of holy places that were covered by the concept.[53] British officials certainly understood their application of the status quo in this manner. The most definitive British report on the status quo, Archer Cust's "The Status Quo at the Holy Sites," an unpublished internal analysis that appeared around 1925, asserted that the status quo referred to the rights at the holy sites that had originally been developed under the Ottomans.[54] It seems more likely though that the idea that this was a well-developed concept during the Ottoman period was a fiction created by mandate experts (such as Cust) who were searching for definitive rules that the British could use as a guide for their own approach to religion. By elevating particular rules or arrangements that operated during the Ottoman period into laws, these experts translated Ottoman policy into concepts that were usable in British administration. Of course, this process, as with any work of translation, involved interpreting and editing the source material in ways that changed its original meaning.

---

[53] Dumper's book offers a succinct description of the evolving meaning that the term status quo has had throughout Palestine's history. See, Michael Dumper, *Politics of Sacred Space.*

[54] See Cust, "The Status Quo at the Holy Places," PRO CO 733/132/2.

The clearest way in which the status quo was reinterpreted was the way in which the concept was extended far beyond the terms of the original firman which covered Christian rights at the Church of the Holy Sepulchre and the Chruch of the Nativity to include other sites, such as the Tomb of Rachel near Bethlehem and the Western Wall in Jerusalem. In fact, the term had, at least informally, a much broader connotation and was used by British officials to refer to a general need to respect religious rights. This is shown clearly in the memoirs of Ronald Storrs, which makes a great deal about the status quo's determinative power in British policy. At times Storrs uses the notion of the status quo in the more limited sense employed by Dumper.[55] However, Storrs also uses the term to refer to British religious and political policy in general. For example, Storrs contends that the great contravention of the principle had been Britain's endorsement of the Jewish national home, a criticism of British policy that has been repeated by many later scholars.[56] He also pushes the concept beyond its conventional meaning by stating that it was the "bedrock of the General's policy (as it must be of any honest military occupation) in *secular* as well as religious matters…"[57]

The inexactitude and confusion in the way in which the term was often applied exasperated later officials who complained that the idea of the "status quo ante" had

---

[55] For example, Storrs boasts about an incident in which he contravened the status quo by removing an "unsightly" wall in the Grotto of the Nativity in Jerusalem that had been constructed by the Orthodox Patriarch. In a typically grandiose fashion, Storrs justified his interference by an appeal to aesthetics. Storrs, *Memoir*, 316.

[56] Ylana Miller for example argues that, "An administration that entered Palestine with a full commitment to support the development of a Jewish National Home could hardly claim to be perpetuating the status quo." Miller, *Rural Palestine*, x.

[57] Storrs, *Memoir*, 312. The italics are mine.

never been defined in British policy. As chapter six will point out, this made the concept unhelpful when it was most needed such as when British officials were trying to sort out Muslim and Jewish rights at the Western Wall in 1928-29.[58] Reflecting the frustration of his administration, the high commissioner wrote to the Secretary of State for the Colonies in London in 1929 to inform him that this dispute could not be solved until experts were able "to define what is meant by the phrases "status quo", "permitted under the Turkish regime", "established practice" and "allowed to take"," as employed in the various white papers that had been devoted to the subject.[59] But in the early 1920s the vagueness of the concept was actually useful, for it left a certain amount of flexibility in its application. In the first years of British rule officials were able to use the concept to justify a range of British policies—their rejection of Weizmann's attempts to purchase the Western Wall, the provision of a "customary" military band at the Nabi Musa festival, the placement of British Muslim guards at the Haram al-Sharif, or the choice to establish an independent Muslim religious authority in Palestine. In fact, it is hard to escape the conclusion that "status quo ante" was an intentionally vague concept that was used to promote particular traditions that were useful to the colonial project. This is certainly the opinion of Ellen Fleischmann who has written that,

---

[58] Officials such as Harry Luke and Norman Bentwich (the acting high commissioner and attorney-general respectively), worked hard to establish what had been the formal rights of the Jewish community at the Western Wall during the Ottoman period, since the Muslim community objected to Jews bringing benches and other objects that were traditionally prohibited.

[59] High Commissioner to Secretary of State, June 14, 1929, ISA, Attorney General Files, Record Group 3, AG359.

The policy was not necessarily benign or passive. The British
maintained certain religious or tribal structures in order to facilitate
administration, mediate conflict, and impose control, retaining those
"customs" or practices that benefited their objectives in certain ways
while creating or developing others that suited their purposes.[60]

This does not mean that the "status quo" was an imaginary concept; rather, it was

invented in much the same way the concept of the nation was, for it spoke for a past

that seemed real but never was.

VIII - The Rise and Fall of the Holy Places Commission

The policy of preserving the status quo could not hope to solve all preexisting

religious controversies. Ironically, the dispute between Christian sects over their

rights at the Church of the Holy Sepulchre was probably the most obvious controversy

that could not be resolved by making a simple reference to the status quo. In the early

1920s the Foreign Office received a letter from the Romanian Orthodox Church that

questioned Franciscan rights:

> L'introduction des Franciscans au Saint Sépulchre est un simple
> accident de l'histoire, et non pas une situation naturalle et continue, en
> ce sens que, si l'invasion des Lieux Saints par les Musulmans n'aviat
> pas en lieu, les Franciscans n'y seraient pas restées les seuls Chrétiens
> et n'auraient pas assume à eux seuls las celebration du culte et la
> defense du Saint-Sépulchre, et que l'histoire, commence en 326 ap. J.C.
> avec Sainte Hélène, aurait suivi son cours normal.[61]

---

[60] Ellen L. Fleischmann, *The Nation and Its "New" Women: The Palestinian Women's Movement,
1920-1948* (Berkeley: University of California Press, 2003), 33.

[61] PRO FO 574/4/1013.

The Franciscans for their part had a very different narrative about past precedent, arguing that by right they should have had even more power at the holy sites. For them, the accident of history was the original Sultanic *firman* that recognized the Greek Orthodox as the preeminent Christian community in Palestine.[62] In other words, they did not see the status quo as valid at all, a problem for a British administration that hoped to use Ottoman precedent as the bedrock of their approach to religion.

Likewise, Muslim and Zionist leaders offered radically different interpretations of the history of the Western Wall that were difficult to reconcile. The Zionist Organization (and the larger Jewish community) viewed the wall as a purely Jewish site and the Muslim neighborhood that abutted the wall as a group of backward and "doubtful" usurpers. Muslims, on the other hand, saw the wall as integral to Muslim history (as the site where Muhammad tethered his horse al-Buraq) and the neighborhood as holy, given its status as the Abu Maydan waqf—for them it was the Jews who were the usurpers.

In both cases the arrival of the British allowed for these disputes to take on new life, for it encouraged all sides to push strongly for a (re)definition of their rights under British rule. Here an appeal to the status quo couldn't really help because past precedent was called into question by all sides. A different approach had to be adopted in this case, so that these controversies would not affect public security and

---

[62] This position was argued in a pamphlet on the Orthodox position in Palestine, and by a book by Albert Rock that was originally published in Palestine during the mandate period. See Albert Rock, *Status Quo in the Holy Places.*

more importantly so that these disputes would not attract the attention of outside powers.

A solution was found in 1919 when the Reverend P. N. Waggett proposed that an international commission be formed to resolve questions involving religious sites.[63] The proposal was initially offered as an alternative to allowing foreign consuls in Jerusalem to advocate on behalf of their coreligionists, as had occurred in the Ottoman period. But it was soon realized that the convening of an international commission would also relieve the mandatory power of the burden of deciding religious controversies on its own and thereby help to immunize it from the criticism of one community or another.

The proposal for an international commission was brought up shortly after that at the San Remo conference in which the territories of the former Ottoman Empire were parceled out amongst the victors of the First World War. Again the French were reluctant to accept the idea of an international commission because they wanted to retain their right of protection of the Roman Catholic community. But a compromise was proposed by the Italian Premier Francesco Nitti, who suggested the establishment of a commission associated with the League of Nations.[64] As a result the creation of an international commission was adopted as part of Article 95 of the Treaty of Peace with Turkey (a.k.a. the Treaty of Sèvres):

---

[63] See Waggett to Chief Political Officer, December 27, 1919, ISA 2/4/140

[64] According to the historian Paul Hanna it was the Italian Premier Francesco Nitti who proposed the formation of the commission. His proposal was a compromise between the French position, which called for the continuation of their protection over the Roman Catholics and opposed the inclusion of the Balfour declaration in the Treaty of Peace with Turkey, and the British position, which was committed to the Jewish National Home and could never accept a French protectorate. See Paul Hanna, *British Policy in Palestine* (Washington: American Council on Public Affairs, 1942), 55.

The Mandatory undertakes to appoint as soon as possible a special
Commission to study and regulate all questions and claims relating to
the different religious communities. In the composition of this
Commission the religious interests concerned will be taken into
account. The Chairman of the Commission will be appointed by the
Council of the League of Nations.[65]

That treaty was never ratified but the proposal lived on in the Mandate for

Palestine (July 24, 1922) which established the guidelines for British rule in Palestine

under the auspices of the League of Nations:

Article 14. A special commission shall be appointed by the Mandatory
to study, define and determine the rights and claims in connection with
the Holy Places and the rights and claims relating to the different
religious communities in Palestine. The method of nomination, the
composition and the functions of this Commission shall be submitted to
the Council of the League for its approval, and the Commission shall
not be appointed or enter upon its functions without the approval of the
Council.[66]

At the same time the 1922 Mandate for Palestine enshrined the protection of the status

quo as the guiding principle in British policy to religious groups in Palestine.[67] This

---

[65] "The Treaty of Sèvres, 1922," *The Treaties of Peace 1919-1923, Vol. II*, Carnegie Endowment for
International Peace, New York, 1924.

[66] "The Palestine Mandate," *The Avalon Project at Yale Law School* <http://www.yale.edu/lawweb/
avalon/mideast/palmanda.htm>

[67] The term status quo was not found in the text of the Mandate for Palestine, nevertheless the concept
of protecting pre-existing rights was strong as shown in the thirteenth article:

Article 13. All responsibility in connection with the Holy Places and religious
buildings or sites in Palestine, including that of *preserving existing rights* and of
securing free access to the Holy Places, religious buildings and sites and the free
exercise of worship, while ensuring the requirements of public order and decorum, is
assumed by the Mandatory, who shall be responsible solely to the League of Nations
in all matters connected herewith, provided that nothing in this article shall prevent
the Mandatory from entering into such arrangements as he may deem reasonable with
the Administration for the purpose of carrying the provisions of this article into effect;
and provided also that nothing in this mandate shall be construed as conferring upon
the Mandatory authority to interfere with the fabric or the management of purely
Moslem sacred shrines, the immunities of which are guaranteed.

effectively meant that early on in the civilian period, the Palestine government's approach to religion had gained international endorsement.

At first, British officials, particularly Lord Balfour, worked to bring the Holy Places Commission into existence and offered various proposals for its composition during 1921 and 1922.[68] The commission they envisioned would not be an academic body but a forum in which representatives of the great powers could debate Palestine's religious future. As one Foreign Office official explained, "Members of the Commission will probably have to be selected rather on account of their suitability to represent the big religious interests concerned than on account of their actual knowledge of the sites of the Holy Places and their history."[69] Given that Article 14 provided the colonial authorities with the authority to determine the composition of the committee, British officials worked to put together a commission who would be sympathetic to the British administration. Officials in the Palestine government and the Colonial Office suggested candidates for the Holy Places Commission that were either anglophiles or clients of the British Empire, such as King Hussein of Mecca, and proposed that the commission be chaired by an American Protestant rather than a Roman Catholic.[70]

Such proposals were rejected by French and Italian representatives and strongly criticized by the Vatican, all of whom sought Roman Catholic chairmanship

---

"The Palestine Mandate," *The Avalon Project at Yale Law School* <http://www.yale.edu/lawweb/avalon/mideast/palmanda.htm>

[68] See PRO CO 733/6/50887, CO 733/10/21965, CO 733/152/5, CO 935/1/1, T 161/118, FO 681/88 and ISA 1/572/1.

[69] FO 371/6388/E598/598/88.

[70] CO 733/10/21965.

of the entire commission or at the very least of the proposed Christian sub-committee.[71] This position was opposed in turn by Orthodox Christian leaders who saw this as an abrogation of the status quo and pushed for equal representation with the Catholics on all committees.[72] Unwilling to bend to Catholic demands and unable to convince the Catholic powers to support their proposals, the British government eventually withdrew their proposal for the formation of the commission in October 1922.

The failure of the holy places commission proposal was not a total failure for the British administration. The protracted negotiations over the composition of the committee (from late 1920 until 1922) gave the Palestine government some space to develop their own approach to religious sites on the ground free from the involvement of foreign powers. And when outsiders tried to involve themselves in local religious controversies, British officials were able to rebuff their efforts by appealing to the authority of the future commission.[73]

The collapse of the commission proposal moved the British authorities to adopt a unilateral approach to governing holy sites. Rather than using an international commission to determine religious rights in Palestine, officials proposed that a

---

[71] British plans for the Holy Places Commission were criticized heavily both before and after the promulgation of the Mandate for Palestine. FO 371/7785 and FO 371/7786 contain more than a score of letters that describe the French, Italian, and Vatican's position.

[72] See for instance Patriarch Daminos to FO, August 9, 1922, FO 371/7786/E7947 or Patriarch of Constantinople to FO, August 24, 1922, FO 371/7786/E8449. A letter from the League of Nations to the Foreign Office, September 8, 1922 includes letters from eleven different Greek Orthodox groups that discuss the proposed commission.

[73] For example when a group of Italian Franciscans demanded the handover of the Coeneuculum in October 1920, the Foreign Office responded that the issue was matter for the future commission to determine. See PRO FO 371/6389/E11552 (October 1920).

Commission of Enquiry made up of British judges resident in London should hear religious disputes. This approach was bolstered by the Vatican's insistence, in opposing British proposals for the formation of a holy places commission, that issues such as the ownership of holy places were judicial matters that should be decided by a British Court of Justice rather than an international commission.[74] It was soon realized that this proposal would be unworkable and it was replaced by a measure that empowered the High Commissioner to have final say in all religious disputes.[75] This was confirmed in the Palestine (Holy Places) Order-in-Council 1924, which stated that "no cause or matter in connection with the Holy Places or religious buildings or sites in Palestine, or the rights or claims relating to the different religious communities in Palestine shall be heard or determined by any Court in Palestine."[76] Instead, the High Commissioner was given the right to decide religious questions, in the absence of the commission proposed in Article 14 of the mandate, and his decision was "final and binding on all parties."[77]

This order gave British officials the authority to determine and fix rights at the holy places, though such rights were qualified by article 13 of the Mandate for Palestine, which obligated the British to protect existing rights and prohibited them from interfering with Muslim holy sites.[78] In 1919, with the status of Palestine

---

[74] PRO FO 371/6389/7786/E10201 (September 29, 1922).

[75] It would not only have been difficult to find judges who had a competent understanding of the religious issues at stake. The proposal would also have meant that religious disputes could not be solved expeditiously.

[76] See Great Britain, *Proclamations*, 30.

[77] Ibid.

[78] See footnote 47.

unsettled, British officials had been unwilling to take on this duty, but in 1924,

confident of their position in Palestine the high commissioner was happy to take on

this responsibility. This effectively gave Britain the same ability to oversee religious

policy that the Ottomans had had before them; however, unlike the Ottomans, that

power was not restricted by the presence of powerful European consuls.

IX – Resurrecting the Millet System

As the definitive British study of the status quo, Archer Cust's "The Status Quo at the

Holy Places," makes clear, the "defense of religious rights" at the heart of the

preservation of the status quo depended upon the recognition of and cooperation with

distinct religious authorities. Given the military and civilian authorities' commitments

to protecting the status quo, direct supervision of religion was not permitted. Nor was

it desired by a colonial administration that sought above all to be streamlined and

efficient. Oversight of religion thus devolved to local religious leaders, which was not

a radical departure from Ottoman precedent, except, as we shall see, in the case of the

Muslim community.

For the Jewish community and Christian churches the existing systems of

religious courts and institutional hierarchies were largely preserved. British policy

was defined early on by Proclamation 42 of April 24, 1918, which explicitly stated

that "the jurisdiction of the Courts of the Christian and Jewish Communities in matters

of personal status of Ottoman subjects shall be as it was before the Occupation."[79]

---

[79] Great Britain, *Proclamations*, 10.

This did not mean that there were no changes. The recognition of two Chief Rabbis for the Jewish community (one Ashkenazi and Sephardic), a practice that continues today in the State of Israel, was a departure from the traditional Ottoman practice of having a single *hakham bashi* (Chief Rabbi) drawn from the Sephardic community. However, this change was more evolutionary than revolutionary since in the later years of the Ottoman period Ashkenazi Rabbis had been recognized by the Ottomans in various cities across the Levant. This change also did little to change the relationship between the state and the Jewish community, for the religious life of the community remained outside the purview or interest of the central authorities and personal status issues continued to be handled by rabbinical courts.

The replacement of Muslim rule by Christian rule also did not radically change the Christian community's relationship with the central state. While the British consulate during the Ottoman period had cooperated closely with the local Protestant community, when Britain took over Palestine it adopted a hands-off attitude towards the Christian community, largely to allay fears that it would favor the Protestant position. This was demonstrated by the administration's lack of support for missionary groups and its curtailment of official representation at Protestant church services.[80] To be sure, the British did become involved with local Christian institutions. After the conquest of Jerusalem, German religious buildings (and moveable property) were taken over by the military authorities. British officials also became involved in adjudicating disputes between Christian sects over their rights at

---

[80] Soldiers and officials were able to attend services provided they attended in a private capacity.

the holy places. The Palestine Government also became involved in leadership battles within the Greek Orthodox Church and even took charge of its finances when it became insolvent.[81] However, these interventions were not intended to alter the balance of power among the Christians in Palestine. Paradoxically British interventions were designed to preserve the pre-existing situation. Government intervention into the financial affairs of the Orthodox Patriarchate, for example, was undertaken in order to head off its financial collapse following the withdrawal of Russian patronage and the arbitration of disputes between the Christian sects was designed to return the sides to existing religious arrangements.

X - Establishing the Muslim Authorities

The replacement of Ottoman rule with British rule had a much more profound impact on the Muslim religious authorities. During the Ottoman period those authorities had been part of the state structure with state institutions in Istanbul overseeing the management of waqf and shari'a law. The Porte through its local agents also retained the right to appoint or dismiss religious officials, with the most senior religious figures (such as the qadi of Jerusalem) filled by officials sent over from Istanbul. In the Ottoman empire, the Muslim religious authorities were not financially, administratively, or politically independent but were intimately tied to the Ottoman state. In short, the Muslim community was not a millet, nor could it have been one.

---

[81] British intervention eventually led to the creation of a commission in the early 1920s to address the financial problems of the Orthodox Church which was formally called, "The Commission Appointed by the Government of Palestine to Inquire into the Affairs of the Orthodox Patriarchate of Jerusalem."

This raised immediate difficulties for British officials. If the transition from Ottoman to British rule had only a minor effect on the administration of the Christian and Jewish authorities, for the Muslim religious authorities it was unavoidably disruptive. The British takeover severed deep financial and administrative ties between Islamic bodies in Palestine and their parent institutions in Istanbul. This raised uncomfortable questions about who should now regulate the shari'a court system, collect and distribute waqf funds, and control religious appointments. Britain was not a Muslim power, making it unthinkable for it to replace the Ottoman government as the head of the Muslim religious hierarchy, even if such a replacement was practicable, which it was not. Of course British officials never had any intention of doing this, for they believed in nonintervention. This was made explicit by the high commissioner in a meeting with Muslim leaders on August 24, 1921:

> Formerly under the Turkish rule there was a Turkish authority in these matters, the Sheikh Ul Islam, in Constantinople. Now Palestine is cut off from the Government of Constantinople and there is a Local Government in Palestine, but this Government in Palestine which is not a Moslem one, is most anxious not to intervene in Moslem religious matters. We want the Moslem population of Palestine to feel that with respect to their Wakfs and Sharia Courts they are to have the management of their own religious affairs...[82]

This commitment to nonintervention meant that the partial administration of religious law or religious institutions by the colonial authorities, as occurred in British

---

[82] Deedes to Colonial Office, PRO CO 733/6.

India was never seriously contemplated in Palestine.[83] It would also explain why the

Palestine government would be reluctant to exert as much control over Islam as it did

in Cyprus, Egypt, or the Sudan.[84] Committed to nonintervention, the Palestine

government chose to create a wholly local religious administration, so that the Islamic

court system and waqf administration could be handled by Palestinian Muslims

themselves. This approach was developed in a series of decisions from 1918 to 1921

that ended up creating an autonomous Muslim religious system that can properly be

labeled as "Palestinian Islam."

One of the first orders of business for colonial officials was the reconstitution

of the local Islamic court system, which had been badly disrupted by the war and the

Ottoman withdrawal. In a proclamation in June 1918 the military authorities formally

abolished the right of recourse to the Ottoman Court of Cassation and the *shaykh al-

Islam*, both located in Istanbul, and proposed the establishment of a Shari'a Court of

Appeal in Jerusalem in their place.[85] This court was duly established on September

13, 1918, and was presented as a simple replacement for the Ottoman court rather than

being something new. This was made clear by the fact that in subsequent

---

[83] In India, the British took control over Islamic religious law by integrating the *shari'a* into a hybrid system dubbed Anglo-Mohammedan, in which judges were empowered to apply either Islamic or common law as the case dictated. British control over Hinduism was even stronger. Franklin Pressler observes that, "A little-recognized aspect of modern south Indian history is that the British colonial state penetrated Hindu religious institutions, both temples and *maths* (monasteries), deeply and systematically. This penetration was something that was neither unknown at the time nor unintentional." He sees this penetration as part of the state's attempt to "spread the administrative net over all religious institutions," due to their belief that religion was a major threat to their power. See Franklin Presler, *Religion under Bureaucracy: Policy and administration for Hindu Temples in south India* (Cambridge: Cambridge UP, 1987), 7-15.

[84] A brief overview of British policy towards Islam in these countries was included on pages 27-29.

[85] This was Proclamation 42, which was promulgated on June 24, 1918. Great Britain, *Proclamations*, 10.

For a further discussion of this early legislation see Eisenman, "Young Turk Legislation."

proclamations that dealt with Islamic law Ottoman legal precedent was used, with the exception that all references to the Court of Cassation were replaced by reference to the shari'a court of appeal.[86] Paradoxically then the preservation of the Ottoman system required the creation of wholly new institutions in Palestine.

The shari'a court of appeal was headed by the mufti of Jerusalem, Kamil al-Husayni, and when he died in March 1921 the position passed to a member of the al-Khalidi family.[87] This established a policy by which Islamic law would be administered by local Muslim authorities and would be distinct from British common law, which was administered by British and local judges in a separate secular court system.

The scope of Islamic law was similar to what it had been during the Ottoman period in that Islamic courts were given jurisdiction in cases that had to do with personal status issues, mainly marriage, divorce, and inheritance cases. But under the British, Islamic law applied solely to Muslims. This was an innovation for Palestinian Islam. During the Ottoman period shari'a courts could hear cases even if the parties in the case were non-Muslim. A good example of this was the fact that Ottoman shari'a courts dealt with the personal status of orphans regardless of religious background. This power was removed from the shari'a courts under the British, who made sure that Islamic law applied only to Muslims.[88] This was an important factor in the

---

[86] For further details on this see Eisenman, "Young Turk Legislation," 65.

[87] Upon his death he was succeeded as Mufti of Jerusalem by his nephew Hajj Amin al-Husayni. At the same time the British appointed Khalil al-Khalidi to the presidency of the Shari'a Court of Appeal. See Kupferschmidt, *Supreme Muslim Council*, 20. The contested election of Hajj Amin to the position of mufti will be discussed in the next chapter.

[88] See Great Britain, *Palestine and Transjordan Administration Report for 1920* (London, 1921), 91-92.

transformation of the Muslim community into something like a traditional *millet*, for the existence of an independent and separate religious court system was one of the central privileges accruing to a recognized *millet* under Ottoman rule.

XI - The Committee for Moslem Religious Affairs

The next major initiative in regards to the administration of Islam was the search for a body to permanently oversee the administration of Muslim law and the waqf system. At first the British adopted a system whereby they appointed a President of the Wakf (sic) Administration and a Director General of Wakfs from the local Muslim community and made sure that the annual budget for pious endowments was reviewed by the Palestine government's finance department.[89] Appointed to head this waqf administration, known more commonly as the Central Wakf Committee, was again the mufti of Jerusalem. This approach replicated British policy in Cyprus where from 1914 onwards Britain had been in control of the appointment and dismissal of all Muslim officials.[90] However, this solution was not popular with local Muslims who complained in private meetings with British officials and in the local press that Britain was exercising too much control over Muslim institutions. In response Herbert Samuel wrote to the Foreign Office in November 1920 stating that he thought the government's approach to waqf needed to be reevaluated given that "the control

---

[89] See Samuel to Curzon, November 14, 1920, ISA 100/649/7.

[90] Kupferschmidt, *Supreme Muslim Council*, 10. As Kupferschmidt correctly points out, the Cypriot experience was frequently referred to by legal experts in Palestine in their search for an Islamic system for Palestine.

exercised by the Government over the Administration of Moslem Wakfs was resented by Moslem opinion."[91]

This reevaluation led to a conference on November 9, 1920 between representatives of the Muslim community and officials in the Palestine government to discuss the administration of *awqaf* and the shari'a courts. British records give no indication of the process by which representatives of the Muslim community were chosen, except that the gathered body consisted "of Muftis, principal Ulema, and Moslem Notables," who met with the high commissioner, the attorney general, the civil secretary, and other British officials.[92] At this meeting three resolutions were reached:

> 1. That the Government should retain financial control over the administration of Moslem Wakfs;
> 2. That appointments to the judicial offices in the Shari'a Courts should be made by a Moslem authority;
> 3. That in order to prepare a scheme to give effect to the above resolutions a Committee should be appointed.[93]

The Committee for Moslem Religious Affairs that was formed out of the third resolution was made up of seven British officials and nine Muslim representatives.[94]

This committee soon proposed that a "Central Moslem Authority" be established to oversee the entire administration of the shari'a court system—that is to say they

---

[91] Ibid.

[92] See Government of Palestine, *The Committee for Moslem Religious Affairs* (Jerusalem, 1921), 5.

[93] Ibid.

[94] The Muslim members on this committee were Kamil al-Husayni (the Mufti of Jerusalem and President of the Shari'a Court of Appeal), Muhammad Murad (Mufti of Haifa), 'Abdallah Jazzar (Mufti of Acre), Asad Kaddourah (Mufti of Safed), Nimr Hamad (Ma'mour of Wakfs, Nablus), Raghib al-Nashashibi (Mayor of Jerusalem), Omar Zaytar (Mayor of Nablus), Abdullah al-Dajani (Jaffa), and Said Shawa (Gaza). The list of members is found in a pamphlet on the conference published by the Palestine government. According to this publication Kamil al-Husayni was unable to attend meetings due to his declining health. See *The Committee for Moslem Religious Affairs*, 5.

envisaged a body that not only supervised the shari'a courts but also controlled the nomination and dismissal of qadis and the approval of muftis.[95] According to this arrangement the decisions of the Central Moslem Authority would be subject to the approval of the Palestine Government, which would also retain financial oversight of its annual budget.[96] An even more independent system was proposed for the administration of awqaf: the same Central Moslem Authority would control the waqf system with the colonial government retaining only financial oversight through a British inspector.

The decisions reached at this conference were not fully accepted by its Muslim participants, who argued that the policy did not give the community the full independence that it deserved.[97] This issue was addressed in a follow-up meeting in August 1921, at which the Palestine Government conceded that appointments to the shari'a courts should be controlled solely by the Central Moslem Authority and that British oversight of the waqf budget would be reduced to an annual review of the waqf budget. It was also at this time that the high commissioner offered his commitment to nonintervention by stating that his government had no intention of taking the place of the *Shaykh al-Islam*.[98]

---

[95] This new body would be made up of the Inspector of the Shari'a Courts and four elected Muslim notables. See Kupferschmidt, *Supreme Muslim Council*, 21-22.

[96] *The Committee for Moslem Religious Affairs*, 5.

[97] Kupferschmidt, *Supreme Muslim Council*, 22.

[98] Ibid.

In other words, by August 1921 Britain had pledged itself to support an independent religious authority. The next chapter will outline how this authority came to be invested in the Supreme Muslim Council.

XII - Conclusion

When it came to the Jewish and Christian religious authorities the role played by the Palestine Government was similar to the role that the Ottomans had played in the eighteenth and nineteenth centuries as a kind of referee of religious affairs in Palestine. British involvement in the appointment of a new Orthodox Patriarch and participation in internecine contests over the Holy Sepulchre, for example, were similar to the involvement of the Sublime Porte in such affairs during the nineteenth century. The British decision to employ a version of the millet system, in which local religious communities were given the right to oversee their own religious properties, their own religious services, and their own religious courts fit with Ottoman practices in the nineteenth century. However, this policy was at odds with the direction of Ottoman reforms of the late-nineteenth century, which had sought to replace a decentralized communal system of rule with a centralized bureaucratic and secular system of governance. Britain's conservative tone was also at odds with its onetime claim to be bringing a civilizing mission to the country's benighted Arab population, although it fit well with its rule would protect the country's religious heritage.

There was of course a major innovation here that broke with Ottoman precedent—the integration of the Muslim community into a British version of the millet system. The early years of the military administration have often been presented by scholars as an inert period in the history of mandatory Palestine, due to the hesitancy of the military authorities to take major policy decisions before the civilian authorities arrived. Gideon Biger, for one, has described the military period as "was a time when little was done in the way of development in order to preserve the *status quo ante bellum*," and contrasts the period with the early years of civilian rule which he calls the period of "Great Ideas" (1920-23).[99] But in terms of religious policy the period was crucial in establishing the basic framework for religion under British rule that guided British policy throughout the mandate period. This was a framework built around the idea that the colonial government would protect traditional religious practices and hierarchies under the policy of protecting the status quo. This led British command to embrace the Ottoman millet system as a model for its relationship with local religious communities and to postpone or avoid dealing with religious disputes that threatened to upset communal relationships.

This division of Palestine's population had also been part of Ottoman policy but only before the Tanzimat reforms, which had worked to break down these distinctions in Ottoman society. The British return to dividing the Palestinian population along communal lines was thus a return to the thinking of an earlier era. Treating the population as being divided between separate Muslim, Christian, and Jewish population was not inevitable, although it is hard now to envision another outcome. In 1919, an alternative shared Palestinian identity had been proposed by

---

[99] Biger, *Empire in the Holy Land*, 248-49.

Reverend R. N. Waggett, in response to the military authorities' request for a solution to communal conflict. Waggett proposed that the concept of "Palestine" be promoted as a way of encouraging the local population to think of themselves as having a shared destiny.[100] This proposal was never seriously entertained, perhaps because it would have conflicted with the division established between Jews and non-Jews in mandatory law. But even more likely is that Waggett's proposal went against the idea that communal divisions were natural in Palestinian society. This was shown in Edward Keith-Roach's observation, while he was drafting a law on municipalities, that it would be useful to "recognize in the law *the division which exists in fact*, and to form separate registers of Mohammadans, Christians, and Jews."[101] As a consequence, communal divisions were built into British census taking, into the adoption of separate communal electoral rolls and proportional representation, and became the prism through which British officials viewed Palestinian society.

Another moment in which a Palestinian identity might have been promoted was with the promulgation in 1922 of a Palestinian constitution and the formal creation of a Palestinian citizenship. This was to be complemented by the establishment of a legislative council that would give the local population a limited form of representative government. However the legislative council never came into being (as explained in Chapter 5) and the Arab and Jewish communities remained politically, socially, and economically separated from each other for the rest of the mandate.

---

[100] Waggett to Civil Secretary, ISA 2/4/140

[101] Keith-Roach to Curzon, February 14, 1921, ISA HC/570/10, italics added.

In terms of religion the division along communal lines would be formally

confirmed in the Religious Communities Ordinance of 1925, which according to

Michael Hudson, "not only perpetuated the Ottoman distinction between Muslim and

Christian Arabs but also enhanced the autonomy of the Jewish community in

education and organizational aspects."[102] Again it should be stated that this following

of Ottoman precedent did not mean a simple continuation of Ottoman practice. As the

next chapter makes clear, the colonial government's treatment of Islam created novel

religious institutions and empowered particular religious leaders in an effort to protect

a religious status quo that had never in fact existed.

---

[102] Michael Hudson, "The Transformation of Jerusalem, 1918-1987," *Jerusalem in History*, ed. K. J. Asali. (London: Scorpion , 1989).

Chapter Four

The Supreme Muslim Council

I – Introduction

When the British arrived in Palestine they encountered an Islamic institutional system that was no longer intact. The Ottoman withdrawal had removed some of the leading Muslim leaders from Jerusalem (such as the Ottoman- appointed qadi of Jerusalem) and had decisively cut off local institutions from the religious bureaucracy of the Ottoman state. As we saw in the last chapter, British commanders quickly replaced these figures and institutions with local equivalents: the O.E.T.A. reconstituted the local law courts, placing them under local Muslim control, and the military governor of Jerusalem, Ronald Storrs, replaced the departed qadi of Jerusalem (a position that had been held by an Ottoman Turk) with the leading local religious figure, the Jerusalem mufti Kamil al-Husayni. Kamil al-Husayni was also made president of the Shari'a Court of Appeal, which was established in Jerusalem in September 1918 as a replacement for the legal authority of the shaykh al-Islam in Istanbul.

al-Husayni's appointment as president of the shari'a court of appeal was indicative of his prominence under the British, a prominence that was unprecedented for a mufti of Jerusalem.[1] During the Ottoman period the office of mufti of Jerusalem was not a preeminent figure in the Ottoman religious hierarchy. It is true that the mufti's jurisdiction extended over the powerful independent Jerusalem district, but he

---

[1] Under Ottoman law the *Shaykh al-Islam* was the final judicial authority in Islam.

190

had no authority over the districts of Nablus and Acre. When British rule unified these Ottoman provinces and established Jerusalem as a colonial capital city for the first time since the Roman period, the muftiship of Jerusalem quickly rose in stature.[2] As the mufti of the colonial capital and then as the president of the country's shari'a court of appeal, Kamil al-Husayni became the putative head of Palestinian Islam. This position was formalized by his elevation to the position of Grand Mufti (al-*mufti al-akbar*) in 1918, which effectively (though not officially) transformed the muftiship of Jerusalem into the muftiship of Palestine. This was a novel position in Palestine. Although there had been a grand mufti of Istanbul in the Ottoman Empire, who also held the position of *shaykh al-Islam*, there had never been an equivalent position in Palestine. According to Uri Kupferschmidt, the decision to create a Grand Muftiship was influenced by the British experience in Egypt, where the *hanafi* mufti of Cairo was commonly referred to by the British as the Grand Mufti of Egypt.[3] This seems plausible, since a number of prominent officials in the military administration had served in Egypt before and during the war, although British files do not directly discuss why the new office was created.

The reason why Kamil al-Husayni was favored by the British came from the fact that he was, in the words of the historian Philip Mattar, "apolitical, amiable, and

---

[2] Jerusalem had been the provincial capital of the Roman province of Judaea-Palaestina.

[3] Kupferschmidt, *Supreme Muslim Council*, 19. For a discussion of the position of the Cairo mufti see Rudolph Peters, "Muhammad al-Abbasi al-Mahdi (D. 1897), Grand Mufti of Egypt, and His "al-Fatawa al-Mahdiyya," *Islamic Law and Society*, Vol. 1., No. 1 (1994): 66-82. In Arabic the mufti's title was actually the *mufti al-diyar al-misriyya* (Mufti of the Land of Egypt) not *mufti al-Akbar*.

cooperative," qualities that made the mufti attractive as an ally for the British.[4] These

qualities were shown early on by the manner in which he "went out of his way to aid

the British occupation authorities, particularly when it came to working out some sort

of suitable arrangement between themselves and the local population," which

according to Yehoshua Porath, "made it very much easier for the latter to get used to

the idea of a Christian power ruling in Jerusalem."[5] Besides his apparent amiability,

the mufti's willingness to work with the British likely came from the fact that he was

part of the older generation of the notable elite, which was used to working with

imperial authorities and less inclined towards the Arabism of the younger generation.

Also important was the fact that he was already acquainted with some British officials,

such as Ronald Storrs.[6]

Of course his receptiveness to the new British regime would have mattered

little, if he was not also a major powerbroker in the new colonial capital of Jerusalem.

As a member of one of the leading notable families of Jerusalem, Kamil al-Husayni

---

[4] Mattar, *Mufti of Jerusalem*, 8. The portrait of the mufti as uninterested in politics is perhaps a little overblown and has much to do with the reputation of his successor Hajj Amin al-Husayni. Tawfiq Canaan (a prominent Palestinian intellectual during the mandate) for example noted that the Grand Mufti protested against the Zionist threat in a dinner given by Ronald Storrs in April 1918. See Tawfiq Canaan, *Conflict in the Land of Peace* (Jerusalem: Syrian Orphanage Press, 1936), 15.

[5] Porath goes on to give specifics about this assistance:

> He saw to it that the question of naming the Muslim ruler during Friday
> prayers did not develop into a political issue, and even his attitude to the
> Jews and his relations with them were friendly and correct. During the
> period of tension that followed the April 1920 disturbances, he appealed to
> the public in the course of a sermon at the al-Aqsa mosque to maintain law
> and order and to rest assured that the British Government, as was their policy
> everywhere, would do nothing to hinder the Muslims in the practice of their
> religion.

Porath, *Emergence*, 187.

[6] Storrs would later claim that when he arrived in the country in 1917 he knew of no one except Kamil al-Husayni and his family. See Taysir Jbara, *Palestinian Leader Hajj Amin al-Husayni*, 27.

was already used to playing the role of an intermediary between the local Arab population and the Sublime Porte. As Philip Mattar put it, "Together with the Khalidis, 'Alamis, Jarallas, and Nashashibis [the Husaynis] constituted the ruling elite of the Ottoman administration in Jerusalem. Members of the Husayni family occupied such positions as delegate to the Ottoman Parliament, district governor, [and] mayor."[7] The family also had a long tradition of holding religious office in Palestine. The first Husayni to hold the position of mufti of Jerusalem had been 'Abd al-Qadir ibn Karim al-Din al-Husayni at the beginning of the 17th century, and the family had held the office of mufti more or less continuously since the end of the eighteenth century. In addition, members of the Husayni family had held other important religious posts such as *naqib al-ashraf* (the acknowledged representative of the descendents of the prophet) and *shaykh al-haramayn* (the keeper of the Dome of the Rock and the al-Aqsa mosque).[8]

As one would expect from Hourani's description of the notable politics, the Husaynis' power was also based upon their extensive landholdings in Palestine. The most religiously important of these landholdings was the waqf of Nabi Musa, which the Husayni family had administered for generations.[9] This gave the Husaynis control

---

[7] Mattar, 7.

[8] Mattar, 6.

[9] For a discussion of the importance of *waqf* properties for Jerusalem's notable families see Gabriel Baer, "Jerusalem's Families of Notables and the Wakf in the Early 19th Century," *Palestine in the Late Ottoman Period: Political, Social, and Economic Transformation*, ed. David Kushner. (Jerusalem: Yad Izhak Ben-Zvi Press, 1986). For a more detailed look at the al-Husayni family in particular consult Butrus Abu-Manneh, "The Husaynis: The Rise of a Notable Family in 18th C. Palestine," *Palestine in the Late Ottoman Period: Political, Social, and Economic Transformation*, ed. David Kushner. (Jerusalem: Yad Izhak Ben-Zvi Press, 1986).

over the annual Nabi Musa festival, which was the only festival in the Palestinian

calendar that brought together Arabs from all around the country. The Nabi Musa

festival, as the name suggests, was an annual festival that celebrated the Prophet

Moses, who Muslims of the region believe to have died near Jericho. The festival was

begun in the nineteenth century by the Ottoman authorities who wanted to have a

Muslim celebration that would compete with the Easter and Passover celebrations. As

we shall see in the next chapter, this festival became a significant site of nationalist

protest in the earliest years of British rule, which was tied to the rise of Arab

nationalism during and after the First World War.[10] For the al-Husyanis control over

the festival allowed them to have contact with a wide variety of people within the

Palestinian Arab community, including Christians who also participated in the

festivities. The festival also had given them valuable experience in working with the

imperial authorities, since putting on the festival required coordination between its

patrons and the Ottoman governorate.

Another factor that contributed to the prominence of the al-Husayni family was

their success in cultivating a good standing in Istanbul and Damascus, which until

1874 had been the provincial capital for the Jerusalem region. This was achieved

according to Butrus Abu-Manneh through such practices as gift giving, the formation

of advantageous marriage alliances, and the creation of political relationships with the

---

[10] For a discussion of the festival see Khaled Marrar, *Maqam An-Nabi Musa: The Shrine of Prophet Moses* (Jericho: Committee for the Promotion of Tourism in the Governorate of Jericho, 1998), Roger Friedland and Richard D. Hecht, "The Pilgrimage to Nabi Musa and the Origins of Palestinian Nationalism," *Pilgrims & Travelers to the Holy Land*, ed. Bryan F. Le Beau and Menachem Mor (Omaha: Creighton UP, 1996), and Ted Swedenberg, *Memories of Revolt* (Minneapolis: U of Minnesota, 1995).

most powerful families in those cities.[11] Kamil al-Husayni and his family were thus

plugged in not only to Palestinian society but to the wider Middle East, an important

quality for a family that sought prominent political and religious office under both the

Ottomans and British.

The final factor that made the British reach out to Kamil al-Husayni was his

religious status. Since he was one of the most learned religious scholars in the country

and one of the most important muftis in Palestine, he was a solid and safe choice for

the position of grand mufti. This was important not simply for the long-term viability

of the position but also in giving the British occupation some form of immediate

religious sanction, a not insignificant factor given Britain's continued fight against the

Ottomans in north of Palestine.

The creation of the grand muftiship placed Kamil al-Husayni in the position of

the official representative of the Muslim community, equivalent to communal leaders

such as the Chief Rabbi or the Greek Orthodox Patriarch, an important first step in the

creation of a recognized Muslim millet. But it is also clear that the mufti was

considered to be a *primus inter pares* by the British, for he was given a higher position

than the Christian Patriarchs and Chief Rabbis of the Jewish community in the order

of precedence at official ceremonies and was alone among local religious and political

leaders in being granted a C.M.G. (Companion of the Order of St. Michael and St.

George) in 1918, an honor given to colonial officials and indigenous leaders for their

---

[11] This is well explained in Abu-Manneh, "The Husaynis: The Rise of a Notable Family in 18th C. Palestine."

service to the empire and was a clear signal of the mufti's importance in British

Palestine.[12]

II - The Muftiship and Politics

Kamil al-Husayni apolitical approach to politics has made him an excellent foil for his

successor Hajj Amin al-Husayni in scholarship about the mandate period. There is no

doubt that the two brothers differed in temperament and upbringing but the difference

between them can be overdrawn. Kamil al-Husayni was less politically active than his

brother, but it is a mistake to describe him as purely a religious figure, just as it is a

mistake to view Hajj Amin as a purely political beast. It would also be wrong to see

these two figures as complete opposites in their relationship with the colonial

authorities, although this is often how they appear in scholarly accounts.

It should be borne in mind that the position of grand mufti was not conceived

as a quietist religious position when it was created by the British. The position was

designed to be a Muslim equivalent of the Greek Orthodox Patriarch, a communal

head entrusted not only with overseeing religious matters and keeping order within his

---

[12] The order of precedence is discussed in ISA, 1/573/3/385.

David Cannadine has argued that awards like the C.M.G extended the British extended the class
hierarchies of British society into their colonies by integrating certain indigenous elites into the British
empire. As such he argues, contra much post-colonial literature, that it was class and not race that
played a decisive role in empire. In the context of Palestine it is difficult not to see the ethnic divide as
paramount, due to the competition between Arabs, Jews, and the Palestine government, though it should
be pointed out that during the military period, when Kamil al-Husayni was granted his award, that this
competition wasn't as strong, or seen as intractable. David Cannedine, *Ornamentalism: How the British
Saw Their Empire* (Oxford: Oxford University Press, 2001).

See Bols report of April 9 FO 371/5119/E5237 and April 14 FO 371/5117/E3158/85/44 and GHQ to
WO, April 18, FO 371/5118/E3474.

millet but also with the task of advocating for the Muslim community.[13] This latter role was clearly what Herbert Samuel had in mind when he stated in 1923 that the job of the mufti was to act as "an intermediary between the Moslems and ourselves."[14] This meant that the responsibilities of the grand mufti went beyond the administration of Islam—the oversight of Islamic courts, the supervision of religious property, the regulation of religious preachers—and involved Kamil al-Husayni in more secular activities, such as serving as a representative of the Muslim community on the Pro-Jerusalem Society (a preservation society) and on other British committees.

Although the mufti's role involved him in politics—in the sense that he became involved in the administration of his community and had a role to play in the wider administration of Jerusalem—it is doubtful that British officials in Palestine would have seen it this way. For them, politics was a contest of power between interest groups and individuals over the governance of Palestine. Since the Britain had been mandated to rule in Palestine, it fell to the Palestine government to govern Palestine, with some assistance from a Jewish agency (as per the wording of the Mandate for Palestine). As a result, Arab political action was seen as unwarranted and unwanted. The Palestine government took a dim view of grassroots Arab political action, preferring that the Arab community work through British-designed political institutions, such as the Advisory Council or the Executive Council, or through private

---

[13] The responsibilities of the grand mufti included the oversight of communal courts, the supervision of religious property, and the regulation of religious preachers, responsibilities that were later taken over by the Supreme Muslim Council, which will be discussed below. But the mufti was also involved in more secular and political roles, such as serving on the Pro-Jerusalem Society and other British committees.

[14] Minutes of Cabinet Committee on Palestine, 9 July 1923, PRO CAB 27/222, quoted in Wasserstein, *British in Palestine,* 133.

representations to the government itself. As I shall discuss in the next chapter, this led to a suspicion among colonial intelligence agents and officials towards any native Palestinian who spoke out or became involved in political and social committees. Such figures were identified as "political," an identification that marked them as troublemakers for working outside the recognized channels. Arabs were unwilling to serve on such colonial councils (particularly the hated legislative council, whose elections were effectively boycotted in 1923) because such participation would constitute recognition of the legitimacy of the mandate. This meant that most Arab politicians were treated with suspicion and were regularly followed by the intelligence service of the Palestine government, which grouped the most problematic onto a top secret "Black List".[15]

Conversely, individuals like Kamil al-Husayni, who mostly worked within the positions defined for them by the colonial authorities, were deemed apolitical. What was interesting is that this perception would remain even if they took positions on political issues, so long as they did not overstep the bounds of their authority. It is often overlooked that Kamil al-Husayni signed on to an anti-Zionist petition that was sent by Arab leaders to the Palestine Government after the violent Nabi Musa festival of April 1920.[16] He also made a major political statement by returning his C.M.G. after British soldiers forcibly searched his house during the Nabi Musa festival. For British officials, these actions were out of character and were deemed part of the chaos

---

[15] It is not clear how long this "black list" was kept, but in the early 1920s , it was used to keep track of the main opponents of the Palestine government within the Arab elite.

[16] See ISA 2/140.

that surrounded the Nabi Musa festival. But it is also possible to see these actions as the acts of a leader whose relationship with the colonial power was souring. These might have been the first of a series of acts of political resistance undertaken by the mufti but we cannot know because the mufti soon took ill and was dead within a year.

III - Replacing the Mufti

The death of Kamil al-Husayni on March 21, 1921 was lamented by British officials, who saw him as an ideal local representative. Their respect for the late mufti was shown in the formal issuance of condolences to the Husayni family and a commitment from the government to provide a stipend for his immediate family.[17] The problem the government faced after his death was that no other Muslim leader had the three qualities that had made him such a useful ally: friendliness with the British, influence in the Arab community, and strong religious qualifications. Shaykh Husam al-Din Jarallah, the inspector of the Shari'a court of appeal, and Shaykh Khalil al-Khalidi, acting-president of the Shari'a Court of Appeal following Kamil's death, had the requisite religious credentials. Both had also shown themselves to be friendly to the British in their positions as religious officials.[18] However, they did not fulfill the third and most important qualification—in the opinion of British officials, they lacked the influence to lead the Muslim community.

---

[17] Porath notes that the pension given to the late mufti's family was far larger than that prescribed by Ottoman law. Porath, *Emergence*, 190.

[18] Shaykh Husam al-Jarallah was the inspector of the Shari'a Court of Appeal. Khalil al-Husayni became the acting head of the shari'a court of appeal after the death of Kamil al-Husayni when the British decided to no longer combine the roles of mufti and qadi in a single office. Three months later he would be appointed to the position permanently. See ISA 2/20/245.

This perception was partly driven by a brilliant campaign of petitions arranged by the al-Husaynis which presented Hajj Amin al-Husayni as the natural choice to succeed his brother as mufti of Jerusalem. This campaign organized numerous petitions of support for Hajj Amin's appointment from groups and individuals throughout the country, creating the perception that he was the both the people's choice and (according to modern parlance) the candidate of inevitability. Indeed, the very same message that formally announced the death of the mufti to the British authorities also declared Hajj Amin to be his designated successor:

> To-day the Mufti of Jerusalem, Kamel Eff. El Husseini, has passed
> away. His death is a great misfortune to the Moslem world. His
> brother Hajj Amin Eff. is his successor. Kindly disseminate the above
> to the Muftis and Cadis of Palestine so that in-memoriam services be
> held, and so that they may rejoice at hearing that a worthy successor
> has been found to the late mufti.[19]

This message from the qadi of Jerusalem was followed by messages and *madhbatas* (petitions) to the Palestine Government calling for Hajj Amin's appointment from the "inhabitants" and "Muslims" of Jerusalem, Gaza, Safed, Tul Karm, Jaffa, Haifa, Jenin, Bani Mura, Hebron, Beisan, Balqa, as well as from the Adwan tribe.[20] The dispatch of petitions from groups throughout the country was an indication that the muftiship of Jerusalem was now a matter of concern far beyond Jerusalem or at the very least showed that the organizers of this letter writing campaign understood how the scope of the position had changed. A letter from the deputy director of police to the civil

---

[19] Muhammad Abu Su'ad al-'Awri to District Governor of Jerusalem, March 21, 1921, ISA 2/10/245. The qadi followed up this note with at least two further requests that Hajj Amin be appointed mufti. Porath notes that his support was somewhat surprising given the fact that al-'Awri was a moderate in his relationship with the government and the Jewish population. Porath, *Emergence*, 190.

[20] These letters of support can be found in ISA 2/10/245.

secretary's office stated that this flood of *madhbata*s from the Husayni camp, was met by petitions from the supporters of Shaykh Husam al-Din Jarrallah, who was supported by the Nashashibi family, the great rivals of the Husaynis.[21] However, these petitions cannot be found in the existing British archives and it seems from British correspondence that the Husaynis were the clear winners in this petition race.[22]

At the same time, the conservatism of British religious policy predisposed the Palestine government to support Hajj Amin's candidacy. To appoint another individual to the position would have been to break with the Husaynis' traditional hold on the office. Granted, religious offices were not technically supposed to be hereditary positions in Ottoman or Islamic law, but to support the candidacy of someone else would have meant upsetting the status quo. Yehoshua Porath and Taysir Jbara have both suggested that the appointment of Hajj Amin was also a means of splitting the leadership of the Arab community, or at least the Arabs of Jerusalem, between the Husaynis who held the muftiship and their great rivals the Nashashibis who held the mayoralty of Jerusalem, following the dismissal of Musa Kazim al-Husayni as mayor for his outspoken words at the 1920 Nabi Musa festival.[23] But it seems more likely that British support for Hajj Amin was based more on inertia and a genuine feeling that he enjoyed the most support of any Muslim figure. British support for Hajj Amin's appointment was shown almost immediately when the Palestine

---

[21] D.D.P.S. to Assistant Civil Secretary (Political), March 23, 1921, ISA 2/10/245.

[22] British correspondence found in ISA 2/10/245 reveals an administration that was impressed by the apparent country-wide support for the mufti.

[23] See Porath, *Emergence*, 192, Jbara, *Palestinian Leader*, 41. There is no direct evidence for this "policy of divide and rule," as Taysir Jbara has called it, unlike in the 1930s when the British supported the Nationalist party of the Nasahsibi *Mu'aridun* "Opposition".

government extended its formal condolences upon Kamil's death not to his son Tahir, as was the conventional practice, but to his brother Hajj Amin.[24]

That Hajj Amin was considered a viable candidate is at first glance surprising. As will be discussed in Chapter 5, Hajj Amin had been among the most vocal advocates for Arab nationalism at the fateful 1920 Nabi Musa festival, at which nine people were killed and a further 244 were wounded after Arab pilgrims at the festival attacked Jewish inhabitants in Jerusalem, leading to four days of violence in the city. In the wake of the riot, Hajj Amin, along with 'Arif al 'Arif and Musa Kazim al-Husayni, was blamed by the British authorities for inciting the crowd to violence. He quickly fled the country and was subsequently sentenced in absentia to ten years in prison. Within months he was granted a pardon by Herbert Samuel, but his supposed act of insurrection raised serious doubts about his political leanings. The Zionist community regarded the British decision to consider, let alone appoint, Hajj Amin as mufti as an act of madness, while senior officials within the Palestine government, such as Norman Bentwich and Wyndham Deedes, agreed that Hajj Amin was unsuitable for the position.

Another factor that worked against Hajj Amin was the fact that his religious qualifications were weak. As explained in Chapter 2, Hajj Amin's education and career path had been more secular than religious. Though he came from a family of 'ulama, his career path was more typical of that of the younger generation of Arab notability, for he had been educated mostly along secular, Westernized lines. And

---

[24] Mattar, *Mufti*, 23.

while he had briefly attended the venerable al-Azhar University in Cairo, where he

had been sent in 1912 by his brother Kamil to gain a religious education, he had spent

much of his time in the city studying under the Muslim reformer Rashid Rida at his

Dar al-Da'wa wal-Irshad (School of Advocacy and Guidance) and involving himself

in Palestinian political societies.[25] Unlike his rivals candidates for appointment to the

muftiship, he was not a learned 'alim. As we have seen, Husam al-Din Jarallah was

the Inspector of the Shari'a Courts and Shaykh Khalil al-Khalidi, was the acting-head

of the Shari'a Court of Appeal, the other candidates were also well-qualified, such as

Musa al-Budayri, the qadi and supervisor of the 'Umar mosque. Compared to them

Hajj Amin was hopelessly underqualified.

Scholars have made much of Hajj Amin's political leanings and lack of

religious credentials, seeing these as factors that should have automatically

disqualified the mufti from consideration. Various reasons have been offered to

explain the appointment: British naivete, the colonial tendency to appease the native

community, the undue influence of the "notorious" pro-Arab official Ernest

Richmond, but none of these accounts is terribly convincing.[26] The problem here is

that these accounts of Hajj Amin's appointment grossly understate why he was

attractive to British officials, while overemphasizing his negatives, or more accurately

backdating his negatives.

---

[25] While in Cairo Hajj Amin was active in the creation of an organization to warn Palestinians about the dangers of Zionism. Mattar, *Mufti*, 9-11.

[26] The last point was made most strongly by Elie Kedourie, who credited Richmond with unduly influencing Herbert Samuel. For a critique of this argument see Mattar, *Mufti*, 26.

Hajj Amin's political leanings, for example, were more complex than is sometimes portrayed. Although a consistent advocate of Palestinian nationalism, he was not a consistent foe of the British occupation. In fact, Hajj Amin had worked for the military authorities as a clerk in the office of Gabriel Haddad, a Christian attaché to Ronald Storrs and in the department of public works in Qalqiliya, and had initially been described in a British intelligence report as being "reliably pro-British." And while it is true that Hajj Amin became a *persona non grata* in Palestine after the Nabi Musa festival of 1920 and would later make it onto the government's "black list", he was not regarded as consistently or radically anti-British until the 1930s.

His religious qualifications were undeniably weak but religious qualification had only been a secondary consideration in the elevation of Kamil al-Husayni to the position of grand mufti. Religious legitimacy was arguably even less important in choosing the mufti in 1921, since the British were merely replacing the grand mufti, not elevating someone to that position. Moreover, the appointment of someone with Hajj Amin's qualifications was not completely unheard of in the late Ottoman Empire, for in later years muftis were chosen who lacked an advanced religious education.[27] The appointment of a religious neophyte like Hajj Amin was thus not as clear a break with precedent as some scholars suggest.

This is not to say that the decision to appoint Hajj Amin was unanimous. Both the attorney general, Norman Bentwich, and the civil secretary, Wyndham Deedes opposed his appointment, whereas the assistant civil secretary, Ernest Richmond

---

[27] Kupferschmidt, *Supreme Muslim Council*, 20.

became Hajj Amin's chief advocate. These two sides represented the divide within the upper echelon of the Palestine Government between pro-Zionists (Bentwich and Deedes) and the pro-Arabs (Richmond). In the end the decision to support Hajj Amin was made by Herbert Samuel, who was motivated by practical politics rather than his own private support for Zionism. For Samuel the appointment of Hajj Amin was a means of curbing his interest in politics. This position was encouraged by the career of 'Arif al-'Arif, who had also been found guilty in absentia for the 1920 Nabi Musa riots. After receiving a pardon at the same time as Hajj Amin al-Husayni, 'Arif al-'Arif was appointed to a government position, in which he became a loyal and quiescent servant to the colonial project.

Samuel's decision also followed Richmond's advice that British support for the mufti would create good will within the Arab community, but it went beyond an attempt to pander. For Samuel the appointment would be used to pacify Hajj Amin by placing him in what was perceived as a non-political office. Samuel's thinking was made clear in his meeting with Hajj Amin on April 11, 1921, when he was able to secure "assurances that the influence of his family and himself would be devoted to maintaining tranquility in Jerusalem."[28] In the end, the high commissioner decided that Hajj Amin's popularity and influence trumped all his other deficiencies, and that it would be far better to reach out and integrate Hajj Amin into the colonial apparatus than allow him to fall into opposition where he was likely to be even more dangerous.

---

[28] This meeting is described in a letter from Samuel to Deedes: High Commissioner to Civil Secretary, April 11, 1921, ISA 2/10/245. Philip Mattar also notes that the high commissioner met with Hajj Amin on April 1, 1921, "to sound him out on his candidacy." Mattar, *Mufti*, 26.

It was therefore practical politics, not naivite or appeasement, which led the British to consider Hajj Amin as his brother's successor.

IV – The Election Debacle

Although Hajj Amin's candidacy was accepted by the British, the process of his appointment was shambolic. The problem lay with the results of an election held on April 12, 1921, to decide which three candidates from a field of six would be considered for appointment to the office of mufti of Jerusalem. This followed the traditional Ottoman practice for electing a mufti, whereby the governing power was charged with appointing the mufti from three candidates chosen by local Muslim electors. The Palestine Government was bound to follow this process by the terms of their mandate for Palestine and fully expected their favored candidate Hajj Amin to emerge as one of the top three vote getters. In the end, however, he finished fourth, behind Husam al-Din Jarallah, Khalil al-Khalidi, and Musa al-Budayri.[29]

The Husayni camp immediately criticized the election results for two different reasons. On the one hand, they argued that the election process was fundamentally flawed since the college of electors that had been put together by the colonial government did not conform to Ottoman practice and as a result was

---

[29] According to Taysir Jbara the breakdown in votes in the election was as follows: 1. Husam al-Jarallah (19 votes), 2. Khalil al-Khalidi (17), 3. Musa al-Budayri (12), 4. Hajj Amin al-Husayni (9), Muhammad Abu Su'ad al-'Awri, qadi of Jerusalem (3), and Amin al-'Awri, member of the Shar'ia court (2). These original figures come from a quote in an article by A. S. Yehuda in the *New York Times*, January 2, 1944 that was republished in Joseph Schetman, *The Mufti and the Fuehrer* (New York: T. Yoseloff, 1965). It is difficult to verify the accuracy of these figures, since there are no official tallies extant. See Jbara, *Palestinian Leader*, 42.

unrepresentative.[30] On the other hand, they accused the Zionists of interfering in the elections by supporting other candidates, particularly the top-vote getter Husam al-Din Jarallah. This latter charge was advertized all over the Old City in posters that were briefly put up by Hajj Amin's supporters on April 19, 1921, which claimed that the election was evidence of a Zionist plot to take over Palestine:

> Wake Up "Moslems"
> The Jews are interfering in the election of the Mufti
> Awake and prevent danger before it occurs. The accursed traitors whom you all know, have combined with the Jews, to have one of their party appointed Mufti on the following conditions:
>
> (1) To assist the Jews in the exchange of Moslem Wakfs and their sale to them specially the Wakf of Abu Maidan near the Wailing Wall
> (2) To assist the jews in killing the national spirit of the country.
> (3) To agree to all Jewish Zionist claims and to accept them on behalf of the Moslems.
> (4) To help in handing over to the Jews the Haram Esh-Sharif, the Dome of the Rock and El Aksa that they might pull them down and build in their place the Temple and the place of Sacrifice as stated by Alfred Mond and the president of the Zionist Commission Dr. Eder. Moslems you must know what you have been brought to in your own country if the Jews mock your religious feelings and public opinion and use their influence in appointing the man of their choice who would be under their orders.
> The pride of Islam is dead, but God wants to punish you for having opposed the Moslem Government of the Caliphate which protected the religion. Will you accept the shame to have a Jewish Zionist Mufti and that your religious affairs should become a plaything in their hands?[31]

---

[30] A minute from Ernest Richmond pointed out that they regarded the late election as "irregular and illegal because it did not proceed from the action of elected Municipalities and elected Administrative Councils. These do not exist and we cannot legally by means of the nominated bodies that have taken their place." See Richmond Minute on "Protest over elections from representatives in Jaffa," May 3, 1921, ISA 2/10/245. The details of this argument are well covered in Porath, *Emergence*, 191.

[31] The text of this proclamation comes from a British translation that is attached to a letter from the district commandant of police in Jerusalem to the district governor of Jerusalem. In that letter the policeman notes that five copies of the proclamation had been posted in the Old City between 11:00 pm and 12:00 am. See A. P. Albina, for District Commandant of Police, Jerusalem to District Governor of Jerusalem, April 20, 1921, ISA 2/10/245.

British officials did not directly engage with either of these criticisms, but their failure

to choose from among the first three candidates threw the election results into doubt.

For a moment, British officials, who were still interested in appointing Hajj Amin al-

Husayni, toyed with the idea of holding new elections, but it was ultimately decided

that the election results could stand if one of the top three vote-getters was persuaded

to drop out. This would enable Hajj Amin to stand in his place as one of the three

final candidates and assure his appointment.[32] When the Nabi Musa festival of 1921

passed without any violence, confirming Hajj Amin's assurance to the Palestine

government that he could make sure that it was peaceful, the Palestine Government

decided that Hajj Amin's candidacy was too important to pass up. They therefore

"persuaded" Husam al-Din Jarallah, who as Inspector of the Shari'a courts was a

government employee, to withdraw his candidacy. This finally cleared the way for

Hajj Amin's appointment as mufti on May 8, 1921.

Uri Kupferschmidt and Yehoshua Porath make much of the fact that Hajj

Amin's appointment was not officially confirmed in writing and that he was not

formally given the title of grand mufti held by his predecessor, seeing it as a sign of

---

[32] Ernest Richmond privately agreed that the elections were invalid and suggested that:

> the following method might be considered. To issue by means of gazette, press and
> possibly notices that the recent election having been shown to be irregular is null and
> void, that in view of the reception by the Government of Mazbatas from the
> Mudarisin, Imams, Ulemas (sic) and numerous individuals throughout Palestine, in
> favour of the appointment of Al Hajj Amin Al Husseini, the Government considers it
> to be clearly proved that the people of Palestine desire the nomination of Al Hajj
> Amin and consequently hereby nominate him.

Richmond Memorandum on the "Grand Mufti", no date, ISA 2/10/245.

official embarrassment over the government's intervention in the election.[33] But the

more significant message of the election debacle was that British support for Hajj

Amin had not wavered; by putting Hajj Amin in power, the High Commissioner had

got his man.

V - The Supreme Muslim Council

With Hajj Amin installed as the new mufti of Jerusalem the Palestine government

could create a more permanent Islamic administration. As we saw in the last chapter,

the Palestine government decided in 1920-21 in consultation with the Committee for

Moslem Religious Affairs to place Islamic affairs under the control of a "Central

Moslem Authority." The functions of this authority, as outlined in a November 9,

1920 meeting between government officials and Muslim representatives, were

threefold:

> (a) To supervise the administration of Moslem Waqfs
> (b) To nominate and dismiss Kadis of the Moslem Religious Court, and the
>   Members of the Moslem Court of Appeal subject to approval of the
>   Government
> (c) To exercise the functions formerly vested in the Sheikh El Islam in regard
>   to the appointment of Muftis, viz. to select one of the three persons elected
>   by the special Electoral College as candidates for the post of Mufti.[34]

As the last function makes clear, the decision to grant these powers to the Central

Moslem Authority was driven by a desire on the part of the colonial power to keep

much of the Ottoman system intact but without creating a British version of the *shaykh

al-Islam*. It was the Central Moslem Authority that would be the replacement for the

---

[33] Kupferschmidt, *Supreme Muslim Council,* 20 and Porath, *Emergence*, 193.

[34] "The Committee for Moslem Religious Affairs," Official Gazette, May 15th, 1921 in PRO CO 742/1.

shaykh al-Islam, a point confirmed in Herbert Samuel's statement on August 24, 1921,

that his government was "most anxious not to intervene in Moslem religious

matters."[35]

It would be more than a year before the "Central Moslem Authority" took

concrete form, owing to the death of the mufti of Jerusalem and the drawn out process

of appointing his successor and the aforementioned negotiations between the

government and Muslim representatives over the functions of the authority.[36] But

once these issues were worked out the "Central Moslem Authority" emerged as the

Supreme Muslim Council, which was created with the Supreme Muslim Council

Order of December 20, 1921.[37]

This order established the council as a five- person body, with a president (also

designated the *rai's al-'ulama*) and four members. Two of these members were to be

drawn from the *liwa'* ("district") of Jerusalem and one each from the *liwa's* of Nablus

and Acre, thereby giving the three former Ottoman districts representation. The act

also called for elections to decide who should serve on the council, laying out a

process that involved the formation of an electoral college chosen by the inhabitants of

each *liwa'* "in accordance with the Ottoman Law of Election to the Chamber of

Deputies."[38] This electoral college met on January 9, 1922, and elected Muhammad

Murad (the mufti of Haifa, for the Acre *liwa'*), 'Abd al-Latif Salah (a Nabulsi lawyer,

---

[35] Deedes to Colonial Office, PRO CO 733/6. A fuller version of Samuel's quote can be found on page 165.

[36] See pages 169-171.

[37] While the order was signed by the high commissioner on December 20, 1921 it was published in the official Gazette on January 1, 1922

[38] See article two of the "The Order Establishing the Supreme Muslim Council Order", Official Gazette, January 1, 1922. PRO CO 742/1.

for the Nablus *liwa'*), Sa'id Shawa (a Gazan landowner, for the Jerusalem *liwa'*), and

'Abdulla Dajani (an *'alim* from Jaffa, also for the Jerusalem *liwa'*). The mufti, Hajj

Amin al-Husayni, was chosen as the *ra'is al-'ulama*, underlining his power as the

leader of Palestinian Islam.

The order gave the council the right to administer and control Muslim

endowments, including control over the annual awqaf budget. This was made

effective by folding the existing General Waqf Committee and the other

subcommittees of the waqf administration into the council as subordinate parts of the

SMC. The council was also given the right to appoint and dismiss the director and

ma'murs (administrators) of the waqf system. At the same time, the council was

granted oversight of the shari'a court system, through its control over the nomination,

appointment and dismissal of all qadis, members of the shari'a court of appeal,

inspectors of the shari'a courts, and court officials. Finally, the council was given the

power to appoint the muftis of Palestine.[39]

This gave the council almost unfettered control over the administration of

Islam in Palestine, which would be further enhanced by the Palestine government's

consistent reluctance to exercise its limited rights of supervision (see fn. 39). The

council also managed more than one thousand religious personnel, annual revenues

---

[39] There were some qualifications involved with these rights. The council's nominees for qadi or for membership on the shari'a court of appeal were technically subject to approval by the Palestine Government, though it does not appear that the government ever exercised this right. The council was also required to send notice to the government of the dismissal of any officials from the waqf administration or the shari'a courts, although again it appears that this requirement was rarely fulfilled or exercised. The council's awqaf budget was also to be sent to the Palestine Government for information purposes. Finally, while the council was given the right to appoint muftis, the election of candidates for each muftiship was to be decided by a proposed independent "Special Election College," or in the case of the mufti of Beersheba, by the tribal shaykhs of the district. See Article 8, *Ibid.*

exceeding £E60,000, a network of educational and charitable institutions, and tens of

thousands of *dunums* of waqf land, all significant assets for whoever was in charge of

the council.[40]

VI - Hajj Amin in Control

It was the SMC and not its president, Hajj Amin al-Husayni, which was the

replacement for the *shaykh al-Islam*. Set up as a five-member council, the president

had to share power with four other elected officials, theoretically ensuring that no one

figure could dominate the council. In practice, however, Hajj Amin was able to

control the body by cultivating alliances with his fellow members. Of the four

councilors elected in the January 9, 1923 elections, Muhammad Murad, Sa'id Shawa,

'Abdulla Dajani, and 'Abd al-Latif Salah, three became strong allies of the mufti. As

Uri Kupferschmidt has detailed, "Sa'id Shawa from Gaza received [from Hajj Amin

al-Husayni] extensive powers in the south of the country, and in the same way

'Abdullah Dajani in Jaffa and Muhammad Murad in Haifa were turned into loyal

allies. Only 'Abd al-Latif Salah of Nablus ventured to voice some opposition, which

---

[40] The Palestine Government report of 1924 stated that the Supreme Muslim Council employed 552 waqf officers, 91 individuals in 15 shari'a courts, and a further 550 marriage registrars (*ma'dhun*s) for a total of 1193 employees. See Kupfershmidt, *Supreme Muslim Council*, 58.

The revenues for the council averaged £E 60,378 during the 1920s. This figure would rise in the 1930s and 1940s, so that over the course of the mandate the average was £ (Egyptian or Palestinian) 76,639. See Kupferschmidt, *Supreme Muslim Council*, 173.

A *dunum* is the Arabic equivalent of the Ottoman Turkish *dönüm*, a measure of area that corresponded during the Ottoman period and for the first decade of British period to 919.3 square meters (9,895 sq ft). In 1928, the measurement was changed to refer to 1000 square meters and is still used as a measurement of land in Israel.

brought him into fierce conflict with the President of the Supreme Council."[41] The

mufti was also able to consolidate power in the council by appointing his extended

family members and loyal deputies to positions throughout the shari'a court system

and the waqf authority.[42]

These moves ensured that the mufti's authority over the council would not be

challenged from within but Hajj Amin's position as president was challenged from the

outside. Hajj Amin and his supporters, commonly referred to as the *Majlisiyyun*

("Councilors", due to their control of the SMC) were opposed by a rival group called

the *Mu'aridun* ("Opposition"), led by the al-Nashashibi family. The al-Nashashibis

were the traditional rivals of the al-Husaynis in Jerusalem and formed the most

important opposition to the al-Husaynis through the mandate. In the early years of the

SMC, the al-Nashashibis sent numerous complaints to the Palestine government about

the nepotism and corruption of the Husayni-dominated SMC and called into question

the idea that the mufti should have control over the religious institutions of the Muslim

community.[43] These complaints were particularly strong in 1925-26 when the SMC

was required by its charter to hold new elections, a moment in which the opposition

hoped to blunt Hajj Amin's power within the council.[44] Although these complaints

were collected by the Palestine government, the documentary record suggests that they

---

[41] Kupferschmidt, *Supreme Muslim Council*, 65.

[42] This nepotism is well detailed in Kupferschmidt, *Supreme Muslim Council*, 69-71.

[43] The complaints of the al-Nashishibis and other complainants are collected in ISA 2/172, ISA 2/6/189, and ISA 2/190.

[44] Article 2 of "The Order Establishing the Supreme Muslim Council" stated that the members of the council would be elected for a period of four years, except for the *Rais al-Ulama* who would be the permanent president of the council. See the "The Order Establishing the Supreme Muslim Council Order", Official Gazette, January 1, 1922. PRO CO 742/1.

fell on deaf ears. The government's positive attitude towards the mufti did not change, and the high commissioner at the time, Lord Herbert Plumer, continued his predecessor's laissez-faire approach to the council. This inaction on the part of the government allowed the mufti to amend the election procedure to ensure that his control over the council was not threatened by this opposition. Pushing through an amendment that reduced the power of the elected members of the municipalities— the "foci of the Opposition," according to Uri Kupferschmidt— Hajj Amin was able to insulate the council against the rising power of the moderate opposition.[45] The success of this maneuver was shown by the fact that after this time, opposition complaints about the council dropped off as the al-Nashashibis looked elsewhere to challenge the power of the al-Husaynis.

The mufti's control over the SMC was therefore not built into its structure from the beginning but was achieved through a grab for power by the mufti and his supporters. British records reveal that the Palestine government showed little alarm over this development. In fact, in 1926 John Shuckburgh, the head of the Middle East department of the Colonial Office, boasted that, "The institution of a Supreme Moslem Council in 1921, has, on the whole, been one of our most successful moves in Palestine. It practically gave the Mohammedans self-government in regard to Moslem affairs."[46]

---

[45] Kupferschmidt, *Supreme Muslim Council*, 29.

[46] Shuckburgh to CO, November 3, 1926, PRO CO 733/13. Sir John Evelyn Shuckburgh had been brought by Winston Churchill from the India Office to head the Middle East Department when it was founded in February 1921.

Why did British officials not react to the mufti's power grab within the SMC? This is an important question because it was his control over the SMC that ensured that he was one of the most powerful figures in the Arab community, which enabled him to eventually emerge as a powerful nationalist foe of the Palestine government. British inaction obviously did not come from ignorance of Hajj Amin's actions, for officials had been made well aware of the issue of corruption and nepotism in the SMC during the election contest of 1925-26.[47] Instead it came from a feeling that Hajj Amin was ultimately working for them. As we have seen, British support for Hajj Amin was based in large part on his ability to keep Palestinian Muslims quiet. This meant that as long as the mufti remained loyal and there was no recurrence of the violence that had taken place at the Nabi Musa festival of 1920, officials were happy to turn a blind eye to corruption and nepotism within the SMC. In fact, the mufti's consolidation of power could be seen as a positive development, since it would enable the mufti to exercise greater control over his community. Such an approach cannot be seen as surprising, for as in other colonial contexts, security was always more important than democratic reform in Palestine. Interestingly, as we shall see in Chapter 6, even when violence did occur under Hajj Amin's watch, as in the case of rioting at the Western Wall in 1929, the Palestine government continued to back their man despite calls from many Zionists, British officials, and even some Arabs for the

---

[47] ISA 2/6/189 preserves a large number of petitions from Arabs who protested the elections during this period.

mufti's powers to be curbed.[48] This was because they saw the mufti as the only person

capable of keeping control of the Muslim community. It was only in 1937, with the

mufti's participation in the Palestine Arab Revolt putting him into direct conflict with

British rule, that British officials took action by removing Hajj Amin from power and

placing the SMC under British control.

Another major factor in this laissez-faire approach was the aforementioned

reluctance of officials to intervene in religious affairs. As we shall see in the next

chapter, British officials policed the political sphere in Palestine in an effort to

minimize political activities that challenged British rule in Palestine. This was not the

case in the religious realm, where the adoption of political positions that opposed the

Palestine government (such as sermonizing against the legislative council elections of

1923) were seen as regrettable but not nearly as dangerous as an unchecked political

sphere. Most importantly, as shown in the appointment of Hajj Amin, religion was

considered by British officials to be a check on the political impulse. According to

this point of view Hajj Amin's concentration of power was not obviously dangerous;

instead it might be useful in creating a strong institution in the Palestinian Arab

community that would divert Palestinian attention away from politics.

In supporting his view that the creation of the SMC was an act of appeasement,

Uri Kupferschmidt argues that the British willingly created the conditions that allowed

for the SMC to become the leading political power in the Arab community. He points

---

[48] Even before the violence at the Wall, representatives from Hebron sent petitions to the Palestine
government claiming that the government was shirking its duty as the mandatory by ignoring the
criticisms of the people against the corruption of the mufti. See ISA 3/293/K/13/31.

out that the SMC became the Arab equivalent of the Jewish Agency and that this development was prefigured in its birth. However, as I have argued, the SMC was initially developed as a solution to the collapse of the Ottoman religious system. The SMC was never imagined as a political institution equivalent to the Arab or Jewish agency; rather, as a kind of neo-millet it would be an institution within which the religious and social affairs of the Muslim community could be self-regulated and self-contained. That it was not intended to be equivalent to an Arab Agency is shown in the fact that British officials proposed the creation of an entirely separate Arab Agency in July 1923, when the SMC had already been in existence for a year and a half.[49] In actuality, the emergence of the SMC as major player in Arab politics came as something of a shock to British officials. Intended in part to blunt Palestinian political aspirations, the council was not supposed to become a voice for Palestinian nationalism.

VII - The Novelty of the Council

The creation of the Supreme Muslim council was certainly a novel development for Palestinian Islam, but was it a "hybrid institution...never conceived of by Islam in the past," as a Zionist political memorandum of the period claimed?[50] J. B. Barron, Director of Revenue and Customs, argued in his 1922 report "Mohammedan Wakfs in

---

[49] According to Ann Mosely Lesch this Arab Agency was "a pale reflection of the Jewish Agency," since it would have had no international standing, no real independence, and few of the powers of the Jewish agency. Ann Mosely Lesch, *Arab Politics in Palestine, 1917-1939: The Frustration of a National Movement* (Ithaca, NY: Cornell University Press, 1979), 186-87.

[50] This quote comes from an undated Zionist memorandum on the SMC, CZA S25/10/373 and is quoted in Kupferschmidt, *Supreme Muslim Council*, 5.

Palestine," that the creation of the SMC grew out of British experiences elsewhere, though he admitted that it differed from British practice in Cyprus (where the corresponding body was appointed by the High Commissioner) or Iraq (where the Department of Awqaf was under the supervision of the Judicial Secretary). He also found a direct precedent for British policy in Palestine in the "Wakf Mohammedan Assembly" of Bosnia and Herzegovina, which had been operating since Austria's annexation of the territory in 1908.[51] In short, it is difficult to see the creation of an independent Muslim-run religious authority as a complete break with imperial precedent.

As mentioned in the introduction to this dissertation, Uri Kupferschmidt has taken a rather different view by arguing that the creation of the SMC was a clear innovation. He argues that not only did British policy obviously differ from the Anglo-Muhammedan law system in India, but it also broke in important ways with the British approach in Cyprus, Egypt, and Sudan, where British administrators established some form of financial and regulatory control over waqf ministries and shari'a affairs.[52] He also argues that Palestine was an "exceptional case" when it came to the British and French mandates set up after the First World War. Elsewhere in the Middle East, the mandatory powers had "retained some measure of control over the Shari'a Courts although they shared this control to different degrees with local

---

[51] J. B. Barron, "Muhammedan Wakfs in Palestine," this is an unpublished draft report, PRO CO 733/20. Barron would later turn this report into a published book on waqf.

[52] See Kupferschmidt, *Supreme Muslim Council*, 6-16.

governments (through Ministries or Departments of Justice) and rulers (e. g. the King

of Iraq and the Emir of Jordan)."[53]

According to Kupferschmidt, "the situation in which [colonial officials] laid

down guidelines and devised solutions regarding the religious rights and status of

these Muslim communities was often repeated [across the colonial world]." For this

reason he contends that, "the uniqueness of the Supreme Muslim Council did not lie in

the historical option by virtue of which it was set up."[54] That is to say, the problem in

Palestine—how to create a workable Muslim religious system—was a problem that

had already been faced elsewhere. (To underline this point Kupferschmidt even

quotes Lord Cromer's statement that the "oriental situation is very much the same

everywhere."[55]) Given that the situation was the same, ipso facto the solution should

have been the same as in other contexts. That the SMC emerged as the most

independent of all Muslim religious authorities can thus only be understood in his eyes

as a departure from colonial precedent. This allows Kupferschmidt to present the

SMC as an innovation that was uncalled for and unnecessarily risky. And for him the

only explanation for why the British would depart from colonial precedent was a lack

of nerve on the part of the colonial government—hence his insistence that the creation

of the SMC was an act of appeasement.

But, this line of argument is undermined by Kupferschmidt's own account of

British and French colonial policy towards Islam. As he points out, there was actually

____

[53] Ibid., 14.
[54] Ibid. 5.
[55] Ibid., 5.

a diversity of approaches in both empires, which were influenced by specific local conditions. The hands-off approach that the British adopted in regards to Islam in Egypt, for instance, was very different from their treatment of Islam in neighboring Sudan. Whereas in Egypt the British were reluctant to intervene in shari'a law, in Sudan they reorganized the shari'a judiciary and established a Board of 'Ulama'. These divergent approaches were influenced by the local political situation: in Egypt deference to local elites made intervention undesirable, while in Sudan the perceived need to quell popular "Mahdist tendencies" among the Islamic leadership led the British to adopt interventionist reforms in the religious realm.[56]

This complicates the idea that the creation of the SMC was some kind of aberrant development, for there was no standard colonial religious policy. The creation of the SMC, just like the creation of the Board of 'Ulama' in the Sudan, was a response tailored to the local context and the demands of the local colonial government. The implication in Kupferschmidt's book and other accounts of the SMC is that it was a problem child from its birth and that the mistake that British officials made was in creating such a flawed institution in the first place. But if we want to understand the failures of the SMC, we need to look at its development over time which transformed its relationship with the colonial government and the Jewish community. This will be the subject of Chapter 6.

---

[56] Ibid., 12.

VIII – Conclusion

Britain's support for Kamil al-Husayni and Hajj Amin al-Husayni and its desire to

build a strong, independent Muslim religious body, was part of a plan to devolve

religious oversight to local Muslims. This would bring the Muslim community into

line with other religious communities in Palestine, which had long enjoyed autonomy

in religious and communal affairs. The alternative would have been to have some

form of direct British oversight in the administration of Islam, an approach that would

have been difficult for local Muslims to swallow. More importantly, this was not a

solution that British officials could countenance. A system of direct colonial control

over religion would have been at odds with the duties of the mandatory power, which

was constrained by its responsibility to protect the status quo. As Kupferschmidt

himself notes, "we have to bear in mind that the Council's establishment came

towards the end of the era of colonial rule and not at the beginning of it."[57] That is to

say, what was possible in the administration of Indian religion in the eighteenth and

nineteenth centuries was very different from what was possible in Palestine in the

twentieth.

At the same time the creation of a British-run Islamic system would have

necessitated the creation of a religious bureaucracy within the colonial administration,

something that the cash-strapped, self-supporting Palestine Government wanted to

avoid. The creation of the SMC enabled the British to pass responsibility for Muslim

---

[57] Kupferschmidt, *Supreme Muslim Council*, 6.

affairs to a body that was, at least initially, friendly to the Palestine government. This suggests that appeasement is the wrong way of framing the debate about the emergence of the SMC. That judgment implies that the concession that granted the Muslim community control over its own affairs was a failure by the Palestine government to play the part of the imperial overseer. But as we have seen this is at odds with the specific interests of the Palestine government, which wanted to construct a stable system that would require minimal intervention on their part into local religious matters.

The appeasement angle may make some sense if we look backwards from the later history of the SMC, when the institution was involved in nationalist politics. This is why Kupferschmidt, for example, highlights Harry Luke's criticism in 1929 (when he was the acting-high commissioner of Palestine) that the "delegation to the Supreme Muslim Council of jurisdiction so extensive and powers so wide as to be to some extent almost an abdication by the Administration of Palestine of responsibilities normally incumbent upon Government."[58] But, if we view the establishment of an independent Muslim administration from the perspective of 1918, a different judgment emerges. I would argue that the emergence of a politicized SMC in the late 1920s could not have been predicted in December 1921, when the Supreme Muslim Council came into being. To understand this evolution we need to move beyond the conditions of its conception and investigate its consequent development. This will be the subject of the final two chapters of this study.

---

[58] Kupferschmidt, *Supreme Muslim Council*, 18.

Chapter Five

Religion and Politics under British Rule

I - Introduction

On the morning of April 4, 1920 violence broke out in Jerusalem during the annual Nabi Musa festival. The fighting began when Arab pilgrims who had recently arrived from Hebron and who had listened to a series of Arab nationalist speeches given by members of the notability began attacking Jewish onlookers. This sparked four days of sporadic attacks by Arabs on the Jewish quarter of Jerusalem, counterattacks by armed Zionist paramilitaries, and a crackdown by British troops. By the time order had been restored, nine people were dead, 244 were wounded, and numerous buildings had been looted or attacked. Jerusalem was placed under martial law for the first time since the opening days of the British occupation.

The violence at the Nabi Musa festival was significant because it called into question Britain's security arrangements in the city and more fundamentally its plans for ruling Palestine. Before the events of April 1920, most British officials operated under a misguided belief that the local Arab population had accepted their occupation. Such naïve ideas were ended with the violence at Nabi Musa, as officials in London and Jerusalem scrambled to understand how the situation in Palestine had gotten so bad and how it could be saved.

Of the two major moments of violence at the beginning of British rule in Palestine—in Jerusalem at the Nabi Musa festival in April 1920 and at Jaffa in May

223

1921—it was the violence of the religious festival that was most upsetting to British officials. Those officials had written home shortly after the conquest of Jerusalem stating that there was an "absence of religious intolerance in Palestine," and that local Muslims were "religious [but] not bigoted."[1] The outbreak of violence at a religious event brought back all the old stereotypes from the nineteenth century about Arab religious fanaticism. The festival's bringing together of religion and politics gave ammunition to those who saw Pan-Islam as a real threat to Britain's position, particularly when it was alleged by some Zionist officials and British intelligence officers that foreign provocateurs had infiltrated the crowd. And, the fact that the attacks were mostly carried out by uneducated peasants seemed to confirm the British stereotype that the fellah was a "noble savage" who could easily be moved to violence through the religious incitement of a crafty notability.

But it wasn't religion that provoked the crowd at the festival, it was nationalism. Palestinian Arab speakers appealed to the assembled crowd to defend the nation not Islam, although at this time the nation was understood to refer to Greater Syria. These speakers were not religious speakers but were individuals involved in Arab politics—Musa Kazim al-Husayni (the mayor of Jerusalem), Muhammad Amin al-Husayni (then a young man involved in anti-Zionist politics), and 'Arif al-'Arif (an educator and editor of the pro-Faysal Arab nationalist paper *Suriyya al-Junubiyya*). As the Palin Commission, a commission of enquiry into the cause of violence at the festival and the reasons for Britain's security failure, later concluded, Arab

---

[1] These quotes come from reports sent home to London early in 1918. See PRO FO 371/3383 and PRO FO 371/3391/37361.

"frustration" had little to do with religion but came from their rejection of the terms of British rule in Palestine, particularly Britain's support for Jewish settlement.[2]

The event was given different names by its participants reflecting different narrative readings of the violence. For the British the event was called the Jerusalem Riots or the Easter Riots, reflecting an official reluctance to present the event as a political act against British rule. To Zionist leaders and the wider Jewish community this was a pogrom—a stunning charge that reflected Jewish mistrust of the military authorities, who they regarded as being pro-Arab. For Arabs, the violence was an unfortunate but understandable reaction to Zionist provocation in Palestine. This explanation of self-defense would be dropped in later Palestinian nationalist accounts, which presented the riots of Nabi Musa as the first Palestinian nationalist revolt against British rule.[3] Despite this difference of opinion, witnesses before the Palin commission and indeed the commission itself agreed that these were not random acts of destruction—the violence was political. The nationalist speeches, the display of a portrait of Emir Faysal, and the chanting of anti-Zionist slogans convinced the

---

[2] The commission was a military court of enquiry since the events occurred when Palestine was still under military control. It consisted of Major-General P. C. Palin (Chairman), Brigadier-General G. A. Wildblood, and Lieutenant-Colonel C. Vaughn-Edwards with Mr. MacBarnet (a judge from the Court of Appeal in Egypt) as Legal Advisor.

[3] For example, the event is described as *al-Thawra al-Ula* (The First Revolt) in the memoirs of Muhammad Izzat Darwazeh. The historian 'Abd al-Wahhab Kayyali calls the event *al-Thawra al-Ashreen* (The Revolt of 1920). See Mohammad Izzat Darwazeh, *Mudhakirat Muhammad 'Izzat Darwazeh* [The Memoirs of Muhammad 'Izzat Darwazeh], Volume 1 (Beirut: Dar al-Gharb al-Islami, 1993), 320 and 'Abd al-Wahhab Kayyali, *Tarikh Filastin al-Hadith* (Beirut: al-Mu'assat al-Arabiyya al-Harasat wa al-Nashar, 1981)

commission and British officials that something more was going on than the usual

tensions of religious celebration in Palestine.[4]

After gathering evidence from some 152 witnesses, the Palin commission

produced a report on July 1, 1921 at Port Said. The report concluded that the violence,

while not justified, resulted from specific Arab frustrations:

> (a) Disappointment at the non-fulfillment of promises made to them by British propaganda.
> (b) Inability to reconcile the Allies' declared policy of self-determination with the Balfour Declaration, giving rise to a sense of betrayal and intense anxiety over their future.
> (c) Misapprehension of the true meaning of the Balfour Declaration and forgetfulness of the guarantees determined therein, due to the loose rhetoric of politicians and the exaggerated statements and writings of interested persons, chiefly Zionists.
> (d) Fear of Jewish competition and domination, justified by experience and the apparent control exercised by the Zionists over the Administration.
> (e) Zionist indiscretion and aggression, since the Balfour Declaration aggravating this feeling.
> (f) Anti-British and anti-Zionist propaganda working on the population already inflamed by the sources of irritation aforementioned.[5]

In some ways these findings were groundbreaking because they recognized the

political commonsense of Arabs. The court of enquiry rejected the stereotype that the

peasant was apolitical and moved purely by emotion, and instead acknowledged an

Arab desire for self determination, although nowhere does the word nationalism

appear. But this finding did not have much influence on British policy because the

report was never published. Official acknowledgment of the fact that the political

---

[4] British accounts of the festival even before the Palin report presented the Nabi Musa festival as a moment of high tension in Palestine. In fact the earliest British report on the festival in April 1918 boasted that while the Ottomans had had to bring in large numbers of troops to police the festival, the British were able to keep the peace with a small contingent of police. See PRO FO 371/3391/92045

[5] PRO WO 32/9614.

aims of the Arab community might in any way be at odds with British rule was considered to be unhelpful and the report was buried in the British archives.[6]

This was also not the first time that nationalist speeches had been made in a public forum; indeed two political demonstrations had taken place in Jerusalem in February and March of 1920. Palestinian Arab political societies and religious leaders had also raised public and private objections to the Balfour Declaration and to British rule well before April 1920. What was significant here was the mass nature of the protest and, most crucially, the violence. The Nabi Musa riot seemed to suggest that political disaffection was found in a wider swath of the Palestinian public than just an educated notable elite. It also demonstrated how nationalist protest could combine with religious celebration, a development that represented a challenge to the British policy of noninterference in religious matters.

This chapter investigates this intersection between religion and politics and how British policy was built around keeping them separated from each other. It will argue that the British approach was built in part on surveillance and intervention into local politics, greater colonial oversight of mass gatherings, and an attempt by the imperial power to divert Arab politics into a regulated system of politics. I contend

---

[6] This was due to the fact that by the time the final report was drafted in mid-July 1920, the newly installed civilian administration had no wish to reopen the controversy. Indeed, High Commissioner Herbert Samuel had already decided to pardon the main protagonists in the event: 'Arif al-'Arif and Hajj Amin al-Husayni, who had been found guilty of incitement, and Vladimir Jabotinsky and his Zionist colleagues, who had organized an illegal Jewish milita. It is also true that the findings of the court of enquiry conflicted with Samuel's personal belief that the political grievances of the Arab community were largely superficial and could be overcome by better British propaganda.

Samuel's superiors in London agreed with his request and that of the Zionist Commission that the report remain unpublished. See WO 32/9614.

that British success in blunting the power of local politicians had the effect of so

weakening Arab political parties that by the end of the 1920s people were searching

elsewhere for a political advocate. Into this political vacuum stepped the SMC, which

will be detailed in the chapter that follows.

II – The Earliest Nationalist Groups

As in other countries of the region, in the territory that became Palestine, the first

major political organizations emerged in the early twentieth century and frequently.

Among the earliest parties were branches of the Committee of Union and Progress

established in order to raise the political consciousness of the local Arab elite during

its takeover of the Ottoman empire.[7] But the CUP's attempts to Turkify and secularize

the Ottoman empire also pushed Arabs to join political societies that advocated for

Muslim and Arab causes in opposition to CUP policies. The Muhammedan Union

Societies, for example, organized Arab opponents to Ottoman reform around the issue

of Islam, and were established across the Levant. The Decentralization Party, which

was established in Cairo by Syrian émigrés in 1913, called for equality and greater

autonomy for Arabs under Ottoman rule, a message that was popular enough in

Palestine to lead to the establishment of branches in Nablus, Jenin, Tulkarm, and

Jaffa.[8] Finally, *al-Jamiyyah al-Arabiyya al-Fatat* (The Youth Arab Society or simply

al-Fatat), an Arab nationalist group that was originally founded in Paris in 1911 and

---

[7] Divine, *Ottoman Palestine*, 148.

[8] For a good discussion of these groups see Muslih, *Origins*, 63.

which called for greater Arab rights, drew Palestinians to its branches in Beirut and Damascus before the First World War.

Other political groups were geared towards more local issues. In 1910 Najib Nassar, the publisher of the nationalist paper *al-Karmil*, founded an association in Haifa to combat Zionist immigration, while Arabs in Jaffa set up "The Patriotic Ottoman Party" for the same purpose.[9] As the name of the latter party suggests, opposition to Zionism at that time did not necessarily equate with support for Arab nationalism, let alone the championing of Palestinian nationalism. The complexity of such positioning is shown in Donna Robinson Divine's comment that, "The threads of an Arab nationalist consciousness can surely be found embedded in the programs and discussion of these nascent political organizations, but so can expressions of absolute political loyalty."[10]

It is important to note, however, that the number of Palestinian Arabs involved in organized Arab nationalist groups before the First World War was, as Yehoshua Porath, has put it, "infinitesimal". As a result their influence on local politics was also small. Perhaps only a score of Palestinians were involved in the major Arab nationalist societies, and none of those societies advocated a separate Palestinian nationalism.[11] Even if we add the individuals involved in political associations like Najib Nasser's group or "The Patriotic Ottoman Party" the number of Palestinian

---

[9] Porath, *Emergence*, 29.

[10] Divine, *Ottoman Palestine*, 162.

[11] Porath counts only 24 Palestinians as active in Arab nationalist societies, while C. E. Dawn puts the number at 22 Palestinians, with a further 10 joining during the war. Porath, *Emergence*, 20; C. Earnest Dawn, "The Rise of Arabism in Syria," *Middle East Journal*, vol. 16 (1962), 148-49.

Arabs involved in political groups was tiny and represented only the most educated elite.

The Arab Revolt and the brutal rule of Jamal Pasha in Syria brought more Palestinian Arabs into politics, although for the most part the political elite remained loyal to the Ottoman empire. It was the collapse of the Ottoman Empire, and above all the occupation of the country by Britain, which supported Jewish immigration to Palestine, that profoundly changed politics in the country. In the wake of the Great War, buoyed by Wilson's promises of national self-determination and the (vague) promise of Arab self-determination in the region, Palestinians began to organize themselves into political societies that expected to play a role in the future of the country.

Two of the most important political parties formed after the First World War were the Muntada al-Adabi ("The Literary Society", founded in January 1918) and the Nadi al-Arabi ("The Arab Club," founded in late 1918). These societies were formed by the younger generation of the country's leading notable families, many of whom had gained experience in Arab nationalist organizations during the war in Beirut, Cairo, and Damascus.[12] For instance, the eventual mufti Hajj Amin al-Husayni had first gotten into politics as a student in Cairo during the war, where he had founded an Arab club opposed to Zionism.[13] When he returned home after the war he used this experience to become a leading figure in the Nadi al-Arabi, which took a similar anti-

---

[12] As Bayan al-Hout points out, the early Arab political societies drew upon the notable youth. Hajj Amin al-Husayni was only twenty-one when he helped found the *Nadi al-Arabi* political society in 1918. Bayan al-Hout, *al-Qiyadat wa al-Mou'assasat*, 86.

[13] Mattar, *Mufti of Jerusalem*, 9.

Zionist stance. Shaykh Abdul Qadir al-Muzaffar, another major figure in the Nadi al-Arabi (he became its president in 1923), had previously been a member of a club of the same name in Damascus.[14] Izzat Darwazeh, secretary of the Nadi al-Arabi in the early 1920s had founded the *Al-Jami'a al-Filistiniyya* ("Palestinian Society") in Damascus after the war.[15] Other politicians such as Naghib al-Nashashibi, who later became the mayor of Jerusalem and was a founding member of the moderate *Hizb al-Watani* (the Palestinian National Party), gained political experience in Emir Faysal's short-lived General Syrian Congress in Damascus. Some politicians even fought for Arab rights while in Europe, such as Awni Abdul Hadi who founded al-Fatat (the Young Arab society) in Paris in 1911 and was one of the organizers of the first Arab nationalist congress in Paris in 1913.[16] Indeed, the two clubs themselves were originally branches of organizations that were already established outside of Palestine: the Nadi al-Arabi being an offshoot of the al-Fatat club in Damascus and the Muntada al-Adabi simply being the Palestinian branch of a society of the same name that was originally founded in Istanbul in 1909 as a place for Arab visitors and residents to gather.[17]

---

[14] See PASSIA, "Palestine Personalities," < http://www.passia.org/palestine_facts/personalities/>.

[15] Darwasah, *Muthakirat*, 320.

[16] The exchange of ideas between Palestine and other regional capitals (particularly Damascus, Cairo, and Beirut) was also carried out through the circulation of newspapers across the region and the reprinting of foreign newspaper articles in local newspapers. The two most important Palestinian nationalist newspapers of the mandate period, Haifa's *al-Karmil* (edited by Najib Nassar) and Jaffa's *Filastin* (edited by 'Isa and Yusuf al-'Isa) regularly reprinted news articles and editorials from papers such as *Alif Ba* (Damascus), *Lisan al-Hal* (Beirut), and *al-Muqattam* and *al-Ahram* (Cairo).

For a discussion of the impact of Palestinian and regional newspapers on Palestinian politics see Khalidi's *Palestinian Identity*, 119-144. Also see Qustandi Shomali, *al-Jarida Filastin 1911-1967* (Jerusalem: Jerusalem Research Center, 1992).

[17] Muslih, *Origins*, 164.

Both the Nadi al-Arabi and Muntada al-Adabi presented themselves as cultural clubs but were ostensibly Arab nationalist societies that strongly opposed Zionism and advocated unification with Syria as a means for protecting Palestinian rights. The main difference between the two clubs was the fact that the Nadi al-Arabi was run by the younger generation of the al-Husayni family and the Muntada al-Adabi by their great rivals, the younger generation of the al-Nashashibi family. As a result, these societies were used to promote the power of these two families in and around Jerusalem. This meant that from the beginning Arab politics was not unified but divided by familial rivalries amongst the elite, no doubt contributing to a 1919 British assessment that the notability was too divided to be politically effective.[18]

This split between the al-Husayni and al-Nashashibi camps, particularly the competition in the 1930s between the Husayni *Majlisi* (Council) faction and the Nashashibi *Mu'aridi* (Opposition) faction, has often been presented as one of the main reasons for Arab weakness during the mandate period.[19] The impact of this division is somewhat exaggerated for the mandate period as a whole but it is quite misleading when assessing the early years of Arab politics. Those years reveal that although the two sides had somewhat different views about the future of the country, the Nadi al-Arabi and Muntada al-Adabi frequently worked together. This is shown in their drafting of joint letters of protest, their co-organizing of demonstrations, and their

---

[18] See Great Britain, Foreign Office, "Syria and Palestine Handbook" (London: 1919), 56-57, in PRO FO 373/5/E132.

For a discussion of the coordination between the two societies see Porath, *Emergence*, 77. A number of their joint petitions and letters of protest can be found in the Israel State Archives, for example, see ISA 2/1/30 and ISA 2/4/140.

[19] The council referred to the Supreme Muslim Council headed by Hajj Amin al-Husayni.

coordination of advocates to appear before the King-Crane Commission in 1919 (the

latter action is described in more detail below). The fundamental problem for the

Arab community at the time, as would be the case throughout the mandate, was not a

lack of unity but a lack of material and military power vis-à-vis the Zionist enterprise

and the colonial government.

IV - Muslim and Christian Cooperation

Al-Jamiah al-Islamiyya al-Masahiyya ("The Muslim-Christian Association," hereafter

MCA) was another political society that was established at the beginning of the

mandate. Founded in Jaffa in early November 1918, the association spread to

Jerusalem two weeks later and then went on to establish some 15 branches throughout

the country over the next year or so.[20] As such, the MCA came to have a greater reach

than the Nadi al-Arabi and Muntada al-Adabi, which remained centered on Jerusalem.

The most important way in which the MCA differed from the other two clubs was that

it was founded by members of the older generation of the Palestinian notability,

individuals whose political experience came from careers in the Ottoman

administration as opposed to recent membership in literary and cultural societies. The

first president of the MCA (and mayor of Jerusalem), Musa Kazim al-Husayni, for

example, had served as the Ottoman *qai'maqam* (subgovernor) of Jaffa, Safad, and

Acre, and also as the district governor of Yemen. His high standing during the

---

[20] al-Hout, *al-Qiyadat wa al-Mou'assassat*, 81.

233

Ottoman period was reflected in the honorific "Pasha" which was attached to his name.[21] And. his successor as president, 'Arif al-Dajani (also recognized as a pasha) had served as the mayor of Jerusalem in the final years of Ottoman rule. Because of its experience of working with the Ottomans, the MCA was more moderate in its tone towards the British, calling for Palestine's independence under British tutelage rather than the country's immediate integration into Emir Faysal's Arab kingdom.

The statutes of the MCA defined it as an organization that aimed to increase the political, economic, and educational power of the Arab community as a means for protecting its national rights "morally and materially".[22] Although the society did not present itself as a political group, it did see its duty as representing the rights of the Palestinian people: "The object of this society is to look after the interests of Palestine generally, and its resolutions are valid to all the districts of Palestine."[23] The joint Muslim and Christian membership was central to the association's attempt to be representative and there is some evidence that a religious quota system operated to ensure that both Muslims and Christians were represented in the organization.[24]

---

[21] <http://www.passia.org/palestine_facts/personalities>

[22] The statutes stated that the "purpose of the society is to elevate the interests of the country (Palestine) connected with agriculture, technics (sic.), economics and commerce, the revival of science and the education of the national youth and the protection of national rights, morally and materially." ISA 2/5/155.

[23] Ibid. Despite this claim the statutes do appear to provide the local districts the ability to reject resolutions made by the association's General Palestine Society. It is for this reason that a number of scholars have decided to talk about Muslim Christian Associations rather than a single Muslim Christian Association.

[24] The Jerusalem branch for example was composed of "forty members 10 of whom are of the Moslem Relief Society, 5 Latins and 5 Greek Orthodox and 10 of the villages," which indicates that some form of religious quota system was in place. It is unclear if this ratio was kept in other branches. Ibid. The Nadi al-Arabi and Muntada al-Adabi also included Christian members, but as Mushammad Muslih has pointed out, Christians were overrepresented in the MCA as compared to their percentage in the wider Arab population. Muslih, *Origins*, 162-164.

For British officials who viewed the local population as being divided into a
Muslim community, a Christian community, and a Jewish community, the mixed
membership was not seen as natural. Both British and Zionist intelligence officers
reported on a number of occasions that the MCA's Christian membership was ready to
bolt the society due to its inability to get along with the organization's Muslim
members.[25] This never happened and it would appear in hindsight that these reports
had been driven by wishful thinking rather than actual evidence.

The British and Zionist expectation that Muslims and Christians would not
easily work together in the MCA was based upon their view that Palestinian society
was inherently divided by religious identity. This ignored the history of Arab politics
in the region, where mixed religious membership in Arab cultural and political groups
was common. The *nahda* had been a cultural movement emphasizing Arab identity
that had brought Christian and Muslim intellectuals together and the political parties
formed by Arabs in the last years of Ottoman rule contained both Christians and
Muslims. The political association that Najib Nasser founded in 1910 is a good
example of this, for while Najib Nasser was an Orthodox Christian his club included a
sizeable Muslim membership.[26] The Nadi al-Arabi and Muntada al-Adabi also
included Christians among their memberships.[27]

---

[25] See CZA S25.

[26] Porath, *Emergence*, 29.

[27] A British intelligence report from February 15, 1921 reported that Jamal al-Husayni suggested at a
meeting of the *Muntada al-Adabi* that the Young Men's Muslim Club be "amalgamated" with the club
and the Christian members be expelled. The report noted that this suggestion was rejected as it would
cause hostility from the Christian population. Quigley to Chief Secretary, February 15, 1921, ISA
2/5/157/2223/10.

The novelty of the MCA then was not its mixed-religious membership but its ability to open up branches in major cities throughout Palestine. The MCA can be considered the first nationwide political party in Palestine. This was shown in a December 1920 intelligence report on Muslim and Christian political parties by the CID of the Palestine government which stated that the party had branches in the districts of Jerusalem (which included Jaffa), Samaria, Gaza, and the Galilee and noted that the MCA had the largest membership of any political organization in Palestine at 650 members (as compared to the Nadi al-Arabi at 400 and the Muntada al-Adabi at 110). Most importantly, the assistant director of the police noted in a covering letter in that the MCA was the only club of the 43 clubs in Palestine and Phoenicia that had been really active in the last year.[28] This observation does not jibe with the reality of the the Nadi al-Arabi and the Muntada al-Adabi efforts in organizing Arab demonstrations in Jerusalem in February, March, and April 1920, but it does suggest that by the end of the year, the MCA had eclipsed these two organizations to become the leading player in Palestinian politics.[29]

VI - Palestinian Arab Congresses and the Arab Executive

Despite having more branches and more members than other political organizations, the MCA was not particularly effective in creating a broad political movement, since

---

[28] See Quigley to Assistant Chief Secretary, December 23, 1920, ISA 2, 5/155/59/CID/S.

[29] These were of course not the only political organizations established in Palestine but they were only organizations that can be said to have made an impact on Palestinian politics. For more details on the various minor Palestinian Arab political parties the reader is invited to look at Yehoshua Porath, *The Emergence of the Palestinian-Arab National Movement 1918-1929* and Muhammad Muslih, *The Origins of Palestinian Nationalism.*

there was "no central system of organization."[30] This was deliberate: the society's

own statutes created an organization in which its branches worked separately to fight

for the rights of Palestinian Arabs.[31] This gave the organization local flexibility but

led to differences of opinion among its membership about the MCA's objectives. One

such difference was over the future of Palestine, with the organization as a whole

supporting what has been called a "Syria- first" policy (i.e. Palestine's unification with

Emir Faysal's Syria, the majority position in Palestinian Arab politics from 1918 to

1920) but with some members pushing for full Palestinian independence. Another

was a difference over how strongly British rule should be opposed.

After the fall of Faysal's government in the summer of 1920, Musa Kazim al-

Husayni, the leader of the MCA called for the convening of a congress of all Arab

political parties in Palestine in order to create a more coordinated nationalist policy.

He realized that with the Syrian option off the table, Arab politicians needed a new

unified national message. This led to the Third Palestine Arab Congress, as the

meeting was known, which gathered in December 1920 in Jerusalem. The congress

was attended by almost all of the major political figures in the country, except for the

al-Nashashibi faction, which chose to boycott the proceedings.[32] The congress'

---

[30] Porath, *Emergence*, 33.

[31] The society's statutes called for the creation of a two-tiered organization, in which the main branch at Jerusalem enjoyed a separate but not a superior position: "The Moslem Christian Society embodies two Societies, the activities of one of them are specially for the Jerusalem District and its name the Moslem Christian Society in Jerusalem. The other Societies devote their activities to Palestine generally under the name of the Palestine Moslem Christian Society." The statutes also reveal that the aims of the society were not completely political, for the society established sub-committees that dealt with education, agricultural and technical development, commercial interests, and moral issues. ISA 2/5/155

[32] The first Palestine Arab congress had taken place in Jerusalem in 1913 and the second congress was considered to be the General Syrian Congress of 1919-20. See Wasserstein, *Britain in Palestine*, 94.

resolutions were hardly revolutionary—they reemphasized Arab opposition to the Balfour Declaration and reaffirmed Muslim-Christian unity—but the congress succeeded in creating a "representative" body of Palestinian Arab politicians, the Arab Executive.[33] Officially called the Executive Committee of the Third Arab Palestinian Congress, this body would play the leading role in Arab nationalist politics throughout the 1920s both in Palestine and abroad, by convening additional Arab Congresses; by dispatching political delegations to London, Egypt, India, the Hejaz, and Switzerland; and by sending out numerous petitions and protest letters to the Palestine Government, the Colonial Office, and the League of Nations.

VII - Religion in Politics

The Arab Executive, like the Muslim-Christian Association, the Nadi al-Arabi, and Muntada al-Adabi, brought together Muslims and Christians under the banner of Palestinian nationalism.[34] But the fact that Arab political groups were non-sectarian did not mean that they were always secular in their politics. To be sure, many of their central arguments about Palestinian had little to do with religion. The Jewish claim to Palestine was attacked on the grounds that Jews constituted a small minority of the population and owned a tiny percentage of the land. Zionist claims that Jews were "returning" to their ancestral homeland were countered by the argument that Arabs had been resident in Palestine for 1,300 years whereas the European Jew was a

---

[33] Given the Nashashibi boycott the claim to represent the Palestinian population was not credible and the body would later be criticized for being a Husayni controlled group.

[34] See Porath, *Emergence*, 382.

newcomer. And British support for the Jewish National Home was assailed for being

in contravention of Britain's obligation to protect the *status quo*, as laid down by the

Hague Convention of 1909, a contradiction of the right to national self-determination

and a betrayal of wartime promises made to the Arabs. These arguments showed

fluency with the language of international law, nationalist politics, and history that put

paid to the idea that the Arab population was hopelessly backward or motivated only

by material interests.

But appeals to religion were also consistently used to make the Arab case. The

Bible was used by Arab politicians to undermine the Jewish historical claim to

Palestine, by arguing that the ancient Jews had only ruled the land for a relatively brief

period, and that their rule which had been marked by war, rebellion, and

disturbances.[35] Arab petitioners also claimed that the Jewish religious connection to

Palestine was weak or even invented, because Jews had no significant religious sites in

the country.[36] Although inaccurate, this argument was not purely rhetorical for Jewish

holy places had had much less significance for the inhabitants of Palestine during the

Ottoman period.

---

[35] This observation was supplemented by claims that European Jews were regularly agitators and
revolutionaries in the modern period, such as in the Russian Revolution, a view shared by the British
military authorities. These ideas of Jews as agitators can be traced back to the notorious Protocols of the
Elders of Zion, which were becoming known in the Arab world at the time. It should be noted however
that a distinction was usually made in Arab thought between these European Jews and the Sephardic
Jews who had been inhabitants of Palestine under the Ottomans.

[36] See "Petition from the Nablus Liwa to the Paris Peace Conference," January 1, 1919, *Watha'iq al-
harakah al-wataniyah al-Filastiniyah*, 11.

VIII - Palestine as Holy Land

Religious history was also used in a positive sense to establish the Arab claim to Palestine. Although the secular language of national self-determination was frequently used to legitimize the Arab right to rule Palestine, it was an argument that was frequently combined with a religious argument that emphasized Palestine's Christian and Muslim heritage. A number of early petitions to the British military authorities asserted that Palestine had a unique identity because it was the birthplace of Christianity and one of the holiest lands in the Islamic world. Palestine was also described as important to Arab Christians because it was the place where Jesus was born, practiced his ministry, performed his miracles, and was buried. At the same time Jerusalem was the first *qibla* (direction of prayer) in Islam and the city from which Muhammad ascended to heaven on his night journey. It was also the site of the al-Aqsa Mosque, the "farthest mosque" mentioned in the Qur'an. In short, Palestine was the most important holy place in Christianity and the third holiest in Islam, after Mecca and Medina.[37] Porath argues that these religious arguments were used to appeal to different audiences: the Islamic character of the country was used to rally the majority Muslim community in Palestine, whereas appeals to Palestine's Christian past were largely used for external propaganda.[38] This seems to suggest that Palestinian politicians were saying one thing to one audience and something entirely different to the other, but the petitions and protests that Arab politicians submitted to

---

[37] For a selection of these petitions the reader is directed to File I and II of "Petitions from the Civil Population of Palestine," ISA 2/1/30 and *Watha'iq al-harakah al-wataniyah al-Filastiniyah.*

[38] Porath, *Emergence,* 42.

the British government and the League of Nations combine both Christian and Muslim claims into a single Palestinian Arab claim. This indicates that Muslim and Christian chauvinistic arguments could comfortably be used at the same time without causing friction between the two religions.

As we shall see in the next chapter, the defense of the Islamic heritage of Palestine would soon become the most important factor in the religious politics of the Arab community, especially the defense of the *Haram al-Sharif* from the perceived threat of a Zionist takeover. But it is striking that both Muslim and Christian claims to the country were emphasized in these early petitions, manifesting a shared religious concern for Palestine.

The emphasis on the Christian heritage of Palestine was not only an attempt to appeal to the Christian backgrounds of British officials but was also meant to appeal to the hundreds of millions of Christians outside the country. Likewise, the appeal to Palestine's Islamic history was not meant just for local consumption. Arab petitions in the military period emphasized that some 350 million Muslims and 750 million Christians looked to Palestine as a holy land, as opposed to only 14 million Jews who saw the country as a holy place.[39] The handing over of the country to the Zionists was thus portrayed as threatening not only the natural communal balance within Palestine or as upsetting the country's religious history but as disturbing Palestine's place as holy land for millions around the world.

---

[39] Porath, *Emergence*, 41.

These religious arguments were more than just rhetoric, for the concept of

Palestine as a holy land resonated with Muslims and Christian in the country. The

most vocal early advocates of an independent Palestine were the editors of *al-Karmil*

(Najib Nassar) and *Filastin* (brothers Yusuf and 'Issa al-'Issa). All three were Greek

Orthodox Christians, whose papers initially were established to cover events within

the Orthodox community but soon became major voices of Palestinian nationalism. It

was no accident that the idea of Palestine as a unique territorial unit was advocated by

Orthodox Christians since the Orthodox community had a concept of Palestine even

under the Ottomans, which corresponded to the Patriarchate's authority over what had

been the three Roman districts of Palestine.[40] This was illustrated in Khalil al-

Sakakini's 1913 book *al-Nahda al-Orthodoksiyya fi Filastin* (The Orthodox

Renaissance in Palestine) in which the word *Filastin* (Palestine) was used to refer to

Palestine and Transjordan, the area over which the authority of the patriarchate

extended.[41]

For Muslims the concept of a holy land identified with Palestine was less

developed. According to Rashid Khalidi and Alexander Schölch, Muslim ideas of

Palestine as a unique holy territory "went back to the "*Fada'il al-Quds*" (or "merits of

Jerusalem") literature, which described Palestine, including Hebron, Jericho,

Bethlehem, Nablus, al-Ramla, Safad, Ascalon, Acre, Gaza, and Nazareth for pilgrims

---

[40] Porath, "Political Awakening of Palestinian Arabs," 359.
[41] Ibid.

and visitors to Palestine, and for the devout and inquisitive elsewhere."[42] Khalidi also

suggests that the idea of a holy territory can be found in Muslim protests to the

Ottoman Porte in 1701 against the arrival of a French Consul in Sidon, which argued

that this incursion violated the sanctity of Jerusalem (referred to as the *Bayt al-

Maqdis*), identified as the first of the two *qibla*s and the third holiest place in Islam.[43]

But the "Merits of Jerusalem" literature and the 1701 protest appear to be rather slim

evidence of a Muslim equivalent to the Christian conception of the Holy Land.

More important in forging a sense of national identity among Muslims was the

Nabi Musa festival, which had originally been established by the Ottoman governorate

as a Muslim alternative to the annual Easter and Passover celebrations. Over time,

however, the festival had become something of a national event, with Muslims and

Christians attending the festival from all three of the Ottoman districts. This

transformation of the festival meant that it became part of what Roger Friedland and

Richard Hecht have called an emergent "civil religion."[44] This festival's national

character continued into the British mandate with Hala Sakakini (a Christian who was

the daughter of the famous Palestinian educator Khalil Sakakini) reminiscing about the

"national day" of Nabi Musa:

> Only once in my life did I attend this exciting pageant. Again it was in
> the company of Aunt Melia, who had many Muslim friends. We sat on
> a high spot on the slope north of St. Stephen's Gate. The place was

---

[42] Khalidi, *Palestinian Identity*, 29. As Khalidi points out, this connection was first made in Alexander
Schölch's *Palestine in Transformation: 1856-1882.*

[43] This opposition to the arrival of the consul was registered in a petition to Sultan Mustafa II that was
signed by more than eighty Muslim leaders. The event is described in Khalidi,*Palestinian Identity*, 29-
30.

[44] This point is discussed in Friedland and Hecht, "Pilgrimage to Nebi Musa," 94.

densely crowded. Everywhere you could see the Arab flag with its green, red, white and black colours fluttering high above the heads. The scene filled us with enthusiasm and national pride. Every now and then strong young men would link their arms together and, forming circles, would start dancing the "*dabkeh*" and singing. It was thrilling to watch and wonderful for the spirit. Although the *Nabi Musa* feast was supposed to be a religious occasion, it was in fact a national day in which all the Arabs of Palestine, Christians and Moslems alike, shared.[45]

The national scope of the festival made it available for Arab nationalist political action and under the British the festival would become a nationalist event.

VIII - Nabi Musa as a National(ist) Festival

As the name suggests, the Nabi Musa festival celebrates the Prophet Moses, whom Palestinian Muslims believe had died and was buried near Jericho. His burial site became a *maqam* or shrine that was an important pilgrimage site during the Ottoman and British mandate periods. The belief that Moses made it west of the river Jordan, i.e. into Palestine, conflicts with Christian and Jewish tradition and the view of most Muslims which holds that Moses died and was buried on Mount Nebo in present-day Jordan. This made the shrine and the festival exclusively local Islamic traditions, an important factor in their transformation into objects of Palestinian national identification.

The shrine itself was constructed upon the orders of the Mamluk Sultan Baybars in 1269 C.E. and was part of a "chain of Islamic shrines built by the Ayyubids and the Mamluks to honor and venerate prophets, the companions of

---

[45] Sakakini, *Jerusalem and I*, 49.

Prophet Mohammad and saints and holy men."[46] According to Khaled Marrar, who

has written a useful tourist guide to the site, the construction of the shrine was

designed to underline the Islamic character of Palestine, especially the desert east of

Jerusalem, which contains a number of Christian holy sites.[47] Traditional pilgrimages

(*ziyarat*) to the site had been occurring since the late-twelfth century—that is to say

even before the construction of the shrine—but it wasn't until the mid-nineteenth

century that the Nabi Musa festival became an organized official festival.[48] As Eddie

Halabi has pointed out in a recent dissertation, the modern festival began when "high-

ranking state and religious officials imposed their order over the ceremonies, invited

Ottoman authorities to participate, and limited the ceremonial role of the mostly

peasant pilgrims."[49] This change was part of centralizing state reforms of the mid-

nineteenth century Ottoman empire, which gave provincial officials greater

bureaucratic and administrative responsibilities and empowered them to take a greater

role in local religious affairs.[50] One important change imposed by the Ottomans was

the fixing of the festival to the solar calendar (specifically the Greek Orthodox Julian

---

[46] Marrar, *Maqam An-Nabi Musa*, 15.

[47] Marrar, *Nabi Musa*, 6, 16.

[48] This has led Eddie Halabi in his excellent account of the festival to classify the shrine's history into two periods, the "traditional *ziyarah*" which occurred from the twelfth to the mid-nineteenth centuries and the "modern *mawsim* (festival)." Eddie Halabi, "The Transformation of the Prophet Moses Festival in Jerusalem, 1917-1937: From Local and Islamic to Modern and Nationalist Celebration," (Ph.D. diss., University of Toronto, 2007), 66.

[49] Halabi, "Transformation of Festival," 77.

[50] Ibid.

Calendar) and not to the lunar religious calendar typically used for Muslim ceremonies.[51]

The festival had a political purpose from its inception, with the Ottomans using the festival to strengthen their control over the Arab community. Unlike other local saints, Moses was, according to Richard Hecht and Roger Friedland, "a public saint whose power was beyond the control of a single family, clan or kin-group." This gave the festival an all-Palestinian quality that was lacking in the festivals of other local prophets such as Nabi Saleh or Nabi Rubin.[52] This quality was exploited by the Ottoman authorities, who used their patronage of the festival to build important political relationships with the local Muslim population, such as through the giving of gifts to visiting pilgrims, a practice unique to this festival, or by partnering with local notable families to put on the festival.[53] As Butrus Abu-Manneh has pointed out, the latter practice allowed those elite families, particularly the al-Husayni family, to use festival to strengthen their own political and social power in Palestine.[54]

---

[51] The *mausim al-Nabi Musa* ("pilgrimage season to Nabi Musa"), would begin on the Friday preceding Good Friday according to the Greek Orthodox calendar and end on the Thursday of Easter week (Maundy Thursday).

 The two best accounts of the festival are Halabi's recent dissertation and Tawfiq Canaan's, *Mohammedan Saints and Sanctuaries in Palestine*, the latter offering invaluable information about local Muslim popular religious practice during the early years of the mandate. Information on the recent history of the site and the festival can be found in Marrar, *Maqam al-Nabi Musa*, 75-82. Gilbert Clayton also wrote about the festival see Clayton to GHQ, Egyptian Expeditionary Force, May 2, 1918, PRO FO 371/3391/92045.

[52] Friedland and Hecht, "Pilgrimage to Nabi Musa," 93.

[53] At most Muslim religious festivals the celebrants are expected to provide gifts. At the Eid al-Fitr, for example, worshipers are required to pay the *zakat al-fitr*, an alms for the month of Ramadan that is distributed to the needy local Muslims. The gifts at the Nabi Musa festival were provided for out of Ottoman state funding. See Friedland and Hecht, "Pilgrimage to Nabi Musa," 93.

[54] See Abu-Manneh, "The Husaynis: The Rise of a Notable Family in 18th C. Palestine."

The first festival under British rule was celebrated in April 1918 without

incident, a success that was immediately celebrated in British propaganda to the

Muslim world. A glowing account from Palestine was sent to the Foreign Office to

assure the world that although the pilgrimage had originally been created to compete

with Easter, "happily the pilgrimage has lost all such significance and is now regarded

purely as a religious exercise."[55] Gilbert Clayton, the chief political officer of the

Egyptian Expeditionary Force, added in another letter that the "impression produced

in Moslem circles has been excellent and on all sides were heard expressions of

gratitude to the Commander-in-Chief and loyalty to His Majesty the King."[56]

A year later the festival took on a very different cast. The 1919 festival was the

first at which pilgrims stopped along the parade route to hear nationalist speeches.[57]

This development was tied to rising expectations of national or regional independence

on the part of Palestinian Arabs, influenced in part by President Wilson's Fourteen

Points, the Paris Peace Conference, and local support for the Egyptian revolution of

1919, which had begun a month earlier. But the most crucial factor was Arab

opposition to the Balfour Declaration, which by then was widely known. The Arab

educator, Khalil Sakakini noted this change of tone in his diary when he lamented

after the violence of the 1920 festival that Palestinian festivals, which used to be

---

[55] FO 371/3391/92045.

[56] Clayton to FO, May 2, 1918. FO 371/3391/78488.

[57] It is unclear who gave these speeches but it is likely that one of the speakers would have been Musa Kazim al-Husayni who was the mayor of Jerusalem and a member of the al-Husayni family that were the patrons of the festival.

religious in character, had by 1919 become nationalist (*qawmi*), as manifested in the appearance of anti-Zionist and Arab nationalist chants.[58]

British officials had been forewarned about the potential for nationalist protest and violence at the 1919 festival. British intelligence officers and Zionist officials had separately cautioned the occupying forces that disorders were probable and the military governor at Tiberias had warned that pilgrims from Nablus and Hebron would have to be closely watched due to their traditional fanaticism.[59] In the end there was no violence but the event did become politicized, with the assembled crowd singing nationalist songs and chanting "Long Live Emir Faysal," and "Long Live King Husayn" during their pilgrimage to the site.[60]

IX – The Nabi Musa Riots of 1920

As it turns out, the violence promised in 1919 would arrive a year later. The fateful 1920 festival was preceded by two political demonstrations against British rule that took place in Jerusalem in February and March, and by a steady stream of petitions and editorials protesting British policy.[61] "The Administration," as the Palin

---

[58] Khalil Sakakini, *Yawmiyat Khalil al-Sakini* [The Diary of Khalil Sakakini], volume 3 (Jerusalem: Muassasat al-Dirasat al-Maqdisia, 2004), 219.

[59] On March 20, 1919, a British intelligence agent, J. S. Camp urgently warned his superiors that "the greatest precautions must be taken if disorder is to be prevented during the period from April 10-25." See Camp to Storrs, March 20, 1919, ISA 2, 1/43. In his response, the assistant military governor, General Waters-Taylor, presciently pointed out that the arrival of the Hebron and Nablus pilgrims would be a moment of potential danger since both towns were renowned for their fanaticism.
The Zionist Commission had even greater fears about the potential for violence, see Wasserstein, *British in Palestine*, 39.

[60] Zionist report, Jerusalem, April 14, 1919. CZA L4/276/Ib.

[61] The demonstrations took place on February 27 and March 8 and included political speeches calling for Arab self-rule. The February demonstration was a response to a speech by the Chief Administrator

Commission report into the riots stated, was also "in full receipt of information from their agents, both as to foreign activities and as to the propaganda carried on by various [Arab nationalist] clubs." [62] Despite this, British officials appear to have been much less concerned about violence in 1920 than they had been a year earlier. Ronald Storrs, who as the military governor of Jerusalem was ultimately in charge of security at the festival, was convinced that the danger was not as great as a year before, a misreading of the situation that was based on a hubristic belief that the power of the colonial presence and the efficacy of the colonial message had already won over the Arab population. This colonial overconfidence led Storrs and his fellow officers to draw the wrong lesson from the 1919 festival, for rather than seeing the festival's protests as a sign of nationalist unease, they concentrated on the festival's lack of violence, which they saw as a confirmation of their policy of minimal security. In fact, the military authorities were so convinced of the efficacy of their security arrangements that they boasted to the press that they had been able to protect Palestine's holy sites without resorting to the massive troop presence that had been part of Ottoman security arrangements. [63] This meant that when violence did break out

---

of the O.E.T.A., Major-General Bols, that reaffirmed the British commitment to the Balfour Declaration. The March demonstration was influenced by Faysal's recent declaration that he was the King of Syria and Palestine. During these demonstrations there were minor clashes between the Arab protestors and local Jews but there was little violence, though the Palin Report noted that, "the attitude of the mob on this occasion was seditious and extremely threatening." See WO 32/9614. These demonstrations were organized by the *Nadi al-Arabi* and *Muntada al-Adabi* political societies, which are discussed below.

[62] WO 32/9614.

[63] This is just one of the many parallels with the security arrangements made by the United States in present-day Iraq.

at the festival, there was little to check its spread through Jerusalem, a reckless

oversight that would later be heavily criticized by the Palin Commission.

Accounts of the outbreak of violence at the festival are conflicting and

confusing. Testimony given by colonial officials and local residents before the Palin

commission presents a number of different explanations for the violence. The mayor

of Jerusalem, Musa Kazim al-Husayni, asserted that a quarrel between a Jewish boy

and an Arab boy had been the catalyst but added that Jews had been provoking Arabs

for weeks leading up to the festival.[64] A British soldier testified that the violence

started after a Jewish youth threw a rock at a banner carried by pilgrims from Hebron,

an observation corroborated by an eyewitness from Hebron.[65] Jewish witnesses

meanwhile argued that Arab attacks were unprovoked and resulted from a

preconceived plan by political agitators to attack the Jewish community.[66]

The most complete account of the outbreak of violence came from the

testimony of a British lieutenant and reserve inspector, L. Harrington:

> On Sunday 4th, inst. about 9:15 am - 9:30 am I came into Jerusalem via
> the Mamilla Road when I reached the Jaffa Gate, coming up the hill

---

The local police force was found to be ineffective in the course of the 1920 Nebi Musa riots, with reports that Arab policemen were reluctant to crack down on Arab rioters and in some cases engaged in attacks of their own.

[64] CZA L4/840

[65] Ibid.

[66] Max Nurock, the head of the Zionist Commission, for example, testified that he had been warned by a British officer that Muslims had planned to use the festival as a means to carry out an anti-Jewish riot. See CZA L4/840. A letter from the Zionist Commission to the Zionist leader Nachum Sokolow was even more explicit, "la situation presente exactement le tableau d'un vrai pogrom. Sont coupables quelques incitateurs arabes et l'attitude hostile d'un grand nobre des autorites locals vis a vis des juis." Zionist Commission (Beirut) to Sokolow, Apri 9, 1920, PRO FO 371/5117/E3017.

This accusation was strenuously objected to by the military authorities and was rejected out of hand by the court of enquiry, which considered it to be a deliberately provocative characterization of the events. See PRO WO 32/9614.

towards the gate I observed a large procession which I recognized as the Hebron pilgrims, whom we were expecting somewhat later. I had been instructed to be on the spot when the procession arrived, and I reined up at the side of the road and watch the pilgrims go by. There was the usual dancing and singing, and when they reached the top of the hill just outside the Jaffa Gate, a man named Aref El Aref addressed the crowd. He also got on a white horse and rode amongst the crowd. The effect of his speech seemed to me to turn the crowd up the Jaffa Road towards the Municipality buildings, and I started to ride with them. Outside the Municipality the crowd stopped and speeches were given from the balcony of the Municipality and from the balcony of the Society known as the Nadi el Arabi. The speeches given from the Nadi El Arabi appeared to me to excite the crowd and I saw the photo of the Emir Feisal held above the head of one of the speakers on the balcony of the Nadi el Arabi.

The exhibition of the photograph was received with great acclamation by the crowd clapping and cheering. Immediately after the speeches the crowed began to move towards the Birket Mamilla, but was instantly checked by the Commandant of the Hebron Police, Moh. El Hajazi and turned towards the Jaffa Gate. They moved in this direction and everything appeared to be going quite smoothly with the usual sword swinging and dancing. I rode about the centre of the procession to the Jaffa Gate until I reached a point opposite the Grand Hotel, then where was a momentary check and Aref El Aref came to me and pointed behind me said "Mr. Harrington, you had better say what that man wants or he will cause trouble." I turned round and looked behind me towards the Jaffa Gate, and saw a small boy running with a Muslim after him. I cannot say whether he was persuing him. Immediately the whole street was in an uproar. Sticks and stones started to fly. People rushed inside the gate from outside and vice-versa. Jews were seized and beaten.[67]

Harrington's account was contradicted in places by other testimony, but contains all of

the elements of the narrative accepted by scholars: the arrival of the Hebron pilgrims,

the speech given by 'Arif al-'Arif and his ride on horseback, the nationalist speeches

given from the balconies of the Municipality building and the headquarters of the Nadi

al-Arabi, and finally the outbreak of violence inside the Jaffa Gate.

---

[67] Testimony of the 27th Witness (unnamed) in front of the Court of Enquiry, L4/837.

A major concern of the commission of enquiry was establishing whether the

riots were planned in advance in order to verify if there was any truth to Jewish claims

of Arab premeditation, as well as the more serious Zionist accusation that the attack

constituted a pogrom against the Jews of Jerusalem. This accusation was significant

because, even though it was rejected by British officials, it brought up a well-known

criticism of the military administration, its perceived lack of commitment to the

Balfour Declaration. And what made the accusation particularly stinging for officials

in the O.E.T.A. was the fact that it was also made by a fellow officer, Richard

Meinertzhagen, the pro-Zionist Chief Political Officer of the Egyptian Expeditionary

Force.[68]

The Palin Commission Report rejected the idea that the attacks were planned

in advance or that British officers cooperated with or condoned the attacks.[69] The

court of enquiry pointed out that the "exact incident which caused the explosion has

---

[68] After the festival Meinertzhagen vigorously argued that event had been a pogrom and that the military authorities were culpable. In truth, Meinertzhagen was an ardent gentile Zionist and prone to exaggeration, if not outright fabrication. He was also prone to overstepping the bounds of his position and undermining the work of his military superiors, which eventually led to his reassignment to the colonial office in 1921. Recent scholarship has addressed Meinertzhagen's biographical fabrications as well as his falsifications and fabrications in his famous ornithological studies. See Brian Garfield, *The Meinertzhagen Mystery: The Life and Times of a Colossal Fraud* (Washington, DC: Potomac Books, 2007), Alan Knox, "Richard Meinertzhagen-A Case of Fraud Examined," *Ibis*, Vol. 135, No. 3, (July 1993): 320-325, and R. Dalton, "Ornithologists Stunned by Bird Collector's Deceit," *Nature*, Vol. 437, No. 7057 (September 2005): 302.

[69] The report stated that "there is, however, no evidence of any definite plan on the part of an organized body of rioters and the whole affair has the appearance of spontaneity." PRO WO 32/9614. Later historians have largely agreed with the commission's findings. Yehoshua Porath for instance devotes two pages to the issue of premeditated violence at the festival and reaches the conclusion that although some Arab politician had planned to use the festival to promote Arab nationalism there was no evidence of a plot to cause violence by members of the major Arab political societies (the al-Nadi al-Arabi, al-Muntada al-Adabi, and *Jam'iyyat al-Ikha' wa-al-'Afaf*("Association of Brotherhood and Purity"). Nor does he find evidence of a British plot to assist in the planning of the violence, despite Zionist claims at the time that officials such as Colonel Waters-Taylor knew about the attacks in advance. Porath, *Emergence*, 98-99.

not been clearly ascertained," arguing instead that the problem had been the unauthorized and unprecedented injection of politics into the festival. It identified three major ways in which politics intruded: through the presence of *agents provocateurs* in the crowd, through the exhibition of a portrait of Emir Faysal, and through the giving of speeches of a "flagrantly political character."[70] This conclusion endorsed the opinions of the local military authorities, who had already publicly charged Hajj Amin al-Husayni and 'Arif al-'Arif with incitement for giving nationalist speeches at the festival. Both men had evaded arrest and fled the country, only to return when Herbert Samuel pardoned them as one of the first acts of his administration.[71] The Mayor of Jerusalem, Musa Kazim al-Husayni, who had also given a nationalist speech from the balcony of the Municipality building, was not so lucky: he was dismissed by Ronald Storrs and replaced by the more moderate Raghib Bey al-Nashashibi, a move that ensured that the mayoralty and muftiship of Jerusalem remained divided between the rival al-Nashashibi and al-Husayni families.[72]

X – Identifying and Controlling Arab "Fanaticism"

The debate about premeditation and incitement in the wake of the violence of 1920 was part of the same discourse that emphasized Arab action as being motivated by

---

[70] Ibid.

[71] At the same time Samuel pardoned Vladimir Jabotinsky (the founder of the right-wing Revisionist movement) and members of his Jewish paramilitary, who had been sentenced to lengthy prison sentences for organizing an illegal militia. Jabotinsky's Jewish Defense Forces had been organized in the wake of the attack on the Jewish settlement of Tel Hai, where the famous Joseph Trumpeldor had been killed.

[72] After his dismissal, Musa Kazim al-Husayni returned to politics, becoming the leader of the Arab Executive.

fanaticism rather than politics that was detailed in Chapter One. In the eyes of the Zionist Commission and a number of British officials, the Arab crowd was not a legitimate political actor but a fanatical mob that had been pushed to violence by unscrupulous notable agitators. Even the Palin commission report, which concluded that Arabs had some political grievances, found that the violence itself was caused by "the determination [that] had been come to by the firebrands of the political agitators to take advantage of any occasion which might offer to raise a disturbance and that agents provocateurs were present at the pilgrimage with that intention."[73] The pilgrims from Hebron (as well as those from Nablus) were regarded by the British as especially volatile, and it was no surprise to the commission that it was the pilgrims from Hebron that were "gradually worked up into a highly inflammatory condition" by the speeches of local politicians and by the exhibition of Faysal's portrait. The resulting violence, which was described in the report as an "explosion", could be traced to a transformation of the pilgrims into a "mob" through the exploitation of their "excited condition" by political operatives.[74]

As touched upon in Chapter One, the view that Arabs were naturally combustible was rooted in the orientalist stereotype of the Arab as religious fanatic. As we saw, this stereotype was spread mostly through the accounts of British travelers to the country before the war, which concentrated on the primitive exoticism of Arab cultural practices, including their celebration of religious festivals. Although, some officials like Ronald Storrs had little interest in the festival and described it as a

---

[73] PRO WO 32/9614.

[74] Ibid.

"rather pointless" event, many others continued to be impressed by the color of the festival.[75] This was shown by the emphasis in British reports placed on the feasting, sword fighting, horseback riding, singing, and dancing of the pilgrims involved in the Nabi Musa festival rather than on the religious significance of the event.[76]

For the members of the military administration the Nabi Musa festival appeared to be just as exotic, loud, and primitive as it had been to British visitors to Palestine before the First World War. The exoticism of these festivals was tied the religious fanaticism of Palestine. As Storrs put it, ""Moslems are far more orthodox here than in Egypt," I had written after my first few weeks in Jerusalem, "so is everybody, worse luck."[77] Sometimes this fanaticism was blamed on history, namely the "bitter hatred of centuries still smoldering, ready to burst into flame again at a later date." But more typically it was based upon what one official described as the fact that the fellah was a salt-of-the-earth character, wholly ignorant of politics but quick to become angry if his honor or that of his tribe was called into question.[78]

This focus on fanaticism undoubtedly contributed to an official blindness towards the nationalist demands of the local population.[79] The local population was

---

[75] Storrs, *Orientations*, 346

[76] Good examples include accounts of the festival in Edward Keith-Roach, *Pasha of Jerusalem: Memoirs of a District Commissioner under the British Mandate* (London: Radcliffe Press, 1994), 160, and in the Palin Report itself, (PRO WO 32/9614).

[77] Storrs, *Orientations*, 346.

[78] See Richard Adamson's personal account of "The Holy Fire in Jerusalem, Easter, 1920," Richard Adamson papers, GB 165-001, Middle East Center, St. Antony's College, Oxford.

[79] Occasionally, British intelligence reported on the real political or economic concerns of the local population, such as General Water-Taylor's report that Jaffa residents were protesting on account of a "local grievance of taxation of their orange groves." However, the vast majority of British reports dismissed Arab protest as the actions of a fanatical population acting out. See General Waters-Taylor to the Chief Administrator OETA, February 7, 1919. ISA 2/5/155/3026(A).

believed to be both uninterested in politics and incapable of understanding it. *The Syria and Palestine Handbook* published by the Foreign Office in 1919 asserted, for instance, that

> The bulk of the population are fellahin, that is to say agricultural workers owning land as a village community or working land for the Syrian effendi. They have for centuries been ground down, overtaxed, and bullied by the Turk, and still more by the Arab-speaking Turkish minor official and by the Syrian and Levantine landowner. They have little, if any, national sentiment, and would probably welcome any stable form of government which would guarantee to them reasonable security and enjoyment of the fruits of their labour.[80]

Officials on the ground had much the same feeling about the local population. The military governor of Jaffa spoke for many of his fellow officers when he argued in May 1919 that: "freedom of speech is not understood in this Country, and the privilege is invariably abused." As a result he asserted that politics as practiced in Europe was unsuitable for Palestine: "Freedom of speech, so innocuous in Europe, is impossible in Eastern Countries, and we are only asking for trouble by allowing it."[81]

Since the bulk of the population did not understand how politics worked it was assumed that they could easily be influenced by agitators. As early as February 1919 a military intelligence officer warned his superiors that a great danger lay in the "fanaticism of the villagers," which could easily be harnessed by French and or pan-

---

[80] Great Britain, Foreign Office, "Syria and Palestine Handbook" (London: 1919), 56-57, in PRO FO 373/5/E132.

[81] Lieutenant-Colonel H. H. Postlethwaite to Civil Secretary Wyndham Deedes, May 29, 1919. ISA 2/5/155/Z/186.

Arabist agents.[82] This attitude very much fit with Lord Cromer's portrait of the

Oriental mind as illogical, childlike, and easily manipulated as opposed to the

European who was "by nature skeptical and requires proof before he can accept the

truth of any proposition."[83] The Palestinian landowner was often implicated in

British thinking as a manipulator the local population. This was not simply through

economic exploitation, as the quote from *The Syria and Palestine Handbook* suggests,

but also through political manipulation. For example, when Herbert Samuel returned

in April 1920 from a visit to Palestine before his appointment as high commissioner,

he dismissed Arab nationalist and anti-Zionist politics as a crude attempt by the

effendi class to maintain its control over the country, an argument that was often made

in Zionist propaganda.[84]

---

[82] J. N. Camp to Advanced G.H.Q, February 15, 1919. ISA, Chief Secretary's Files 2, 5/155 M/56.
Captain Camp was reporting on a meeting of members of various Muslim-Christian societies in
Jerusalem from January 27-February 10, 1919.

[83] Cromer, *Modern Egypt*, vol. 2, 146.

[84] Samuel to Curzon, April 2, 1920. ISA 100, 649/6.
The argument that the ignorant fellah majority was being preyed upon by a greedy effendi class was
particularly strong in Zionist propaganda, where it was often used as a means for downplaying the
political common sense of the villager. Such a view often came from a patronizing and racist view
towards Arabs. For example, in a letter to Alfred Balfour, Chaim Weizmann urged the British to take
concerted action to control the Arabs, since:

> The Arabs, who are superficially clever and quickwitted, worship one thing, and one
> thing only—power and success. Hence, while it would be wrong to say that British
> prestige has suffered through the military stalemate, it certainly has not increased. In
> the bazaars and cafés people wander [sic.] what is happening, and enemy agents are
> quick to seize the opportunity and to whisper into the ears of the credulous that the
> Turk is all powerful, is only biding his time and waiting for an opportunity which is
> bound to come very soon. It is not exactly dissatisfaction, but is an uncertainty, a lack
> of firm ground—a haziness in the outlook and a sitting on the fence. This has
> naturally made the British Authorities rather nervous, and, knowing as they do the
> treacherous nature of the Arab, they have to watch carefully and constantly that
> nothing should happen which might give the Arabs the slightest grievance or ground
> of complaint. In other words, the Arabs have to be "nursed" lest they should stab the
> Army in the back. The Arab, quick as he is to gauge such a situation, tries to make

To be sure, not every British official agreed with Samuel's assessment that Arab nationalism was a superficial and artificial movement. The assistant civil secretary (political), Ernest Richmond, argued that Arab political demands needed to be considered in British planning and rejected the idea that Arabs were apolitical. Wyndham Deedes, the civil secretary, shared Richmond's views, although he was not sympathetic to the Arab position. Finally, the Palin report made a point of rejecting the idea that Arab politics were superficial:

> It has been said by the Zionists that the popular excitement is purely artificial and largely the result of propaganda by the effendi class, which fears to lose its position. It is sufficient to quote the evidence of Major Waggett with which the Court finds itself in full accord, when he says: "It is very important to realize that the opposition is by no means superficial or manufactured, and I consider this a very dangerous view to take of the situation."[85]

Even so there was a general tendency to see the Arab population and particularly the fellahin as being easily led. This led the British authorities to monitor and guard against attempts by local politicians from the MCA, the Nadi al-Arabi, or the Muntada al-Adabi, and the Arab Executive to influence the population.

This attempt to protect or immunize the population from effendi influence was shown in the preparations of the O.E.T.A. administration in the build-up to the arrival of the King-Crane commission in the spring of 1919. Originally billed as the Inter-Allied Commission to the Near East, the commission proposed by President Woodrow

---

the most of it. He screams as often as he can and blackmails as much as he can. -- Weizmann to Balfour, May 30, 1918. CZA L3/310.

[85] PRO WO 32/9614.

The report did however view the presence of agents provocateurs and local agitators as a major factor in the violence of the Nebi Musa festival.

Wilson had been pared back to a two-person fact-finding mission after the French and British refused to participate (they had already decided the future of the region in the Sykes-Picot agreement).[86] Nevertheless the arrival of the commission was met with eager anticipation by local Arabs who coordinated a list of three demands: unity of Palestine and Syria, independent Arab government, and the repudiation of the Balfour policy.[87]

For British officials, the King-Crane commission was problematic because it would necessarily raise difficult questions about the future direction of the country and the place of Britain in that future. Particularly disconcerting was the fact that the commissioners planned to speak directly to the people, who officials feared would be influenced by provocateurs to speak out against the British occupation. (They could see no other reason why Arabs would speak out against British rule). To counter this, local military governors were instructed by headquarters in Jerusalem in April 1919 to hold educational meetings with the local population, so as to head off any "demands for complete autonomy independent of any mandatory or protecting power," and were warned about the potential for local meetings to be "diverted to illegal purposes or fanatical demonstrations." They were also given wide latitude to threaten "the authors of illegitimate and fanatical propaganda" with 1) deportation if they were non-residents, 2) internment in Egypt, without trial, if they were residents, "known to be inflaming the minds of the people," or 3) prosecution "where direct evidence is

---

[86] The two-person commission was made up of Dr. Henry King, the President of Oberlin College and Charles Crane, a Chicago businessman and was sponsored by the United States government.
[87] Wasserstein, *British in Palestine*, 40.

obtainable of actions and expressions subversive of law and order or tending to excite disaffection."[88]

The existence of such policies goes against Bernard Wasserstein's contention that news of the commission's arrival "produced an immediate relaxation of the political atmosphere in Palestine."[89] In fact this was a tense moment in the early history of British Palestine, for the King-Crane commission gave Arabs an unprecedented opportunity to speak out against British rule. The British response, as in other moments of tension during the mandate, was to disregard freedom of speech and political action in order to make sure that security was kept up.

In the end, however, the King-Crane commission mattered little for its report was shelved by the allied powers at the Paris' Peace conference. Its recommendation that Palestine be unified with Syria under the administration of the United States or Britain is interesting for the scholar because it reflected a genuine attempt by a western commission to accommodate the views of Palestinian Arabs in the future of the Middle East, but the recommendation made no difference to European policy for it was summarily rejected by Britain and France.

XI - The Khutba Scare of 1920

Another moment of tension, which was mentioned at the beginning of this dissertation, was what I call the "khutba scare", which involved what some officials

---

[88] Lieutenant-Colonel A. A. to Military Governors of Jerusalem, Jaffa, Haifa, Gaza, Hebron, Beersheba, Nablus, Jenin, Tulkeram, Tiberias, no date [most likely April, 1919], ISA 2/5/155/5588/P.

[89] Wasserstein, *British in Palestine*, 39.

saw as a politicization of the mosque in Palestine. As we have already seen British officials believed that one of the most potent ways of influencing the minds of the local population was through Islam. This is what made Pan-Islam so worrying for some officials and why the Nebi Musa violence of April 1920 was taken so seriously. Six months later another episode scared British officials, when the sermon, or khutba, at the traditional Friday prayers in Jerusalem and elsewhere appeared to become politicized. British concerns centered on the person to whom the sermon was dedicated, i.e. who received the blessings, in Muslim history traditionally the caliph or sultan or the local Muslim political leader.

As Uri Kupferschmidt has put it, "the use of mosques and khutbas for purposes which would commonly be defined as political had never been foreign to Islam."[90] Since the khutba was, as still is today, often used by the imam to address moral, political, and social issues of the day, it was by nature more than a simple religious sermon. (It should be noted that this isn't wildly different from religious sermons in Christianity.) The dedication was one aspect of the sermon that was inherently political since it was meant to express loyalty to the political leadership. Because of this the dedication could be seen as a challenge to the British administration if it was given to a Muslim leader who was not a British ally. This was the case in 1920 when imams in Palestine decided to dedicate the khutba to the Ottoman sultan, who in his position as caliph, was the leading religious figure in Sunni Islam. Interestingly, this decision, which British intelligence officers viewed as a dangerous innovation, was a

---

[90] Kupferschmidt, *Supreme Muslim Council*, 230. Consequently, the interest of the political authorities in the Friday prayer was also not new.

return to the practice before the British occupation, when blessings had traditionally been given to the Ottoman sultan.

In the British mandate in Iraq sermons had continued to be dedicated to the Ottoman sultan after the British occupation but for the first three years of British rule in Palestine the khutba was a non-issue, as it appears that blessings were not given to any outside Muslim leader. This changed in October 1920 when the Palestine police reported that they had received intelligence that the Muslim authorities were planning to reintroduce the sultan's name into the Friday prayers. On October 4, Colonel Quigley of the Criminal Investigation Department (CID) warned his superiors that the "Pan-Islamic movement" was active in Palestine and "a significant move is proposed in furtherance of the agitation. So far no mention has been made in the Friday prayers of the Sultan, but in the near future prayers will be offered for him as Kaliph (sic.)."[91] This intelligence proved accurate for on October 30 prayers were offered to the last Ottoman sultan and caliph, Mehmed VI Wahid al-Din, at the al-Aqsa mosque under the direction of the Grand Mufti of Jerusalem.

This development generated a debate within the Palestine government about what the dedication meant and what steps the British should take in response. Some officials saw the development as harmless. Harry Luke, the acting-district governor of Jerusalem, was one of the first officials to offer an opinion when he argued that the Palestine government should do nothing, since blessings offered to the sultan were

---

[91] Quigley to Civil Secretary, October 4, 1920. ISA 2/5/163/78/CID/S. Quigley viewed the leading figures in this movement as 'Arif al-'Arif (who had been a central figure in the Nabi Musa riot) and Shaykh Abdul Qadir al-Muzafar (a member of the *Nadi al-Arabi* political society and later a member of the Arab Executive).

preferable to expressions of support for the Turkish nationalist forces of Mustafa Kemal.[92] The Civil Secretary's Office disagreed and felt that the reintroduction of the sultan's name could cause trouble and therefore asked the police and district governors to report on 1) the effect of the introduction of the caliph's name on the population, and 2) any information they had about the individuals or groups behind this development, as a means for developing a long-term approach to this unwanted development.[93]

The police adopted an alarmist tone and warned that the re-introduction of the sultan's name was causing pro-Turkish feeling to grow. They argued that it was part of a scheme by pro-French Arab notables to discredit the sharif of Mecca, who had been Britain's chief Arab ally since the Arab Revolt of 1916.[94] Only C.H.F. Cox, the district governor for Galille, agreed, stating his belief that it would be a dangerous mistake to allow the sultan's name to be introduced in the khutba.[95] All of the other district governors were unconvinced and expressed their doubts that any conspiracy or outside influence was involved, some of them arguing that the reintroduction of the sultan's name should not be viewed as a political act at all.[96] These governors also

---

[92] Luke to Civil Secretary, November 2, 1920. ISA 2/5/163/1523/DG.

[93] Richmond to District Governors, December 9, 1920. ISA 2/5/163.

[94] Ghowne to Civil Secretary, December 10, 1920. ISA 2/5/263.

[95] Cox admitted, however, that the political effect had been minimal for his district. Cox to Civil Secretary, December 14, 1920. ISA 2/5/2631/523/DG.

[96] In Jerusalem, Harry Luke contended that even if French agents had been involved, the impetus for the reintroduction was a pro-Muslim/anti-Zionist sentiment shared by pro-Sharifians as well as those loyal to Turkey. The District Governor of Jaffa, W. F. Stirling, discounted the idea that French agents could be against the candidature of the Sharif to the caliphate, "unless they are very ignorant."

In Samaria, H. H. Postlethewaite went further and argued that politics had nothing at all to do with the reintroduction: "I do not connect the revival of this custom with any conspiracies or intrigues. It has been the rule from time immemorial to mention the Caliph's name in prayers and it is natural that this

were nearly unanimous in stating that the introduction had had little effect on the local

population, only Harry Luke, the acting district governor of Jerusalem, enigmatically

noting that the incident had caused some interest in the city.[97]

For his part, the mufti of Jerusalem, Kamil al-Husayni, denied that he had any

political aim in reintroducing the sultan's name. He stated that he would have

preferred to have held off making such a decision until a proper peace with Turkey

had been concluded but had finally given into pressure from local Muslims.[98] Given

his close working relationship with the British authorities, there was little reason for

British officials to doubt his explanation. But it is also true that the reintroduction was

regarded as an assertion of Muslim power by the Arab community itself.

In the end the debate within the Palestine government was decided by Herbert

Samuel, who concluded that he was "disinclined to attach undue importance to either

---

custom, which lapsed temporarily since our occupation, should be revived." The District Governor in
Beersheba agreed, when he stated that he had no reason to suspect that the Grand Mufti had any
political motive in reintroducing the caliph's name. Finally, in Haifa, G. S. Symes covered all bases by
saying that that the reintroduction was a revival of an older tradition but may also have been a political
act.

  See Luke to Civil Secretary, December 13, 1920. ISA 2/5/263/1523/DG, Stirling to Civil Secretary,
December 15, 1920. ISA 2/5/2631/523/DG, Postlethewaite to Civil Secretary, December 13, 1920. ISA
2/5/2631/523/DG, F. F. Kerry-Levack to Civil Secretary, December 27, 1920. ISA 2/5/2631/523/DG,
G. S. Symes to Civil Secretary, December 19, 1920. ISA 2/5/2631/523/DG.

[97] This suggests that events in Jerusalem did not have much influence on national politics in the early
1920s, which was also seen by the fact that the Nabi Musa violence of 1920 had little effect outside of
Jerusalem, especially when compared with the spread of violence after the 1929 Western Wall Riot. By
the same token it suggests that although the Mufti of Jerusalem had been elevated to the Grand Mufti of
Palestine his influence was still largely limited to the Jerusalem district. This would change with the
creation and growing strength of the Supreme Muslim Council in the 1920s, which enabled the Mufti to
build a greater political presence in the country. This transformation will be discussed in the next
chapter.

[98] The Mufti's account is briefly covered in a telegram from the High Commissioner to London,
January 1921, ISA 2/5/2631/523/DG.

cause or effect of [the] recent change."[99] Much like the concern that the British had

with the King-Crane commission, the khutba scare turned out to be more smoke than

fire. The introduction of the sultan's name in the blessings had no impact of

Palestinian affairs. Palestinians never rallied around the sultan and there is no

evidence of Palestinian outrage or sadness when Mehmed VI was removed from

political power in 1922 and religious office in 1924. Nevertheless, it is significant that

for three months at the end of 1920 the re-introduction of a simple and traditional

blessing in a traditional Muslim ritual had caused the British authorities so much

concern and confusion. As with the Nabi Musa festival six months earlier, officials

fretted during the khutba episode about an apparent infusion of politics into religion.

They also again worried that foreign agents had influenced Palestinian religious

practice and were forced to confront the fact that the truth was far more complex.

XII – Arab Criticisms of British Religious Policy

While religious arguments and demonstrations were most often used to challenge

Zionism, British colonial rule itself was also occasionally criticized on religious

grounds. As we saw in Chapter Three, in the opening years of the mandate,

Palestinian Muslims were critical of Christian control over the affairs of the Muslim

community. Their complaints about British oversight of wakf and shari'a law did not

challenge Britain's right to rule Palestine but did call into question one of the central

justifications of British rule, the claim that the Palestine government was protecting

---

[99] Ibid.

the religious status quo. As such the argument was seen by British intelligence as a

political use of Islam, which could be used to undermine the British position in

Palestine.[100] Such criticism naturally died down when the British decided to grant the

SMC control over Muslim religious affairs, but other criticisms persisted throughout

the mandate period.

One of the most important of these was the argument that the Palestine

government was not doing enough to protect Muslim holy sites. This criticism was

built around the Arab belief that Zionists were actively trying to takeover of the

Haram al-Sharif. This belief was encouraged by Weizmann's attempt to buy the

Western Wall in 1918 and by comments from militant Zionists that the Jewish temple

would rise again over the Temple Mount, although no serious attempt was ever made

by the Zionist community to take control of the Haram. The fact that British officers

had not initially been opposed to Weizmann's plan gave the impression that Britain

might be amenable to a Jewish takeover of the site as part of its commitment to the

Balfour Declaration. As we shall see in the next chapter, this particular criticism of

British action would be especially important in the 1929 Western Wall conflict.

Even British urban planning was criticized for its effect on sacred Muslim and

Christian land in Jerusalem. A 1925 memorandum submitted to the League of Nations

by the Arab Executive, for example, charged that British urban planning was

---

[100] British intelligence saw the argument as evidence of a Pan-Islamic agenda on the part of Muslim leaders. As I point out in the next section this was a misreading of the situation. CID to Chief Secretary, October 21, 1920. ISA 2/5/163/301/CID/S.

adversely affecting the Muslim and Christian communities in Jerusalem, thus demonstrating that Britain was unfit to rule over Palestine.[101]

One of the Arab Executive's complaints was over the Palestine Government's treatment of the Mamilla Cemetery, Jerusalem's oldest Muslim burial site. In the early 1920s, following the explosive growth of new neighborhoods around the cemetery, the British had urged the SMC to close the cemetery—in other words to discontinue burial there—for public health reasons. Explaining that medical experts had found nothing wrong with the tombs, the Arab Executive accused the Government of using the public health explanation as a pretext for controlling the use of "the only Muslim Cemetery in the neighborhood of Jewish quarters."[102] A second complaint centered on the response of the British authorities to the overflow of waste from a sewerage system that had been built in and around the Jewish neighborhood of Mea Sha'arim in 1920 with funds from the Zionist Executive. As the Arab Executive noted in its letter to the League of Nations, this overflow had caused the contamination of "the Muslim quarters of Shaikh Jarrah, Wadil Joz and Babil Zahira [sic], and the very sacred vicinity of St. Mary's Tomb," in January 1922.[103] The Arab Executive accused the Palestine government of ignoring calls for help from local Arabs, and charged it with favoritism towards the Jews because of its unwillingness to fix the sewerage system, even though his had been recommended by a British expert brought in from Egypt. Finally, the Palestine government was accused of unlawfully selling of sacred

---

[101] Executive Committee of the Palestine Arab Congress to League of Nations, April 8, 1925. ISA, 2/6/176.
[102] Ibid.
[103] Ibid.

land in Jerusalem as part of its disposal of the landholdings of the Greek Orthodox

Church in the New City. This disposal of Greek Orthodox controlled land was part of

the Palestine government's attempt to keep the Orthodox Patriarchate solvent but was

seen by the Arab Executive as a way for ensuring that the land could be bought by

Zionist land purchasing agencies at a reduced rate.

Naturally, such policies were contrasted with what had taken place under

Ottoman rule.[104] In Arab petitions in the 1920s, the British approach to local religious

communities was frequently compared to Ottoman control and found wanting,

particularly in terms of Britain's lack of support for Islam. Complaints about Britain's

waqf policy and cavalier attitude towards holy sites operated alongside criticisms of its

alleged political and economic favoritism towards the Jewish community to create a

picture of a colonial power that was not working in the interests of its subject

population but of an outside force.

As we shall see in the next chapter, these kinds of criticisms would eventually

be voiced by the SMC itself, as it became the most vocal advocate for the Muslim

position in Palestine.

---

[104] British intelligence saw this mostly as a function of religious identity:

> It is however certain that there has been a revulsion of feeling in favour of the Turks
> and this must be attributed partly to disappointment with conditions since the Turks
> were driven from Arab territories and also to propaganda. It is easy to work upon
> Moslem sentiment to forget past grievances and remember that the Turkish
> Government was a Mohammedan one and therefore to be preferred to a Christian one.

Brunton to Government House, June 11, 1921. ISA 2/5/163.

XIII – Islam in the Service of Nationalism

Religious arguments were also used to motivate fellow Arabs, both within Palestine and in the larger Arab world, to support the Palestinian nationalist cause. The Jewish threat to the Haram al-Sharif, for instance, was central in pro-Palestinian propaganda that was sent to Muslims outside Palestine. In the 1920s, for instance, the Arab Executive, the MCA, and eventually the SMC sent delegations to various parts of the Muslim world to publicize the Palestinian cause. These delegations used the issue of the holy places as a means to convey the danger that Palestine faced from Zionism. An address to the Egyptian people on July 1922 by Shaykh 'Abd al-Qadir al-Muzaffar (one of the most outspoken of Palestinian nationalist politicians) was typical:

> The Islamic Palestinian people, who have stood guard over the Al-Aqsa Mosque and the Noble Rock for 1,300 years, proclaims to the Islamic world that these Holy Places are in great danger from Zionist aggression...We, as vigilant loyal guardians charged by God with preservation of the Third of the Holy Precincts...have devoted ourselves to its protection...It is to the aid of the Faith that we call you, Egyptians and Muslims, with constant and breaking hearts.[105]

His concentration on the holy sites was designed to present the Palestinian problem as an Islamic cause and thus worthy of support from Muslims throughout the world. This helped raise the profile of the Palestinian cause, while at the same time it enhanced the prestige of the Arab Executive, the self-proclaimed "vigilant, loyal guardians charged by God with preservation of the Third of the Holy Precincts." Such claims would help the Arab Executive, and later the SMC, to secure moral and

---

[105] *'Al-Ahram*, 4 July 1922., as quoted in Nels Johnson, *Islam and the Politics of Notables* (London: Keegan Paul, 1982), 27.

material support from the wider Muslim community at the expense of rival Palestinian political groups.[106]

There is also some suggestion that Arab politicians used religious sermons to rally their base. Zionist intelligence claimed that the MCA paid *khatibs* (preachers) to give particular sermons and accused the religious authorities of allowing mosques to be used by Arab politicians to organize opposition to the Jewish National Home.[107] This cooperation between the religious authorities and Arab politicians was also noted by British intelligence, particularly in 1923 when religious leaders preached against a British plan to create a legislative council (this will be explained in greater detail in the next chapter).

The use of the holy places to motivate Muslim support must thus be seen as part of the attempt, discussed by Nels Johnson, "by the Palestinian *a'yan* (the landed notability) to use Islamic belief and institutions to further their own brand of Palestinian nationalism."[108] It is for this reason that Arab politicians connected with the Nadi al-Arabi and Muslim-Christian Association used the Nabi Musa festival of 1920 to deliver their nationalist message and why many of the Arab Executive's reports, speeches, and press messages during the 1920s were populated with images of and allusions to Muslim holy sites.[109] It is also, as we shall see in the final chapter,

---

[106] Such as the Nashashibi faction headed by Ragheb Bey Nashashibi, the Mayor of Jerusalem, which opposed many of the Arab Executive's policies (such as their call for a boycott of the Legislative Council Elections) and enjoyed a closer relationship with the Palestine Government.

[107] CZA L4/737 and CZA L4/738.

[108] Johnson, *Islam and the Politics of Notables*, 29.

[109] For example, pictures of the Dome of the Rock were distributed to the notables of Egypt with a report on the Palestinian situation, a general proclamation to the Muslims was sent with further pictures of the holy places, and Zionist pictures showing the *Haram al-Sharif* adorned with Jewish iconography

why the Supreme Muslim Council, came to use religion to politically challenge

Zionism and the Palestine government.

XIV – The British Response

This blurring of the lines between religious and political language in Arab protests and

petitions challenged British ideas of how religion should operate in the colony. As we

saw in Chapters Two and Three, British officials saw religion as a communal matter

that should not infringe on the public sphere. This was based upon their idealization

of the Ottoman millet system, which as I have argued did not fit with the reality of the

Ottoman past. The question that faced British officials was what should or could be

done to curb what they saw as the introduction of religion and religious actors into

politics.

The Intelligence Department of the Palestine Police Department treated the use

of religious language as a very serious development and advocated for British action

to stop the mixing of politics and religion. As has been mentioned, they saw this as a

sign of the local population's sympathy for Pan-Islam or worse yet as evidence of the

infiltration of Pan-Islamic agents into Palestine. This was why the Criminal

Investigation Department of the Palestine Police reported to the Civil Secretary in

October 1920, when the Sultan's name was reintroduced in the khutba, that

> Moslem leaders in Palestine and their followers have answered eagerly
> the call of pan-Islamism, most of them ignoring the fact that the

---

were distributed by the Arab Executive to notables in the Hejaz and shown to Bedouin tribesmen in
Transjordan. See ISA 2/6/168 "The Arab Delegation (Wafd)" for an account of the activities of the
Wafd.

movement was being fomented by the French. Seeing that the anti-Zionist movement alone had very little chance of success, the Palestinian leaders adopted the religious agitation as the only means for forcing the hands of the Government being convinced that an-all-Moslem agitation will receive the support of the whole Moslem world principally in India.[110]

In 1921 Intelligence agents again warned of Pan-Islam's grip on local politics: "The powerful bond of Islam and the hatred and distrust aroused in the Arab mind by the policies of France in Syria and Britain in Palestine have been sufficient to counterbalance the war-time bitterness against the Turks. We are therefore now confronted by a Pan-Islamic movement."[111]

The "proofs" offered by the Palestine police, however, turned out be largely conjectural, with intelligence officers seeing almost any form of religious language used by politicians as evidence of an affinity with Pan-Islamic ideals. This caused intelligence agents to consistently misread the local religious and political situation. For example, evidence for Pan-Islam was found in the "systematic campaign against the Government interference in the Administration of Moslem Wakfs and Sharia Courts."[112] But as we saw in Chapter Three, the motives driving the Muslim demand for control over the waqf system had nothing to do with international politics but were based upon a purely local desire for these sites to be placed under Muslim control.[113]

---

[110]CID to Chief Secretary, October 21, 1920. ISA 2/5/163/301/CID/S.

[111] Brunton to GHQ, Egypt, February 29, 1921. ISA 2/5/163/2026P.

[112] CID to Chief Secretary, October 21, 1920. ISA 2/5/163/301/CID/S.

[113] This demand also made sense within the strictures of the *status quo* policy, which is why British officials were ultimately receptive to the proposal to create a wholly Muslim body to oversee the *waqf* system.

For the rest of the government, the police's sensationalistic claims about Pan-Islam were treated with great suspicion. As noted in Chapter One, officials in the Palestine government and the Foreign Office saw these claims as unsubstantiated fear mongering. District governors in Palestine also rejected the notion that Pan-Islam was a problem in their reports on the khutba scare. At the height of the CID's concern about Pan-Islam, the assistant political secretary, Ernest Richmond, argued that he could no longer receive police intelligence, since "these reports (and I have had several similar) are unsatisfactory in the sense that while on the one hand they denote a serious situation on the other (a) there are no proofs or even very convincing arguments + (b) they do not accord with my reading of the situation (for what it is worth)."[114] Most importantly, the analysis offered by the police was not accepted by High Commissioner Herbert Samuel, who tended to view Arab protest as fomented by frustrated local landowners rather than outsiders.

Though the Pan-Islamic peril was largely discounted by the Palestine Government, officials still worried about religious language being used to challenge British rule. The violence of the Nabi Musa festival seemed to confirm their fears about the lethal nature of combining religion and politics. As a result, the Palestine government developed three main approaches to combat this threat: 1) political agitators would be identified and pacified; 2) religious ceremonies would be policed

---

[114] The report from the Assistant Director of Public Security, E. P. Quigley, which reported that the Pan-Islamic movement was "assuming the character of a general religious upheaval," also included marginal notes that asked for proof in bold letters. See Quigley to Chief Secretary November 4, 1920. ISA 2/5/163.

more stringently and political groups monitored more thoroughly; and 3) counter-

propaganda would be offered to reassure the local population about British intentions.

The first of these approaches can be seen in the previously mentioned

identification and conviction of the individuals who gave political speeches at the

Nabi Musa festival: Hajj Amin al-Husayni, 'Arif al-'Arif, and Musa Kazim al-

Husayni. The first two fled Palestine when the British authorities issued a warrant for

their arrest and were subsequently convicted in absentia for their role in the riots,

while Musa Kazim al-Husayni was not convicted of any crime but was removed from

his position as mayor of Jerusalem and replaced by Raghib al-Nashashibi.[115]

The second prong of this response was manifested in the drawing up of new

security plans for the Nabi Musa festival and increased surveillance of Arab political

groups. As Edwin Samuel put it, after the 1920 festival the Palestine government

adopted a more organized "management of religious ceremonies."[116] This involved a

rerouting of the parade route so that Muslim pilgrims were kept away far from the

Jewish quarter, an increase in the British troop presence, and a ban on the carrying of

unauthorized banners.[117] The Palestine government also reached out to Hajj Amin al-

---

[115] This was not the first time that Musa Kazim had gotten in trouble for his participation in politics. In 1918 he had been forbidden by Ronald Storrs to serve as leader of the MCA, and along with 'Arif Hikmat al-Nashashibi (the General Administrator of the *Awqaf*) was given the choice of remaining in government employment or choosing a life in politics. As a result he chose to remain in the administration. In 1920 the choice was made for him by the British authorities, with Musa Kazim al-Husayni becoming the leader of the MCA after his ouster from the mayoralty. See Porath, *Emergence*, 33.

[116] Edwin Samuel, *A Lifetime in Jerusalem: The Memoirs of the Second Viscount Samuel* (London: Vallentine, Mitchell, 1970), 59.

[117] For a description of British policy towards festivals in the 1940s see Gibbs Papers GB165-0117, Middle East Center Archive, St. Antony's College, Oxford.

Husayni before the 1921 Nabi Musa festival to make sure that he used his influence to keep the crowd under control.

That would not be the last time the British looked to the mufti to moderate local popular feeling. The British also worked with the SMC to control the giving of political speeches at Palestinian mosques. This approach was necessitated by the fact that the Palestine government was not prepared to intervene in religious matters directly but could lean on the SMC, because it was technically a branch of the Palestine government (even if it was autonomous in practice).

At the same time, an increased vigil was placed upon the use of religious language in Palestinian politics by the intelligence department of the Palestine government. This led to a glut of intelligence reports about Pan-Islam in 1920 and 1921, and contributed to the scare about the introduction of the sultan's name in the khutba. Surveillance of such groups as the MCA and the Arab Executive even went beyond Palestine, as British officers collected information about Palestinian Arab delegations that traveled to Egypt, India, and Europe.

Less significant was the third prong, which was to produce counter propaganda that could be used to blunt this mixture of religion and politics. One approach was to use local religious leaders to repudiate or oppose anti-British and anti-Zionist rumors that periodically emerged in Palestine. Another involved the issuance of reports that showed British religious policy in a favorable light.

This three-pronged response was similar to the policy prescriptions of the forgotten Palin Commission report on the Nabi Musa festival of 1920, which had argued that Britain needed to weed out agitators, maintain an increased troop presence in Palestine, and educate the Arab population about the benefits of colonial rule. And we can see such policies, with varying degrees of success, being applied by British officials throughout the mandate period. But of course all of these approaches did not address the underlying problem that the Arab community had with British rule, the fact that British support for the Jewish national home fatally undermined the possibility of Palestinian Arab self-determination.

For their part Palestinian political groups denied playing any kind of "religious card". A joint declaration by the Nadi al-Arabi, the Muntada al-Adabi, the Muslim Benevolent Society, the Greek Orthodox Benevolent Society, the Greek Catholic Society stated in November 1918 that "the people of Palestine in general and Jerusalem in particular...are the last persons to rouse religious feeling," and emphasized the great relationship that Arabs and Jews had enjoyed under Arab and Ottoman rule.[118]

XV - Conclusion

That religion was a factor within Palestinian nationalism does not make it a unique or backward form of nationalism. While it may not fit the ideal type of secular nationalism developed by Benedict Anderson, it does represent the complex reality of

---

[118] ISA 2/4/140. This nostalgia for the past was reinforced by a distinction that was frequently made in Arab political discourse between the respectful traditional religious Jew and the pushy, chauvinistic, and immoral Zionist. Although it should be pointed out that this distinction did not last very long and in short time being Jewish was considered synonymous with being a Zionist, a melding of identities encouraged by the Zionist Commission's claim to represent the entire yishuv.

national politics outside of Western Europe. Indeed, as the work of Peter Van der

Veer reveals, Anderson's argument that nationalism is an inherently secular movement

relies on a crude form of essentialism that does not fit the actual practice of

nationalism, even in Europe.

> As the argument goes, nationalism belongs to the realm of legitimate
> modern politics. Nationalism is assumed to be "secular," since it is
> thought to develop in a process of secularization and modernization.
> Religion, in this view, assumes political significance only in the
> underdeveloped parts of the world—much as it did in the past of the
> West…Based partly on this philosophical notion of the rationality of
> the West is the current but much less sophisticated idea that Western
> Europe and the United States have had a unique historical experience of
> secularization, whereas Asia (and South Asia in particular) has had a
> history of dangerous politicization of religious difference. This
> impression is plainly wrong, since it perpetuates the old, mistaken view
> of the great divide between the modern West and the backward Rest.[119]

Van der Veer's and Hartmut Lehmann's edited work on European and Asian

nationalism, *Nation and Religion: Perspectives on Europe and Asia*, offers a useful

corrective to the view that "nationalism comes thus in a package with individualism

and secularism, as required by the industrial transformation of an agrarian world," a

position taken by the major theorists of nationalism, such as Hobsbawm, Gellner, and

Anderson.[120] But historians of Palestine do not need to look at such modern

investigations of secularization to understand that "Nationalism feeds on a [religious]

symbolic repertoire that is already available but also transforms it in significant ways,"

for the history of Zionism shows how religious identity and sacred history could easily

---

[119] Peter van der Veer and Hartmut Lehmann, "Introduction," in *Nation and Religion: Perspectives on Europe and Asia*, ed. Peter van der Veer and Hartmut Lehmann (Princeton: Princeton UP, 1999), 3.

[120] Van der Veer, "Introduction," 5.

be integrated into, or perhaps more accurately be appropriated by, a national movement.

Nevertheless it is true that this mixing of religion and politics was greeted with great suspicion, bordering on fear, by British officials in Palestine. Rocked by the events of the Nabi Musa festival of 1920, the Palestine government closely monitored the political activities of religious figures and the use of religious arguments by politicians. As mentioned in the last section, the Palestine government also put into place measures that were designed to ensure that there would be no repeat of the events of 1920.

The fact that it would be nine more years before religion and politics came together again in such an explosive fashion, with a struggle over the Western Wall in 1929, seemed to reassure British officials that religion would not be a major factor in Palestinian politics. In some ways they were correct. Arab political groups, particularly the Arab Executive that dominated Palestinian politics in the 1920s, were far more likely to use secular arguments to make the Palestinian case than religious arguments and their protests and political actions were not centered on religious issues. But in another important way they turned out to be wrong, for politics became important within the religious realm. As the next chapter will make clear, it was the Muslim religious authorities that became politicized.

The political agenda of Hajj Amin al-Husayni was one important factor in the politicization of the SMC but another significant cause, which I will discuss here, was the weakening of Arab political parties over the course of the 1920s as a result of a

British crackdown on their activities and of their own failure to wrest any meaningful concessions out of the mandatory government.

The free-wheeling nature of Palestinian politics that marked the earliest years of British rule was an early target of government surveillance and intervention. Various strategies were used to control Palestinian political activities: Palestinian political parties were monitored by British intelligence, a blacklist of political agitators was kept by the Palestine government, nationalist newspapers were occasionally censored, some members of Palestinian secret societies were exiled to Egypt, and government employees were warned about participating in political parties. At the same time the Palestine government attempted to channel Arab politicians into what were considered to be more legitimate forms of political participation. For instance, Arabs were encouraged to become members of the government's advisory council and executive council. There was also a proposal to form a recognized Arab Agency as a balance to Britain's commitment to supporting a Jewish agency that was provided for in article four of the Palestine Mandate.[121] But the centerpiece of this approach was a

---

[121] Article four of the mandate stated that,

> An appropriate Jewish agency shall be recognised as a public body for the purpose of advising and co-operating with the Administration of Palestine in such economic, social and other matters as may affect the establishment of the Jewish national home and the interests of the Jewish population in Palestine, and, subject always to the control of the Administration to assist and take part in the development of the country.
>
> The Zionist organization, so long as its organization and constitution are in the opinion of the Mandatory appropriate, shall be recognised as such agency. It shall take steps in consultation with His Britannic Majesty's Government to secure the co-operation of all Jews who are willing to assist in the establishment of the Jewish national home.

As Ann Mosley Lesch has pointed out, the Arab Agency would have had none of the same powers as the Jewish Agency. In particular, as Rashid Khalidi has pointed out, this agency would not have had

proposal in 1923 to create a legislative council, which would give Muslims,

Christians, and Jews, a role in the governance of their country. The legislative council

was envisioned as an elected representative body of the Palestinian population that

would replace the preexisting advisory council, a body whose membership was

nominated by the Palestine government.

"Representative" turned out to be a misleading term. British officials

proposed giving Arabs ten out of the twelve seats available to local representatives in

recognition of their demographic majority in Palestine. As we might expect, the

membership was organized along religious lines, with eight seats allocated to

Muslims, two to Christians, and two to Jews. But this would be balanced out by ten

positions allotted to government officials plus the high commissioner's place at the

head of the body. This ensured that a bloc Arab vote could be outvoted by a unified

British vote, with or without Jewish help.

The legislative council was proposed by the Palestine government as a means

to mollify the Arab community by giving it some form of representative government.

This proposal was based on a misperception that was common among British officials

in the early 1920s that Arab opposition to the Balfour Declaration could be overcome

by reassuring the Arab population that its rights would be protected. This was shown

in the Palin Commission's naïve contention that at the root of Arab violence was a

"misapprehension of the true meaning of the Balfour Declaration and forgetfulness of

---

the recognized international standing of the Jewish Agency, which was "entitled to diplomatic
representation in Geneva before the League of Nations Permanent Mandates Commission, in London,
and elsewhere," on the strength of Article Four's recognition of the agency as a "public body for the
purpose of advising and cooperating with the Administration of Palestine." See Lesch, *Arab Politics in
Palestine*, 186-87 and Khalidi, *Iron Cage*, 44-45.

the guarantees determined therein."[122] It was also at the heart of Herbert Samuel's approach to the Arab community during his tenure as high commissioner, which was built around the idea that Arabs could be reconciled to the mandate and Jewish immigration if they could be made to understand the true nature of the British commitment to Arab rights. This is why British officials in the early-1920s emphasized, the mandate's "dual obligation" to Jews and Arabs (who weren't actually mentioned as a people in the text of the mandate or the Balfour Declaration), as did the Churchill White Paper of 1922.

This idea that Arabs could be reconciled to the British mandate simply by giving them an Arab agency or seats on a legislative council thoroughly underestimated the depth of Palestinian Arab opposition to the Balfour Declaration. Since the beginning of the mandate Arab politicians had consistently pushed for an end to the British commitment to the Jewish National Home, which Arabs correctly identified as an obstacle to their own nationalist aspirations. Inspired by Wilsonian ideas of national self-determination and the promises contained in the Hussein-McMahon correspondence, Arab politicians consistently argued in their petitions and private meetings with British officials that Arabs should have the right to decide their own political destiny.[123] And, when the Palestine government did not compromise its position, Arab delegations were sent to London and Geneva to present the Palestinian

---

[122] PRO WO 32/9614.

[123] I will leave the discussion of what exactly McMahon promised to Hussein to others, but what is important here is that Palestinian Arabs believed that Britain had made a commitment to Arab rule in Palestine. For their part, British officials in Palestine, when they were aware of the correspondence, were unsure if Palestine had been promised to the Arabs or not.

case, such as the 1922 *wafd* (delegation) to London organized by the Muslim-Christian Association to fruitlessly press for a rescission of the Balfour Declaration.

It was not surprising then that the Arab community rejected the proposal for the Arab agency and legislative council out of hand, for they recognized that to participate in these schemes would be to recognize the legitimacy of the mandate. The rejection of the legislative council proved to be significant for the relationship between the colonial government and Palestinian political parties, because it effectively ended British attempts to reach out to Arab politicians.

It was the nature of the Arab rejection that made it particularly profound. Officially proposed as part of the Palestine Order-in-Council of August 1922, the legislative council was supposed to come into being after a two-stage election process that would take place within six months. In response, Arab politicians put together a campaign to boycott the elections, which became a *cause célebre* within the Arab community. This campaign involved political campaigning by the Arab Executive and the MCA throughout the towns and countryside of Palestine in the spring of 1923. It turned out to be one of the most successful anticolonial protests during the mandate period because it brought about a widespread boycott, with only about 10% of the Arab population voting.[124] This forced the government to call off the second stage of

---

[124] The reason why it is not often remember is that it was a victory that didn't really change the dynamic in Palestine but continued the standoff between the British authorities and Arab politicians. An editorial in the Hebrew paper *Doar HaYom* ("The Daily Mail"), which was associated with the Revisionist Zionism of Vladimir Jabotinsky, illustrated the general Zionist view that Arab political unity was illusory by arguing that, "not only is there no boycott on the elections but there is actually a true election fight amongst the Arab leaders." See *Doar HaYom*, March 9, 1923 as reprinted in ISA 2/10/242 II.

the election and soon afterwards the proposal for an elected legislative council was

scrapped.

While the collapse of the legislative council elections and the failure of the

Arab Agency proposal were victories for Arab politicians, they came at a high price.

By the end of 1923 Arab political groups had little space for operation or chance of

success in their fight for Palestinian rights. Delegations sent to Europe by the Arab

Executive in 1922 had been ignored by the British government and the Permanent

Mandates Commission, a sign of the fact that "Palestinians had no international

standing whatsoever, and indeed were often dependent on the hostile and

unsympathetic British for such unsatisfactory diplomatic representation as they could

obtain in Geneva and elsewhere."[125] In Palestine their petitions were ignored and with

the Palestine government unwilling to cooperate with them after the legislative

election debacle, there ended up being few opportunities for Palestinians to affect

change in the political system.[126]

There would be other Palestinian Arab political congresses in the 1920s,

although as time went on they occurred with less regularity, as Arab politicians found

themselves increasingly divided. By the end of the decade Arab political parties were

---

[125] Khalidi, *Iron Cage*, 45.

[126] An obvious question that Rashid Khalidi asks in his book *The Iron Cage* is why the Palestinian
population was unable to create a political movement regardless of British intransigence. He argues
that the answer lies in the adherence of the educated Arab notability to the modern legalistic arguments
of their colonizers, which functioned as a de facto cooperation with the mandate. As he puts it,

> In spite of facing this unyielding stonewall of British rejection of their national
> claims, and indeed of their national existence, these Palestinian notables were for far
> too long unable to find a means to disentangle themselves and their people from the
> legal and constitutional constraints that Great Britain had forged for them. They
> could never get out of the iron cage fashioned by their British masters.

Khalidi, *Iron Cage*, 47.

seen by the general population as ineffectual, for they offered little to challenge the

colonial power. This left a space for a new political actor to emerge, the Supreme

Muslim Council.

Chapter Six

The Mufti as a Political Figure

I - Introduction

In 1945 the Foreign Office published a retrospective report on Hajj Amin's political

and religious career. The title of the report, "Colonial Renegades – Palestine: The

Mufti of Jerusalem," indicates how far Hajj Amin's reputation had fallen during the

mandate period. As the report makes clear, the mufti had gained his renegade status as

the leader of the Arab Higher Committee (AHC) during the Palestine Arab Revolt of

1936-39. This was the most serious insurgency of the British period and one of the

most significant anticolonial rebellions in the British empire since India's Sepoy

Rebellion of 1857-58. As in the Indian rebellion, Palestinian insurgents had managed

to threaten British colonial rule by taking over large swathes of the countryside and by

forcing British troops to briefly withdraw from major cities, such as Jaffa, Jericho, Bir

Sabe', and most significantly the Old City of Jerusalem. They also met much the

same fate for they were soon crushed by a British counterforce, a reinforcement of

thousands of troops from Egypt. The AHC played a leading role in this revolt by

organizing a six-month general strike from April to October 1936 that preceded the

outbreak of armed rebellion in 1937.[1] As the leader of the AHC, Hajj Amin al-

---

[1] As Rashid Khalidi has pointed out, this general strike was the longest anticolonial strike up to this
point in history. The strike was built around an Arab boycott of those parts of the economy that were
run by British or Zionist enterprises combined with the withholding of labor by Arab workers. Although
the strike succeeded in hurting the general economy, this action ended up hurting the Arab community
more than the yishuv or the Palestine government, principally by forcing the Jewish economy to
become even more self-sufficient and by shifting some of the economic and infrastructure investments
made by the Palestine government away from the Arab community (such as in the development of the

285

Husayni, emerged as the face of the rebellion. He would not last long in this role, for

British officials, embarrassed by the success of the general strike (as they had been by

the Arab boycott of the legislative council elections of 1923) and angered by the

AHC's seeming inability or unwillingness to curb the attacks of Arab peasant

guerillas, outlawed the AHC in September 1937 and exiled a number of its leaders to

the Seychelles.[2] Hajj Amin was able to escape arrest by first taking refuge in the

Haram al-Sharif and then by fleeing to Beirut disguised as a bedouin (or as a woman

according to some accounts).

For his role in the rebellion Hajj Amin al-Husayni was stripped of his

presidency of the SMC and also lost his title as mufti upon his flight from the country.

This would have profound effects on the structure of the SMC, which came under

much greater government control during the final years of the British mandate. These

changes will be touched upon in my concluding chapter, but here I am interested in

understanding how Hajj Amin emerged as such a central figure in Palestinian politics.

For some authors, the mufti's role in the rebellion was simply confirmation of

his character. According to this point of view religious office had never changed Hajj

Amin's political ways. As mentioned in the introduction of this dissertation, this kind

of argument informs the popular Zionist portrait of Hajj Amin al-Husayni as a slippery

Arab politician, whose participation in politics began with the Nabi Musa festival in

---

port of Tel Aviv alongside the port of Jaffa). For more information about the revolt and its long term
consequences see Rashid Khalidi, "The Palestinians and 1948: The Underlying Causes of Failure," *The
War for Palestine*, eds. Eugene L. Rogan and Avi Shlaim (Cambridge: Cambridge University Press,
2001), Khalidi, *Iron Cage*, 105-124, and Swedenberg, *Memories of Revolt.*

[2] Even before the disbanding of the AHC, the Palestine government had imprisoned a number of Arab
politicians involved with the AHC, some of whom served out their sentences in concentration camps
established during the revolt.

1920 and continued unabated throughout his tenure as mufti and president of the SMC. But as the 1945 Foreign Office report makes clear, there was a great difference between his political activities in the 1920s and 1930s. This point is borne out in an investigation of official documents of the period, as well as in later British and Arab memoirs, which reveal that Hajj Amin moved from being a hesitant and inconsistent political actor in the early and mid-1920s to becoming a more confident political actor at the very end of the decade.

This chapter investigates how the mufti became a leading political figure in the Palestine community and how by extension the SMC was politicized. It is an attempt to get beyond the ahistorical, flattened account of the politicization of Islamic institutions that is often found in scholarly literature. The SMC was not born as a political group (as many Zionist authors and some Palestinian nationalist authors would argue) but grew into that role because of particular events that occurred in Palestine. It was a product of the competitions and frictions that occurred between the Jewish, Arab, and British communities over the course of the 1920s, which came to a head in one particularly profound moment—the struggle over the Western Wall of 1928-29.

II – A Quiet Council

Before explaining the politicization of the SMC it is important to note that I am not trying to argue that the SMC moved from being a completely apolitical organization to becoming a purely political institution. As mentioned earlier, the mufti of Jerusalem was intended by the Palestine government to be the communal head of the Muslim

community. This meant that the office holder would be more than just a religious

figure; like the *millet bashi*s (heads of the millets) of the Orthodox Christian, Latin, or

Jewish communities during the Ottoman period, the mufti was expected to both

administer and control his community—tasks that involved some proficiency in

communal politics as well as religious affairs.

The SMC thus never limited itself to the "the control and management of the

Moslem Awkaf and [Shari'a] affairs in Palestine" that was assigned to it in the

Supreme Muslim Council Ordinance of 1922.[3] As Uri Kupfershmidt has written, the

council saw its jurisdiction as covering many additional aspects of Muslim religious

life: Muslim holy places, mosques, *zawiyas* and *takiyas*, Islamic festivals, preaching,

and other Islamic affairs. Such areas of the religious life of the community would

have been under the control of a millet during the Ottoman period. In the Palestine

government's neo-millet model, the SMC's oversight of these aspects of Muslim life

was perfectly acceptable, which is why British officials saw no problem in regarding

the president of the SMC as being equivalent, as Harry Luke put it, to an "ethnarch."[4]

It is for this reason that British officials did not object as vociferously as we might

expect when the mufti and his council became involved in what the 1945 Foreign

Office report termed "political intrigue." A good example of the British attitude can

be seen in Ronald Storrs' letter to the chief secretary of the Palestine government in

1924 which explained that, "It is generally believed throughout the Jaffa District that

---

[3] Kupferschmidt, 57. The quote comes from the *Palestine Official Gazette,* 1.1.1922.

[4] Luke to High Commissioner January 14, 1929 CO 733.172.

the Council is at least as active in political as in religious affairs and surprise is from time to time expressed that the Government should tolerate this almost overt intervention in politics on the part of persons in the receipt of official emoluments," before adding that this "was to be anticipated, and though deprecated, and as far as possible lessened, should be discounted and to a certain extent excused."[5]

By the same token when I talk of the politicization of the SMC, it should not be assumed that this meant that the council abandoned its administration of religious affairs. Indeed the reason why officials like Storrs could accept the political activities of SMC officials was that the council was otherwise faithfully discharging its administrative duties to the Muslim community. This was important because it confirmed to British officials that Herbert Samuel's decision to rehabilitate rather than punish Hajj Amin after the 1920 Nabi Musa festival had been a sound decision.

Accounts of the career of Hajj Amin al-Husayni often overlook the fact that he kept a low profile in Palestinian politics in the years that followed his appointment as mufti and his election to head the SMC. In the early to mid 1920s the SMC did not take public stands on political issues that affected the Arab community, choosing instead to indirectly engage with these issues. A case in point was the SMC's activities during the Arab boycott of the legislative council elections of 1923. As I pointed out in chapter five, the legislative council proposal had collapsed due to a highly effective election boycott by the Arab community. The campaign to boycott the elections was put together by the Arab Executive and the various branches of the

---

[5] Storrs to Chief Secretary, January 4th, 1924, ISA 2/6/172, "The Moderate Party."

Muslim-Christian Association. The mufti offered no formal endorsement of the campaign and there is no evidence that he publicly came out in opposition to the proposed council. There is some evidence, however, of the SMC offering assistance to the campaign behind the scenes. British intelligence reported that Shaykh 'Abd al-Qadir al-Muzaffar, a close ally of Hajj Amin, was a leading figure in the campaign, although it should be pointed out that al-Muzaffar was not an employee of the SMC. It was also reported that the council's mosques were used by al-Muzaffar and other preachers to propagandize against the election.[6] This included the al-Aqsa mosque, where in March 1923, a crowd of some 4,000 listened to al-Muzaffar preach against the elections. That led the Palestine government to warn the mufti against the use of places of worship for political propaganda.[7]

The SMC's indirect participation in the campaign was also attested to by British district commissioners who informed the high commissioner that the council had exceeded its powers during this period.[8] Despite these observations no official action was ever taken against the SMC, as the high commissioner decided in consultation with Ernest Richmond, the government's main liaison with the Arab community, to wait for the affair to blow over, which it shortly did.[9]

The mufti and his organization were also accused of other clandestine activities during the early 1920s that are more fanciful and consequently more difficult to verify.

---

[6] See Quigley to Storrs, "Daily Intelligence Summary", February 22, 1923, ISA 2/10/242 I.

[7] Samuel to Colonial Office, March 9, 1923, PRO CO 733/43/133ff. Porath notes that the mufti responded positively to this request but only after he was warned a second time after al-Muzaffar preached again at the al-Aqsa mosque. Porath, *Emergence*, 154.

[8] See Kupferschmidt, *Supreme Muslim Council*, 38.

[9] Ibid.

According to a Zionist intelligence agent, Chaim Kalvarisky, the mufti's nephew Tahir al-Husayni (son of the late mufti Kamil al-Husayni) claimed in 1923 that his uncle had been behind not only the violence at the Nabi Musa festival in 1920 but also the May Day riots in Jaffa in 1921 as part of an organized plan to take over the country from the British. Perhaps because of the fantastic nature of these claims, the unreliability of the informant, or even the unreliability of the agent, this information was never followed up by the Palestine government.[10] The SMC was also accused by British intelligence officers of assisting members of what they identified as the "Moslem self-sacrificing society," an organization that first emerged in Haifa in 1924 before opening up cells in Nablus, Jerusalem, and Gaza.[11] British intelligence agents reported that members of the Jerusalem branch "have sworn to sacrifice themselves for Haj Amin and act as his body guard and carry out propaganda in his favour among the Moslem inhabitants," and claimed that its members received jobs in the SMC or the al-Aqsa mosque.[12] It is not clear from British intelligence reports how these cells were related to each other or to the SMC or whether this intelligence was accurate, for no follow up action was taken against these groups. Although it is plausible that the mufti would have supported these organizations, the historical evidence does not make it clear how

---

[10] Tom Segev, *One Palestine Complete: Jews and Arabs under the British Mandate* (New York: Metropolitan Books, 2000), 278. Kalvarisky was a quixotic figure who was involved in his own private project to win Arab support for Zionism through bribery. For more information on Kalvarisky, see Neil Caplan, "Arab-Jewish Contacts in Palestine after the First World War," *Journal of Contemporary History*, Vol. 12, No. 4 (Oct. 1977), 635-668.

[11] See ISA 2/5/166, "Moslem Self-Sacrificing Society".

[12] Broadhurst to Chief Secretary, May 7, 1924, ISA 2/5/166.

important these groups were or if they were anything more than products of the active

imagination of intelligence officials.

III – Representing Muslims at Home and Abroad

A more significant way in which the SMC involved itself in politics was by using its

religious reputation to expand its presence in Palestine and beyond. In the mid-1920s

the mufti was active in expanding the SMC beyond its limited role as a local

ecclesiastical body. The mufti transformed the council in two different ways: by

raising its prestige in the wider Muslim world and by embarking on economic and

social ventures that broadened the council's mission at home. This was part of what

Hajj Amin identified in 1922 as one of the main duties of the SMC, which was "to

represent the Muslims of this country honourably and properly inside and outside the

country."[13]

Projecting power abroad

Hajj Amin's campaign to enhance his reputation in the Muslim world was built upon

the SMC's oversight of the Haram al-Sharif, the third holiest site in Islam. The most

famous way in which the mufti used the site was his defense of the Haram al-Sharif

and al-Buraq (the edifice known to non-Muslims as the Western Wall) during the

Western Wall dispute of 1928-29. This defense will be discussed at length below but

here I would like to concentrate on an earlier way in which the religious site was used

to appeal to Muslims beyond Palestine: the mufti's campaign to repair the Dome of

---

[13] Kupferschmidt, 57. The quote comes from the *Palestine Official Gazette,* 1.1.1922.

the Rock. This campaign led the SMC to send out six delegations, which visited Egypt, the Hijaz, India, Iran, Iraq, Kuwait, and Bahrain in 1923 and 1924, two of which were headed by Hajj Amin himself. These delegations helped the SMC to raise funds and forge relationships with Muslim groups outside of the country.

The impetus for repairing the Dome of the Rock originally came from the British. As mentioned in Chapter Two, the O.E.T.A. authorities commissioned a study of the Dome of the Rock in the first months of British occupation. Richmond's study was mainly driven by Ronald Storrs' and C. R. Ashbee's passion for preservation but also fit nicely in the British desire to protect (or to be seen to protect) the religious heritage of Palestine. The report stated that the bones of the structure were fine but that its "skin" needed to be replaced and so the British authorities decided to repair the outside of the dome as a gesture of goodwill towards the Muslim community. As usual in such occasions another motive was also at play. As Herbert Samuel explained in a letter home to Lord Curzon, "I earnestly hope it may be possible to take up this matter, for there is no doubt that the effect throughout the Moslem world, of which this is the third most sacred shrine, would be favourable and instantaneous."[14]

At first the Palestine government considered funding and carrying out the repairs on its own but was soon reminded by Lord Reading, viceroy of India, and Lord Curzon, the British foreign secretary, that this would be seen by Muslims as a British

---

[14] Samuel to Curzon, 24.8.1920, ISA 2/6/184.

attempt to take control of the holy site.[15] The government therefore encouraged the mufti to organize funding from the Muslim world and to help find Muslim artisans to complete the repairs. The mufti also recognized the effect that the repairs would have on the Muslim world—and the opportunity that this presented for raising his profile— and readily agreed to cooperate. The project thus became a joint effort between the government and the SMC. The government provided Richmond's architectural study of the dome, offered technical knowledge, built and funded a workshop for making "traditional" tiles (an Armenian potter was brought in from Kutiye, Turkey), and protected the site through urban planning and antiquities ordinances. Meanwhile, the SMC provided funds, helped find Muslim craftsmen and, most importantly, became the public face of the project.

Hajj Amin was no stranger to using the Haram al-Sharif for his own ends. In his 1921 campaign to become the mufti of Jerusalem, he had accused Jews of interfering in the elections and alleged that the leading candidate (Husam al-Jarallah) would "help in handing over the Jews the *Haram Esh-Sharif*, the Dome of the Rock, and El Aksa that they might pull them down and build in their place the Temple and the place of sacrifice as stated by Alfred Mond and the president of the Zionist

---

[15] Samuel's plea to Curzon to take up the matter of the repair of the Dome of the Rock included a request to open up public subscriptions in Britain and across the Empire to fund the repairs. Samuel to Curzon, 24.8.1920, ISA 2/6/184. The Viceroy of India reminded Curzon that British funding would be looked upon as a sign that the British were taking over the Muslim holy places, especially given that the Khilafat Committee (a nationalist organization of Indian Muslims) was using the fact of British control over the sites to motivate the Muslim population of India against imperialism. See Viceroy of India to Curzon, 2.11.20, ISA 2/6/184.

Commission, Dr. Eder."[16] The British decision to work with the SMC in repairing the Dome of the Rock gave him the chance to again use the holy site to his advantage.

Because of his partnership with the Palestine government in the preservation project, the mufti's 1923 public appeal for funding for the project (the mufti's "General Appeal to the Muslim World") emphasized the historical need to protect the Islamic "art treasures," "precious tiles," and "gift mosaics" of the Dome of the Rock.[17] But, a rather different message was presented by the SMC's fundraising delegations to the Muslim world, which portrayed the repair of the dome as part of a defense of the site from Jewish takeover. A Foreign Office report in September 1923 warned that a delegation sent by the Mufti to the Hijaz was carrying out pan-Arab propaganda based on the "stock rumor" that the Dome of the Rock was being placed under the control of the Jews by the British.[18] A month later another telegram from British intelligence in Cairo argued that a separate mission that was travelling to India via Egypt was part of a propaganda campaign organized in concert with the Indian Khilafat Committee and the Turkish government in Ankara.[19] Further telegrams from India revealed that the issue that was central to this propaganda was the threat of a Jewish takeover of the *Haram al-Sharif.*[20]

---

[16] Quoted in Monk, *An Aesthetic Occupation*, 53 and Wasserstein, *The British in Palestine*, 99.

[17] ISA 2/6/184. Such language endeared the SMC to officials such as Ernest Richmond who saw this as a sign that Muslims were developing "a more appreciative outlook regarding" monuments. See Abu El-Haj, *Facts on the Ground*, 69.

[18] Oliphant to His Majesty's Consul, Jeddah, 13.9.23, ISA 2/6/184.

[19] Scott to Foreign Office, 9.10.23, ISA 2/6/184. This delegation was headed by Jamal al-Husseini, a leading figure in the Muslim-Christian Association, indicating the close relationship that the SMC had with Arab political groups.

[20] ISA 2/6/184.

These intelligence reports and contemporaneous newspaper accounts show the SMC using pan-Arabist and pan-Islamist language in its fundraising campaign to renovate the Dome of the Rock, but it would be a mistake to assume that the campaign was part of any larger movement. The aim of the campaign was more parochial than that, for its goal was to raise the profiles of Hajj Amin and his organization in the Muslim world and the use of pan-Islamist and pan-Arabist language was an effective means to that end.

By promoting the SMC as the sole defender of the holy site, Haj Amin was able to draw large donations from political and religious figures throughout the Muslim world, not all of which would be used for the preservation of the Dome of the Rock.[21] The campaign also allowed the SMC to effectively position itself as the main organization in Palestine dedicated to defending the Muslim position in Palestine, thereby supplanting the Arab Executive which had also presented itself as the defender of Muslim rights. The relationship forged between the SMC and the Khilafat Committee, which had been identified by British intelligence in Cairo, was another consequence of this positioning.[22] Indeed, the fundraising campaign of 1923-24 was foundational in the SMC's engagement with the wider pan-Islamic movement at the

---

[21] Philip Mattar gives some rough figures in his book about the mufti:

> A delegation to Hijaz was sent in July 1923 (during the hajj) raising P£12,000 and to India in October, raising another P£22,000. Delegations in 1924 to Hijaz, Iraq, Kuwait, and Bahrain raised the total sum to P£84,000. Contributing to this success were King Fu'ad of Egypt, who gave P£10,000, Nizam al-Haydarabad of India, who contributed P£7,000 and King Faysal of Iraq, who gave about P£6,000.

Mattar, *Mufti of Jerualem*, 29.

[22] The Indian Khilafat Committee would remain a strong supporter of the mufti throughout the rest of his tenure. The relationship was so close that one of its main leaders Muhammad 'Ali was buried at the Haram al-Sharif upon his death in 1931, a burial that was criticized by the Zionist officials.

1920s, by giving the council oversight of a prominent cause in the Muslim world.[23]

This engagement was soon shown by the SMC's dispatch of a large Palestinian

delegation to the Congress of the Islamic World, which was held in Mecca during the

hajj of 1926, and would be further demonstrated by the SMC's convening of Muslim

congresses in Jerusalem in 1928 and 1931.

Campaigning at home

This desire to raise the profile of the SMC in the wider Middle East was

complemented by efforts within Palestine to present the SMC as the champion of the

Muslim community. Since the SMC had been recognized by the Palestine government

from its establishment as the organization in charge of Muslim affairs, this would

seem to have been unnecessary. But the political competition between the al-Husayni

and al-Nashashibi families had become more heated in the mid-1920s following the

creation of the moderate *hizb al-watani* (National Party) in November 1923. This

party came to offer a credible Opposition alternative to the al-Husayni controlled Arab

Executive, which not only went after the Arab Executive but also Hajj Amin, accusing

him of being unqualified for religious office and rejecting his claim that the SMC

represented Palestine's Muslims. In fact, as Yehoshua Porath notes, the National

Party's first attack against the al-Husaynis was not directed against the Arab Executive

---

[23] Palestinian participation in the Muslim congresses of the 1920s is outlined in Martin Kramer, *Islam Assembled: The Advent of the Muslim Congresses* (New York: Columbia UP, 1986), 124. The mufti's interest in the Muslim Congresses led to his organization of a Muslim congress in defense of the holy places in Jerusalem in 1928 and a larger General Islamic Congress in 1931, also in Jerusalem.

but against the SMC.[24] Petitions sent by the party to the Palestine government at the end of 1923 complained that the SMC was being used by the al-Husayni family to strengthen its position at the expense of its rivals, that the council was overstepping its duty as a religious body, and that its leader was patently unqualified for office.[25] And as we have seen in Chapter 4, the opposition also complained vociferously about the SMC during the council's elections of 1925-26.

The SMC's defense of the holy places was a useful counterpoint to these criticisms because it allowed the council to cut through this noise and show itself to be the only organization in Palestine that was doing something to protect Muslim rights. For this reason the SMC promoted its protection of the holy sites in *al-Jamia al-'Arabiya* (the mouthpiece of the SMC), in discussions during Friday prayers, and eventually through the creation of an organization called the "Society for the Defense of the Mosque of al-Aqsa and the Holy Places" (which will be discussed in more depth below).

Another important way in which the SMC strengthened its position in the Palestinian community was through its supervision over Islamic festivals. The al-Husayni family's role as one of the traditional patrons of the Nabi Musa festival made it easy for the council to use the festival for its own ends. The festivals that followed 1920 were not violent but they retained the political character of that earlier festival with nationalist songs and slogans being raised against Zionism, colonial rule, and in

---

[24] Porath, *Emergence*, 231.

[25] These petitions can be found in ISA 2/172, ISA 2/189, and ISA 2/190.

favor of Hajj Amin al-Husayni.[26] In the view of at least one member of the opposition, the existence of such slogans attested to the reality that this "national" festival was actually being used by the SMC to hail its president.[27]

This desire to exploit the cultural, economic, and political potential of Muslim festivals was revealed in the SMC's annual statement for 1922-23, in which the council argued that it "has been happy to revive [these festivals], has worked to refine them, to reorganize their management, to increase their amenities. It has attempted to turn some of them into cultural and educational fairs and industrial exhibits, in order to encourage Arab culture and national crafts."[28] It is not clear exactly how industrial exhibits and educational fairs were integrated into religious festivals but this broadening of the festivals' purpose was novel. In part this was a defensive reaction to the actions of the Palestine Zionist Executive, which was active in promoting Jewish cultural and economic development, but it was also a means for developing a Palestinian nationalism that was centered upon Palestine's Muslim heritage, a heritage preserved by the SMC.

The Supreme Muslim council also built various charitable, cultural, and economic institutions in order to strengthen the Arab community and its own role in local life. A network of Muslim private schools was established and subsidized by the SMC; an Islamic orphanage was built in Jerusalem in 1923 to give Arab children vocational training (it became well-known for its printing press which printed the

---

[26] Kupferschmidt, *Supreme Muslim Council*, 233.

[27] Kupferschmidt, *Supreme Muslim Council*, 231.

[28] Quoted in Kupferschmidt, *Supreme Muslim Council*, 234.

various publications of the SMC); an Islamic museum was established on the grounds of the Haram al-Sharif in 1922; libraries were established in Jerusalem, Jaffa, Gaza, Hebron, and Acre in the 1920s; and pharmacies were set up in Jerusalem (1924) and Hebron (1928).[29] The SMC also provided financial assistance to the Arab community, such as in the provision of subsidies to Arab peasants and funding for Arab craft industries. Although many of these projects failed, they represented a real attempt by the SMC to build private Arab institutions of the kind that were being created by the Zionist Organization and various foreign Christian bodies. But maybe even more importantly, such subsidies were a form of largesse that was used to ensure the loyalty of the Palestinian population.

One project that clearly showed the ambitions of the SMC to be more than just a religious body was the ambitious decision to construct a modern hotel in Jerusalem in the early 1930s. The Palace Hotel was partly funded by donations that had not been used for the restoration of the Dome of the Rock and was intended to be the premier hotel of Jerusalem when it opened in 1931. However it was soon eclipsed by the King David Hotel, which opened shortly thereafter, and was never used for its intended purpose. The hotel was the most visible of the many commercial and infrastructure projects—others included the construction of shops, water systems, and electric systems—that the SMC undertook on its waqf properties during the 1920s and 1930s. These projects were clearly not religious in nature but were intended to diversify and

---

strengthen waqf finances, which were crucial to the SMC's ability to fund its other projects.

This diversification of the mission of the SMC placed the organization in a good position when other groups within Arab community faded away or lost popularity. The various political and economic projects enabled Hajj Amin al-Husayni to build his prestige in the country and a system of patronage that tied the local community to the council. In this way the council became a national institution for the Palestinian Arab community.

IV - British Non-interference

Why did the Palestine government not intervene to stop the SMC when it overstepped its role as a religious institution? This is the crucial question for scholars today, as it was for Zionist officials at the time, who have criticized the government for not stepping in before the mufti could play a role in the Western Wall riots of 1929 and the Palestine Arab Revolt of 1936. As we have seen, the government's decision not to intervene has often been presented as a dereliction of duty by the naïve and weak colonial power. I think that it tells us something different about Britain's approach to Islam.

One thing that is immediately obvious is the fact that British inaction was not due to any lack of knowledge about the SMC's activities, for British intelligence monitored the council in Palestine and abroad and was fed further information by Zionist intelligence agents and by the mufti's opponents in the National Party. Nor would it have been due to an unwillingness to abrogate the status quo, for officials had

shown that they were willing and capable of intervening in the political sphere to

police Arab politics. Instead the evidence suggests that British officials did not regard

these political activities as serious because the SMC was otherwise fulfilling the tasks

that it was created to do.

An argument can be made that views like those of Storrs were due to the fact

that those political activities were subtle enough that evidence about the council's

political activities tended to be based on circumstantial or second-hand evidence. This

is clear from the testimony of the governor of Gaza, who accused Hajj Amin in

December 1923 of being influential in putting out propaganda against the National

Party but conceded that he did not know whether local imams and *khatibs* (preachers

who give the Friday sermon) had been given orders from the SMC to take a particular

political line.[30] A similar point was made at the same time by the district governor for

Samaria, who charged the SMC with pushing a political line among its membership

but noted that he had no evidence that it was ordering people to propagandize from the

mosques.[31] Or, as the district governor for Haifa put it, "It is certainly *believed* by

Moslems as well as Christians in this part of the country that the organization of the

Supreme Muslim Council is actively supporting the efforts of the Executive Council

of the Palestine Executive."[32] This did not mean that this evidence was wrong—in

fact all signs point to the SMC being actively involved in such political activities—but

---

[30] District Governor of Gaza to Chief Secretary, December 12, 1923, ISA CS 6/172.

[31] District Governor of Samaria C. H. F. Cox to Chief Secretary, December 11, 1923, ISA 2/6/172.

[32] District Governor of Haifa G. S. Symes to Chief Secretary, December 6, 1923, ISA 2/6/172. Italics added.

that the fact that these activities were taking place behind the scenes meant that they could be ignored, by administration officials, especially by those who were sympathetic to the Arab community, such as Ernest Richmond.[33]

Even more important was the fact that Hajj Amin was fulfilling the main duties required of him. The shari'a court system and the waqf administration were functioning without the need for British oversight, which was why the SMC had been created in the first place. Though there were occasional criticisms about the corruption and imperiousness of the SMC, there had been a welcome drop in the number of complaints about the administration of Islam under British rule since Muslim religious affairs had been placed in the hands of a Muslim run institution. For the Palestine government, which had never had any intention of directly administering Muslim affairs, this arrangement was working. At the same time, Hajj Amin was genuinely considered by British officials to be a reasonable and moderating voice in the Arab community in the mid-1920s. This was based upon his apparent ability to ensure that no further violence occurred at the annual Nabi Musa festival and his generally cordial relationship with British officials during this period.

Another significant factor was that even if the SMC was involved in politics, its activities were not directed against the Palestine government at least until the late 1920s. The mufti was not defending the Haram al-Sharif against British takeover but against Jewish takeover; the SMC was not reinventing itself as an economic and political player to compete with the Palestine government but to compete with the

---

[33] Richmond's incredulity at British intelligence reports about Pan-Islam is discussed in Chapter Five.

Zionist organization; and it was far more common to hear anti-Zionist slogans at Muslim festivals than expressions of anticolonial anger. To be sure, the Zionist presence was intrinsically linked to the British presence in Palestine, so political slogans directed against Zionism were indirectly (and sometimes directly) aimed at British colonialism. But British officials generally preferred to see Arab anger towards Jewish immigration as being linked to the actions of the Zionist organization or Jewish settlers rather than the iniquitous nature of British colonial rule.

Whatever the reasons, it seems clear that up until the late 1920s British officials in Jerusalem and London were satisfied with the SMC and had no desire to interfere with its affairs. Although this positive opinion of the SMC was not shared by all officials, the prevailing opinion of the council was summed up in a memorable comment by John Shuckburgh, head of the Middle East section of the Colonial Office, who stated in 1926 that "the institutions of a Supreme Moslem Council in 1921, has, on the whole, been one of our most successful moves in Palestine."[34] It is for this reason that it is hard to argue against Mattar's, Jbara's, and Khalidi's conclusion that Hajj Amin al-Husayni was a moderate Arab leader who was more willing to compromise with the colonial authorities than oppose them.

V - The Beginning of the Western Wall Struggle

Only four years later, Shuckburgh's glowing comments about the SMC were replaced by despair, with Harry Luke, the acting-high commissioner, complaining to his

---

[34] Shuckburgh to CO, November 3, 1926, PRO CO 733/13.

superiors that the Muslim religious authorities had been granted a "jurisdiction so

extensive and powers so wide as to be to some extent almost an abdication by the

Administration of Palestine of responsibilities normally incumbent upon

Government."[35] What had changed by 1930 was that the SMC had emerged as the

principal political voice of the Arab community and in doing so had transformed itself

into a public opponent not only of the Zionist organization but of the Palestine

government it served under.

The event that transformed the SMC's relationship with the government and

transformed its position in Palestine was the struggle between Arab and Jewish groups

over the Western Wall in 1928-1929. This struggle began with a dispute over the use

of a screen during Jewish prayers at the Western Wall on Yom Kippur 1928 that

developed into a year-long contest between the Jewish and Muslim communities over

their rights at the Western Wall, leading in October 1929 to violent attacks (mostly by

Arabs against Jews) in Jerusalem, Safad, and Hebron. This conflict, which caused 133

Jewish and 87 Arab deaths, ended eight years of relative peace that the country had

enjoyed since the Jaffa riots of 1921 and served as a brutal reminder to British officials

that the Arab population of Palestine had not been reconciled to the construction of a

Jewish national home.

The *Report of the Commission on the Palestine Disturbances of August, 1929,*

more commonly known as the Shaw Commission report, concluded that the events of

1929 did not result from a straightforward contest over religious rights but were

---

[35] Harry Luke memorandum enclosed in HC to Secretary of State for the Colonies, June 18, 1929, PRO
CO 733/172.

caused by what it identified as the "racial antipathy" that existed between Arabs and Jews. While "racial antipathy" was an overblown description of what was at base a national conflict, the report was correct in its assessment that neither Arabs nor Jews had accepted the political aspirations of the other side. As the report put it:

> From the beginning the two races had no common interest. They differed in language, in religion, and in outlook. Only by mutual toleration and by compromise could the views of the leaders of the two peoples have been reconciled and a joint endeavour for the common good have been brought about. Instead, neither side had made any sustained attempt to improve relationships. The Jews, prompted by eager desire to see their hopes fulfilled, have pressed on with a policy at least as comprehensive as the White Paper of 1922 can warrant. The Arabs, with unrelenting opposition, have refused to accept that document and have prosecuted a political campaign designed to counter Jewish activities and to realize their own political ambitions.[36]

This frank and pessimistic assessment (which laid the blame squarely at the feet of the two protagonists and not at their government) was much bleaker than the optimistic opinions of British officials in the early 1920s. The events of 1929 were a wake-up call for the Palestine government, which could no longer hope or pretend that the Arab and Jewish populations could work together. Or, as Bernard Wasserstein has put it, "there was no immediate dramatic change in the balance between the rival political forces in Palestine after 1929. But the riots had a marked effect on the political outlook of the three main protagonists, the British, the Arabs, and the Jews, the combined long-term consequences of which spelt the doom of the mandatory structure

---

[36] Great Britain, *Report of the Commission on the Palestine Disturbances of August, 1929*, Cmd. 3530, (London: H. M. Stationery Office, 1930) [*Shaw Commission Report*].

of politics."[37] Although it took until 1937 for the colonial authorities to propose partition, it was in 1929 that the one-state solution died.[38]

The roots of the Western Wall confrontation can be traced back a decade earlier to the beginning of the mandate period when the Zionist leader Chaim Weizmann approached the O.E.T.A. authorities with a proposal to purchase the wall from the Muslim community.[39] Weizmann was not religious, but like other secular Zionists he saw the wall as a national symbol. As he explained in a letter to Lord Balfour, the wall was the only religious site in Palestine that was "in some sense left to us" and was frustrated that in 1918 the "Wailing Wall is not really ours."[40] For Weizmann the purchase of the wall would not only ensure that the Jewish community would own one of the few concrete symbols of the Jewish heritage of Palestine but would also be a great victory for Zionism that would help to rally "all the Jews, especially the great masses of orthodox Jewry in Russia, Galicia and Roumania, as well as England, Germany and America round the platform which we have created, namely a Jewish Palestine under British auspices."[41] In other words, Weizmann and other Zionists viewed the Western Wall in much the same way as the Arab community

---

[37] Wasserstein, *Britain in Palestine*, 88.

[38] The proposal to partition Palestine was made in the report of the Royal (Peel) Commission on the causes of the Arab revolt of 1936.

[39] The price offered was reputed to have been 70,000 Palestinian pounds. Ilan Pappe, "Hajj Amin and the Buraq Revolt," *Jerusalem Quarterly File*, 6:6 (Spring 2003), 8. Yehoshua Porath points out that this was not the first attempt by the Jewish community to purchase the wall, since Nissim Bechar and Baron Edmond de Rothschild had attempted to buy the wall before the First World War. Those attempts had not led to tensions between the Arab and Jewish communities of Palestine. Porath, *Emergence*, 258, 259.

[40] Weizmann to Balfour, May 30, 1918, CZA L3/310.

[41] Ibid.

thought of the *Haram al-Sharif*, as a site that had transcended religion to become a universal nationalist symbol.

Weizmann was well aware that his proposal challenged the religious status quo. Although the wall is what remains of the western wall of the Second Jewish Temple in Jerusalem, and as such is the holiest site in Judaism, it is also a retaining wall of the Haram al-Sharif and is considered part of the Haram complex. The Haram has been under Muslim control since the seventh century, except for a brief period when the Crusaders controlled Jerusalem in the twelfth century. Muslim ownership of the wall was formally recognized by Muslims, Christians, and Jews and would therefore be protected by the British commitment to the status quo.[42] Weizmann, however, had little interest in protecting the status quo, even though he conceded that this is what governed British policy:

> The British Administration here is guided by one fundamental principle
> laid down in the Hague convention, that in Occupied Enemy Territory
> the status quo has to be preserved. It is not for me to express an
> opinion on the advisability of applying to Palestine rigidly a formula
> which has been violated by every belligerent Power during this war,
> and has lost all relation to reality. We have only to accept the fact and
> to see what we can achieve within the limits set by the status quo.[43]

To work within those limits, he proposed that the concept of the religious site be reinterpreted, so that there would be a clearer delineation between sacred and profane space at the site. This was explained by Weizmann in a statement that he made before the Zionist Commission on March 14, 1918,

---

[42] Of course not everyone agreed with this position in the Jewish community or even among British officials. The Western Wall struggle made it clear that what was said in official statements was often quite different from what was said in newspaper editorials or in individual statements.
[43] Ibid.

The Jews do not wish to touch the Christian and Moslem sanctuaries.
We should however like to feel that Palestine was not wholly composed
of holy places. There must be territorial limits placed to these holy
places, so that we should know exactly what they are. The Jews should
retain the Wailing Wall in Jerusalem, and [we] would like the
Commission to fence it round, and to mount a Jewish guard round it…[44]

Weizmann's proposal to buy the wall in 1918 was an attempt to put this plan

into action by legally separating the wall from the Muslim site. This view ignored both

the religious significance of the site to the Muslim community and the connection that

local Arabs had with the neighborhood at the base of the wall. The wall, known to

Arabs as *al-Buraq*, was not only a retaining wall of the Haram al-Sharif but also the

site where Muhammad stabled his horse (*al-Buraq*) before his Night Journey to

heaven.[45] At the same time, the wall abutted an Arab neighborhood that had been

established as the Abu Madyan waqf during the reign of Saladin, to accommodate

Moroccan pilgrims to Jerusalem. This had led the neighborhood to become known

simply as the Maghribi neighborhood, from the Arabic term for Moroccan. In

proposing his takeover of the wall, Weizmann made clear that this neighborhood was

a blight that needed to be removed:

[The Western Wall] is surrounded by a group of miserable, dirty
cottages and derelict buildings, which makes the whole place from the
hygienic point of view a source of constant humiliation to the Jews of
the world. Our most sacred monument, in our most sacred city, is in
the hands of some doubtful Moghreb (sic) religious community, which
keeps these cottages as a source of income. We are willing to
compensate this community very liberally, but we should like the place

---

[44] Minutes of the second meeting of the Zionist Commission, March 14, 1918, CZA L3/285.

[45] The site is referred to in the seventeenth sura of the Qur'an, which refers to Muhammad's visit to the
"further mosque," considered by Muslims to be a reference to the al-Aqsa mosque.

to be cleaned up; we should like to give it a dignified and respectable appearance.[46]

Weizmann's plan was presented to Ronald Storrs, the military governor of Jerusalem at the time, who responded positively. This might seem surprising given that the plan went against the status quo and threatened Britain's promise that its support for the establishment of the Jewish National Home would not threaten the civil and religious rights of non-Jews. But one of Storrs' great passions was the preservation and restoration of historical and religious sites. In his previous posting in Egypt, Storrs had worked on a preservation commission and shortly after his appointment in Palestine he created the Pro-Jerusalem Society, which was dedicated to preserving the religious and historical architecture of the city. One of the major projects of that society would to be the removal of buildings and structures that, in the view of British experts, "infringed" upon the walls of the Old City, and so Weizmann's plan to "clean up" the site in 1918—in reality the eviction of the Arab residents—resonated with Storrs' views about how Jerusalem should look.[47]

However this proposal was strongly opposed by the inhabitants of the neighborhood, who feared for their homes, and by the general Arab community, which saw it as evidence of a Zionist plot to take over Palestine. The strength of Arab

---

[46] CO 733/132/44051-053442 cited in Mary Ellen Lundsten, "Wall Politics: Zionist and Palestinian Strategies in Jerusalem, 1928," *Journal of Palestine Studies*, Vol. 8, Issue 1 (Autumn, 1978), 7.

[47] For information about these projects see *Jerusalem 1918-1920: Being the Records of the Pro-Jerusalem Council during the period of the British Military Administration.* Ed. C. R. Ashbee. London: John Murray, 1921 and *Jerusalem 1920-1922: Being the Records of the Pro-Jerusalem Council during the period of the British Military Administration.* Ed. C. R. Ashbee. London: John Murray, 1924. Information can also be found in the Ashbee papers (Boxes 361 and 362) at the Jerusalem Municipal Archives.

opposition convinced the British authorities that the sale of the wall would cause

instability in Jerusalem and the Foreign Office quickly urged the Palestine government

to drop the matter. As a consequence, Muslim ownership of the wall was reconfirmed

by the British authorities and the Zionist Executive was forced to give up its attempts

to buy the wall.[48] The British authorities also recognized that the Maghribi

neighborhood at its base needed to be protected from encroachment, since the

"pavement in front of the wall, the courtyard and the dwellings…and much of the

surrounding property all form part of the Abu Madian Waqf, a Moslem religious and

charitable trust which is said to have been founded in the time of Saladin for the

benefit of a sect of Moslems of Moroccan origin known as the Mughrabis [sic]."[49]

VI – Holy Places in Jewish and Arab Politics

Competition over the site between the Arab and Jewish communities was not ended

with the failure of Weizmann's proposal. This failure did not change the fact that that

Muslim rule in Palestine had been replaced by a Christian administration sympathetic

to the Zionist project, which encouraged Jewish leaders to expect that the site would

---

[48] This did not completely end attempts by the Jewish community to buy the wall. Ilan Pappe mentions a second attempt by Weizmann to purchase the wall in 1928 but was warned against pursuing the proposal by High Commissioner John Chancellor. A year later Chancellor suggested to the mufti that he might allow the Jews to buy the area in front of the wall in order to establish a place of worship. See Pappe, "Buraq Revolt," 8 and 11.

The sale of the wall was also suggested was in 1929, when Prince Muhammad Ali Pasha (a member of the Egyptian royal family) suggested the sale of the wall to the Jewish community for £100,000 as a means of placating the Arab community. This solution was not followed up.

[49] *Shaw Commission Report*, 28.

This was not the position of the Palestine Zionist Executive, which made an attempt in 1926 to lease the Abu Madian waqf. This was intended as a first step towards evacuating the Moroccan residents from the area and demolishing their houses. This project came to nothing. See Wasserstein, *British in Palestine*, 227.

eventually end up as Jewish property. The fact that the Palestine government had initially been receptive to Weizmann's proposal acted as further encouragement because it suggested that the government was open to a reevaluation of religious rights at the site.

As a result, competition between the Arab and Jewish communities over the wall would continue unabated throughout the 1920s.

Mary Ellen Lundsten's article, "Wall Politics: Zionist and Palestinian Strategies in Jerusalem, 1928," offers a useful discussion of the way in which the wall became a political cause for the two communities. She points out that one of the more important ways in which the wall became significant was as a symbol in Zionist fundraising. According to Lundsten, "the Jewish National Fund issued stamps in booklets portraying Jewish symbols at the Wall and signifying the relationship between Jewish jurisdiction over the 'Holy Places' and Zionist land acquisition throughout Palestine."[50] Other Jewish publications were even more provocative, with foreign Jewish newspapers publishing pictures of the Dome of the Rock with a Star of David on top, an image that suggested that the entire haram would eventually come under Jewish ownership.[51] As we have seen this mirrored the use of holy sites in fundraising by the SMC, in fact these very same images were used by the SMC to prove that Jews planned to take over the Haram al-Sharif.

---

[50] Lundsten, "Wall Politics," 8.

[51] Examples of these pictures as well as a discussion of how they were used in Zionist and Arab propaganda can be found in Monk, *Aesthetic Occupation*, 126+.

Important figures in Jewish and Zionist circles also spoke of a Jewish takeover of the Haram al-Sharif. The Askenazi Chief Rabbi of Palestine, Abraham Kook, argued in 1919 that the Temple Mount (Haram al-Sharif) was "bound in the end to revert to us" and called upon the British to let the Jewish community protect the Wall.[52] In London, Sir Alfred Mond, the British Minister of Health and a strong financial backer of Jewish immigration, proposed in the spring of 1921 that a new "edifice" needed to be erected where "Solomon's Temple once stood," a speech that was reported in the *Daily Telegraph* and reiterated in a Parliamentary note.[53] This statement was quickly explained away as "figurative" speech by High Commissioner Herbert Samuel and Under-Secretary of State William Ormsby-Gore.[54] But even if it was simply a rhetorical flourish intended to rally donors to give to the Zionist cause (Mond's speech occurred at a dinner for the Palestine Foundation Fund), it was still a provocative statement that sharply broke with official government policy, which is why Samuel and Ormsby-Gore were forced into damage control. As with Zionist pictures of the Haram under a Star of David, Mond's statement was held up by nationalist Arabs as incontrovertible proof that the Zionists intended to take over the Haram al-Sharif. This is shown in the posters that allies of Hajj Amin al-Husayni put up in the Old City during the elections for the muftiship of Jerusalem (see page 190-91), which referenced Mond's statement as proof that Jews were interfering in the election as part of their attempt to take over the Haram al-Sharif. It is difficult to

---

[52] Kook's words were reproduced in the Palin Commission report, PRO WO 32/9614.

[53] Lundsten, "Wall Politics," 9.

[54] Ibid.

know whether this fear-mongering resonated with the Arab population but it does suggest a familiarity on the part of Hajj Amin and his audience with Zionist writings and pronouncements.

VII – Debating Rights of Ownership and Access

Once the wall had become an issue of contention between the Muslim and Jewish communities, activities at the site began to be heavily scrutinized by both sides. In 1920 Muslim religious authorities (this was before the formation of the SMC) attempted to repair portions of the Western Wall but immediately came under heavy criticism by the Palestinian Zionist Executive, who saw the action as a deliberate attempt to "annoy Jews who chose to exercise their customary right to pray at the Wall."[55] Instead of permitting the waqf authorities to conduct repairs, Zionist officials also argued that the government should transfer maintenance responsibilities to the Jewish community.

Such a transfer would have gone against traditional practice, since as the recognized owners of the Wall, the waqf authorities, had the sole right to conduct repairs on the site. In Palestine, the right to maintain and clean areas of religious space was a sign of ownership, as evidenced by the intense disputes among Christian sects over the right to clean as small an area as a single step of the Church of the Holy Sepulchre.[56] The call for the transfer of maintenance responsibilities was thus another

---

[55] Quoted in Lundsten, "Wall Politics," 8.

[56] British records from the mandate period have a number of files on disputes between these Christian sites, which typically baffled British officials. For a good introduction to this competition see L.G.A.

attempt to appropriate the Wall by the Zionist Executive. Although, the Palestine Government did not consent to this change, they introduced an innovation by placing some of the repairs under the supervision of the Department of Antiquities. In the end, the waqf authorities were permitted to repair the upper courses of the Wall (built during the period of Muslim rule), while the Department took over the repair of the lower (Herodian) and middle (Greco-Roman) courses.

This division of the wall only added to the uncertainty of its ownership and opened a new area of competition between the Muslim and Jewish communities. As a result this dispute was followed by other disputes over the renovation of religious sites. In 1921 Muslims complained about repairs by Jews at the Tomb of Rachel near Bethlehem, which eventually led to the Palestine government completing the repairs itself in 1925.[57] And various quarrels between Christian sects over their respective rights at the Church of the Holy Sepulchre and the Church of the Nativity, led the Palestine government to propose the formation of an international holy places commission before deciding that the high commissioner would resolve all such issues (see Chapter 3). But whereas these other disputes abated after the British settled in as the rulers of Palestine, the Western Wall struggle persisted, mostly due to the growing strength of the Jewish community.

Cust, "The Status Quo at the Holy Places," PRO CO 733/132/2 and Rock, *Status Quo in the Holy Places*), although the latter displays a pro-Franciscan bias.

[57] Muslim complaints led the Government again to offer to undertake the repairs itself. As a result the Jewish community decided to withdrawal their application for repairs. Repairs were again proposed in 1925 and the Public Works Department was given permission to undertake structural repairs, however they were not allowed to conduct interior repairs.

A more protracted dispute over ownership arose in 1922 when Muslims complained about Jewish worshippers bringing benches to the wall. At first glance the provision of benches at the site would seem to have nothing to do with ownership. As the Jewish authorities explained, these benches were simply used by worshippers as a place to rest in an area that was otherwise devoid of places to sit. But in the view of the Muslim authorities, the appearance of benches or any other large items of religious paraphernalia were an attempt by the Jewish community to establish a permanent presence at the wall by making it a Jewish space.

The issue became especially significant because the Arab and Jewish press engaged in a lively discussion about whether Jews had the right to bring benches to the wall, a foreshadowing of the heated media dispute that increased tensions between Arabs and Jews in Jerusalem in the run up to the riots of August 1929. A British political report from May 1922 noted that the Palestine government had no choice but to ban benches at the site, since they had been "officially forbidden during the Turkish regime." But the report went on to state that "it would appear that this prohibition has not been observed for since the military occupation, and apparently before it, benches had in fact been introduced by means of monetary arrangements with the neighboring Muslims," and held up hope that the issue would eventually be resolved by the holy places' commission, which at that point was still slated to come into existence.[58]

This tension between formal rights of worship and what occurred in practice became the key issue in the Western Wall dispute. As the British political report

---

[58] PRO CO/733/22.

explained, the Muslim community took a rigid view of the matter and looked to the Palestine government to enforce the existing rules. For Muslim groups, such as the SMC, the status quo was embodied in Ottoman regulations, such as a 1910 letter from the Ottoman government to the waqf administration which stated that, "The place which is designed for prayer by Jews shall be used by them as in previous times. No chairs, curtains, tents, or other articles are to be brought or laid at the place."[59] The Jewish conception of the status quo was different. Jews viewed conventional practice as the best measure of what was permitted at the site, as opposed to what they regarded as static regulations that had been made by a government remote from Palestine and which in any case no longer existed, a reasonable perspective that recognized the gap between the letter and spirit of the law.

The conflict between these two interpretations of the status quo caused great confusion for the Palestine government, which was unable to figure out the various rights of worship that had been formally or informally extended to the Jewish community during the Ottoman period. It was therefore proposed, shortly after the 1922 dispute over benches, that an inquiry, chaired by the Chief Justice of Palestine, Sir Thomas Haycraft, should look into the matter. Its task would have been to establish what were the existing Muslim and Jewish rights at the wall, so that the British could precisely define their respective rights of ownership and access under British rule. This may have helped to lessen the later competition between the two

---

[59] This correspondence was brought to the attention of the military governor of Palestine in 1920 by Mufti Kamil al-Husayni and was later quoted in notes by Attorney General Norman Bentwich on the "Memorandum on the Western or Wailing Wall, 1928," ISA 3/359.

sides over the site, at least that was the hope of British officials, but no inquiry was ever held. There is no indication in British records for why the government failed to follow through on this proposal. One reason might have been that British officials didn't want to make a decision when there was the possibility that this question could be brought before the proposed international holy places commission, which in 1922 was still a viable possibility. Or maybe those officials simply though that the issue would go away on its own and worried that the enquiry could only perpetuate competition over the site.

In September 1925, on the Yom Kippur holiday, dispute over benches broke out again. This time the Supreme Muslim Council became involved when it complained to the Palestine government that benches had once again been placed on the pavement in front of the Western Wall. As in 1922, the government decided that the benches were not permissible and a member of the Jerusalem District Commissioner's staff removed the benches. This led to protests by the Zionist Organization about the intervention of the Palestine government in the religious practices of the Jewish community on the holiest day in the Jewish calendar, and the dispatch of a formal complaint about the Palestine government to the Permanent Mandates Commission of the League of Nations.[60] As with previous Arab and Jewish protests to the Permanent Mandates Commission, this did little to change British

---

[60] Ibid.

policy.[61] According to the terms of the Holy Places Order in Council of 1924 it was

the high commissioner who had the right to decide religious disputes and so it was

well within his rights to bar benches at the site.

The SMC's emergence as a champion of Muslim rights at the Wall was to be

expected. By 1925, the mufti had already sent out delegations of his own to the

Muslim world to raise money for the repair of the Dome of the Rock and both at home

and abroad the mufti had presented himself as the rightful steward and defender of the

Haram al-Sharif. By 1925, he emerged as the lead protector of Muslim sites. The

Arab Executive, whose delegations had also claimed to be the defenders of the haram

in 1922 and 1923, was not as powerful an organization two years later and took less of

a role in defending the sites. Crucial here was Hajj Amin's position as the president of

the SMC, which put him in charge of the waqfs of Palestine—the most important

being the Haram al-Sharif.

VIII – Removing a Screen in 1928

By 1928 the competition over the Western Wall had been going on for around ten

years. In some ways the dispute was a microcosm of the larger battle between

Zionism and Arab nationalism in Palestine. The dispute revolved around an attempt

by the Zionist authorities to take control over a site that was under Arab control, an

attempt that was made possible by the occupation of Palestine by a European

---

[61] In the first years of the British occupation of Palestine, the government showed genuine concern about these kinds of petitions but by 1925 it had become apparent that the League of Nations would always defer to the British authorities when it came to the governance of Palestine.

(Christian) power. This brought about an Arab opposition movement, which used the wall issue to combine religion and nationalism into a powerful message of opposition to Zionism and British support for the Jewish National Home. Finally, the dispute led to a hesitant response by the government, which attempted to placate both sides but did little to solve the situation.

But the situation also differed from the larger conflict between Zionism and Arab nationalism. Here the Palestine government did not make a commitment to supporting the Zionist position. British officials recognized that the Western Wall was Muslim property and, apart for a brief flirtation with the idea of a Zionist purchase of the site, it made it clear that it had no intention of allowing a Zionist takeover. But this did not mean that the Muslim authorities had free rein to do what they wanted with the site. As, Ronald Storrs pointed out in a letter to the Secretary of State in October 1925, the Palestine government fully supported Jewish rights of worship at the wall:

> Such is the strength and continuity of the tradition that the Jews may be said to have established an absolute and acknowledged right of free access to the Wall for purposes of devotion at any hour of the day or night throughout the year. Although it is sometimes asserted by Moslems that they could legally erect a wall debarring public approach, no Mandatory Government could countenance so flagrant an infringement of the status quo. On the other hand, the Jewish right is no more than a right of way and of station, and involves no title, express or implied, of ownership either of the surface of the Wall or of the pavement in front of it.[62]

---

[62] The letter is quoted in the notes by Attorney General Norman Bentwich on the "Memorandum on the Western or Wailing Wall, 1928," ISA 3/359.

In theory, this meant that Muslim ownership of the site was recognized by the colonial authorities but Muslims would not be permitted to infringe on Jewish rights of worship. Jews had the right to visit and worship the wall at any time, as they did under the Ottomans, but in return could not do anything that would challenge Muslim ownership of the wall. The problem in practice was that there was a gray area in which certain actions at the wall could be interpreted either as part of the ritual of worship or as an attempt to challenge the ownership of the wall. For most of the 1920s it was the act of bringing benches to the wall that fell into this gray area; in 1928 it was the placement of a screen to divide male and female worshippers that reopened the dispute over Jewish rights at the wall.

This dispute began on September 24 when a screen a British police officer removed a screen that had been set up for the Jewish holiday of Yom Kippur. As with the removal of benches on Yom Kippur three years earlier, British action came in response to a protest from the SMC, which informed the government on the eve of the holy day of the illegal presence of the screen. This prompted a visit to the wall by the deputy district commissioner of Jerusalem, Edward Keith Roach, who was assured by the Jewish beadle on duty that the screen would be removed by the next day. When it was discovered the next morning that the screen was still in place, the police issued a request that it be removed, which was denied owing to the prohibition on Jews doing work on the Day of Atonement. As a result the screen was a forcibly removed by the police, who had to struggle against the congregation's efforts to prevent its removal.

The government's actions led to letters of protest being sent by the Zionist Organization (along with supporting letters from Chief Rabbis Kook and Meir) to the Permanent Mandates Commission, which complained about the government's heavy-handedness of the government on such a holy day, as well as articles of condemnation in the Hebrew press. But unlike in 1925, the issue did not end there. What began as a relatively innocuous issue became a major political conflict between the Jewish and Muslim communities, or, as the White Paper of November 1928 put it, "public opinion…definitely removed the matter from the purely religious orbit and…made of it a political and racial question."[63]

X – The Mufti's Role

Hajj Amin al-Husayni would become central to this dispute and he is presented in the conventional narrative as the figure who caused this escalation. Yehoshua Porath, Uri Kupferschmidt, and Bernard Wasserstein, have all argued that the mufti exploited the event for his own selfish reasons and that it was his overreaction that caused the breakdown of relations between the communities that led to the riots at the wall in August 1929. This argument closely follows allegations made by Zionist officials in their testimony before the Shaw commission of inquiry (the commission of enquiry that was sent in 1930 by the British government to Palestine to investigate the reasons for the violence) that the mufti had used the moment to incite violence against Jews.[64]

---

[63] *The Western or Wailing Wall in Jerusalem, Memorandum by the Secretary of State for the Colonies,* Cmd. 3229 (London: November 1928).

[64] *Shaw Commission Report,* 73.

Hajj Amin has also been presented as the main protagonist by nationalist Palestinian

writers, such as 'Izzat Darwaza, who praised the mufti for bringing about a nationalist

uprising against the Palestine government and its unjust support for the Jewish

national home.[65]

The Shaw Commission report, in contrast, did not portray the mufti as a

nationalist leader, nor did it find him guilty of incitement.[66] The commission did

agree that the mufti was the person most to blame for transforming the issue into a

political conflict and drew a stark comparison between the mufti's aggressive defense

of Muslim rights at the wall and what it saw as the pacific attitude of the Zionist

Organization and the Va'ad Leumi (the National Council of the Jewish community).

As I will later argue this narrative is somewhat misleading, for the difference

between the two sides was not as great as has been portrayed. There is little doubt

however, that the mufti did take a hard line in response to the wall issue. On

September 30, 1928 he held a large demonstration at the Haram al-Sharif to protest

Jewish actions at the wall at which a strident appeal was made to the Muslim

community:

To All Our Muslim Bretheren

You are aware that there has been during these days an attempt against
the *Buraq*...that the people who are anxious to usurp the western

---

[65] This is shown in the description of the struggle over the wall and the resulting violence as the *thawra al-Buraq* (the al-Buraq revolt). See Mohammad Izzat. Darwazeh. *Muthakirat Muhammad 'Izzat Darwazeh* [The Memoirs of Muhammad 'Izzat Darwazeh]. Volume 1. Beirut: Dar al-Gharb al-Islami, 1993.

[66] The official title of the commission—The Commission on the Palestine Disturbances of August 1929—was a clue to the kind of sober middle ground that the commission intended to stake out. By calling the event "disturbances" the British carefully avoided drawing attention to either the Arab view that the event was a national uprising or the Jewish view that it was a pogrom.

<blockquote>
portion of the wall of *al-Aqsa* have made up their mind to take very step in order to infringe upon your right and that of all Muslims…Religious duty demands that every Muslim look with watchful eyese upon the imminent danger menacing the Muslim community.[67]
</blockquote>

Two days later the SMC dispatched an angry memorandum to the government that protested Jewish plans for the wall. This was followed up by a meeting on October 8th between Hajj Amin and Harry Luke (who was the officer administering the government of Palestine during the absence of the high commissioner John Chancellor), during which the mufti submitted another memorandum that accused the Jews of trying to take possession of the Western Wall and implored the government to stop Jewish propaganda.[68]

At the same time, the mufti made an appeal to Muslim groups outside Palestine, relying on the relationships he had cultivated with such groups over the course of the previous five years. On October 17, 1928, for instance, he sent a letter to his Muslim allies in India requesting assistance in his defense of al-Buraq.[69] More importantly on November 1, 1928 he convened a conference in Jerusalem to defend Muslim rights at the western wall, which was intended to bring Muslims from around the world to Jerusalem in a show of strength. In the end the conference ended up only being attended by Muslims from neighboring countries, who sent a formal letter of protest to the Permanent Mandates Commission of the League of Nations, which

---

[67] *Al-Jami'a al-'Arabiya*, October 1, 1928.

[68] The text of this memorandum is reprinted in the Shaw Commission Report, 31.

[69] Hajj Amin to Shawkat Ali, October 17, 1928. PRO CO 733/173/67314/26. Bernard Wasserstein, who makes reference to the letter, notes that the letter never reached its destination since it was intercepted by British intelligence in India and was forwarded to the Palestine police. Wasserstein, *British in Palestine*, 229.

accused Jews of attempting to take over the wall. The conference also led to the creation of what was called "the Society for the Protection of the Moslem Holy Places," an organization that became the loudest champion of Muslim rights at the Haram al-Sharif.[70]

The dispute between the Muslim authorities and the Jewish community took place not only in newspapers and in competing letters of protest but also at the wall itself. In the months that followed, the SMC introduced a number of innovations to Muslim practice at the wall and changes to the structures that abutted it that were designed to be provocations. These included such changes as the reconfiguration of a wall that overlooked the area where Jews worshipped, which led to a great deal of noise and the occasional dropped brick. The SMC also created a new entrance to the pavement from the Haram complex, turning the pavement in front of the wall into more of a thoroughfare, causing Jewish consternation at what they saw as a violation of their place of worship. The establishment of a *zawiya* (a religious school) near the wall at which a loud *dhikr* ceremony (a sufi devotional act that involved repeated recitation of the names of God) ceremony was performed also disrupted Jewish worship at the site. It was also reported that there was an increase in the volume of the call to prayer from mosques near the wall.[71] These practices were described by the Shaw Commission as being "primarily designed to annoy the Jews," and certainly raised tensions between the two communities.

---

[70] *Shaw Commission Report*, 32. The report also noted that a similar organization called "The Committee for the Defence of the Buraq el-Sharif" had been established before then.

[71] *Shaw Commission Report*, 74, Wasserstein, *British in Palestine*, 229.

XII – Escalating Rhetoric

Despite all of these changes, the Shaw Commission did not find the mufti to be the cause of the violence of August 1929. Instead it found the most significant cause of the "disturbances" to be a Jewish demonstration held on August 15, 1929, at which a crowd led by the ultranationalist Beitar youth movement (allied to Vladimir Jabotinsky's militant "revisionist" Zionists) raised the Zionist flag, sang the Hatikvah (the Jewish national anthem), and raised shouts of "the Wall is ours," "shame on those who profane our holy places," "shame on the government," and other deliberately provocative statements. [72] Later historians, such as Kupferschmidt, Porath, and Wasserstein, basing themselves on the Shaw Commission report, have generally reached a different conclusion. They shift to the earlier provocations of the mufti and present the Jewish demonstration of August 15, 1929 as an unfortunate but inevitable consequence of the mufti's incitement.

But these later accounts, and indeed the report of the Shaw commission itself, downplay the provocative actions of the Jewish community itself during 1928 and 1929, which also contributed to the escalation of the dispute. It is clear from a memorandum that the SMC delivered to Harry Luke on October 8, 1928 that Muslim actions were in part a reaction to Zionist actions in the wake of the British removal of the screen at the Western Wall:

---

[72] Beitar or Brit Trumpeldor was a revisionist Zionist group that took its name from a Jewish settler Joseph Trumpledor who was considered an early martyr for Zionism having lost his life in an attack of the village of Tel Hai by a bedouin tribe in 1919. *Shaw Commission Report*, 54 and 155.

<blockquote>
The Moslem Supreme Council meet you to-day concerning a very serious matter to which, it hopes, you will pay the greatest attention in consideration for its grave consequence over the present and future of the country. The matter in question is the agitation and active wide-spread propaganda undertaken by the Jews with a view to influencing the London Government and other Powers, as well as the League of Nations in order to take possession of the Western Wall of the Mosque of Aqsa, called al-Burak, or to raise claims over that place.[73]
</blockquote>

Although quoted in the Shaw Commission report, there is very little investigation of what sort of agitation that the Jewish community was undertaking. Instead, as I mentioned above, the report praised the Zionist organization and the Va'ad Leumi for their peaceful role in the struggle. It even argued that the Hebrew press, unlike the Arab press, did not really raise tensions over the wall until July 1929. [74]

Philip Mattar has rightly argued that this is a selective and misleading reading of Jewish actions at the wall.[75] He contends that the conventional narrative ignores the days that immediately followed the removal of the screen in 1928. For the first six days after the removal it was the Jewish community not the Arab community that was up in arms. Not only were letters of protest sent to the Palestine government and the Permanent Mandates Commission, but large demonstrations were held by the Jewish community in Jerusalem, a general strike was declared, and angry articles appeared in the Hebrew press. Ilan Pappe has argued that such actions explode the myth of Zionist moderation and complicate the idea that the mufti was mostly to blame for politicizing the issue,

---

[73] *Shaw Commission Report*, 31.

[74] Specifically, the report stated that, "No evidence was brought before us of any intemperate articles appearing the Hebrew Press in Palestine prior to the resumption of the building operations in the neighborhood of the Wailing Wall on the 20th July last [i.e. 1929]." *Shaw Commission Report*, 42.

[75] See Mattar, *Mufti of Jerusalem.*

The Mufti was not the first to drag the opponents into the battlefield. It was the World Zionist Federation [sic] which, shaken by the incident, charged the British police with aggression against the Jewish worshippers who refused to dismantle the arch and the screen they had set up. Four days later a big Jewish demonstration took place in Jerusalem, in which the more extreme elements threatened to seize the policeman who had dismantled the screen and tear him limb from limb. Then a general strike was declared. The Hebrew papers poured fire and brimstone on the gentiles—specifically the Muslims—and the national poet H. N. Bialik bemoaned the desolate Western Wall. Subsequently Harry Lock [sic] of the government Secretariat stated that "Jewish public opinion has turned what was essentially a religious matter into a political-racial one."[76]

What is interesting is that Bialik (who had moved to Palestine from Germany in 1924 and was already famous for his Jewish nationalistic poems), the Hebrew newspapers, and other champions of the Jewish position engaged their audience with the same emotional argument that the SMC used in regards to the holy site: that the Western Wall was in grave danger and that the Jewish community's place in Palestine was dependent upon its protection. It not surprising then that the Jewish community produced their own version of the aforementioned Muslim "Society for the Protection of the Holy Places", the Jewish "Pro-Wailing Wall Committee."[77]

For six days the mufti did nothing in response to these Zionist actions: no formal protests were sent to the Palestine government, no protests were convened, and his mouthpiece, *al-Jamaa al-Arabiya,* did not print any angry articles in response. Such actions were unnecessary because the removal of the screen was essentially a victory for the SMC and there was little need to intervene in what was a dispute

---

[76] Pappe's text should read Harry Luke not Harry Lock. Pappe, "Buraq Revolt," 9.

[77] The Pro-Wailing Wall committee was formed by Dr. Klausner, a lecturer at Hebrew Univerity.

between the Jewish community and the Palestine government. It was only on

September 30, 1928, nearly a full week after the removal of the screen that the mufti

reacted by convening a rally at the al-Aqsa mosque, where his allies gave speeches

opposing a Jewish takeover of the wall.[78] This sequence of events suggests that the

mufti did not take up his defense of the Western Wall out of an irrational fear or for

purely cynical reasons, as the Shaw Commission and the conventional wisdom posits,

but because he was reacting to Zionist protests or perhaps more accurately to the

inability of the Palestine government to silence another Jewish challenge to the status

quo at the western wall.

XIII - The Mufti Arrives

Even though the conventional narrative needs to be rethought, there is no question that

the mufti emerged as the most important Arab actor in the struggle over the Western

Wall. It also remains clear that the event was used by the mufti to transform the SMC

into a major political force in Palestine. The SMC's position as the supervisor of the

Haram al-Sharif and the Abu Madyan waqf allowed the mufti to position the SMC as

the leading political voice of the Arab community. For the duration of the dispute, it

was the SMC and not the Arab Executive or the moderate Arab opposition that

engaged most consistently with the Palestine government and the Zionist Executive.

Equally significant was the fact that the SMC was successful in asserting its rights at

---

[78] Ibid.

the site through action, as opposed to passively waiting for the Palestine government to protect its rights.

Bernard Wasserstein is right to argue that the emergence of the SMC as the major voice in Arab politics at this time was enabled by a shift in power that was going on in the Arab community at the time. By the late-1920s the power of the Arab Executive had waned—by 1927 its office in Jerusalem had closed— and the moderate opposition, in the form of National Party, had emerged as a strong rival.[79] The strength of the moderate National Party had been shown in its success in the municipal elections of 1927 and its ability to control the agenda of the seventh Palestine Arab Congress of June 1928. This represented a blow to the political fortunes and prestige of the al-Husayni bloc that controlled the Arab Executive. It was also a blow to the mufti, as mentioned earlier, whose rule was increasingly called into question by the al-Nashashibi Opposition.[80]

For Wasserstein the mufti's involvement in the wall dispute was thus an attempt to push back at this political threat to the al-Husayni's preeminent position in the Palestinian Arab community.[81] There may be some truth to his argument but the mufti was hardly being opportunistic in defending the wall in 1928 for he had been presenting himself as the defender of the Haram al-Sharif since at least 1922. The

---

[79] Wasserstein, *British in Palestine*, 222.

[80] This had even led the opposition to successfully push for the invalidation of the 1926 election results to the SMC, which ended up weakening Hajj Amin's authority over the council. These elections were required because members of the SMC, except for its president, were elected to four-year terms. The new elections led to the creation of a council with three members drawn from the *majlisiyiin*—Hajj Amin al-Husayni, Muhammad Murad, and Sa'id Shawa—and two members from the Opposition—'Abd al-Rahman al-Taji and Amin al-Tamimi, although the latter eventually became a great ally of Hajj Amin.

[81] See Wasserstein, *Britain in Palestine*, 220-225.

SMC had protested against Jewish practices at the wall, as the mufti explained in his memorandum of October 8, 1928, on two occasions in 1922, two occasions in 1923, four occasions in 1926, and twice in 1928.[82] The mufti was no stranger to the wall issue and it can hardly be surprising that he once again rushed to defend the site.

Where the transformation of Arab politics in the latter part of the 1920s matters is that the disunity and fractiousness of the Arab nationalist movement meant that the movement lacked a focus. The Western Wall conflict gave the movement an issue to focus on and a new leader to rally around. But none of that would have been possible unless the Zionist movement hadn't also chosen to make the Western Wall conflict a national issue after the screen was removed in 1928. The intense Zionist response to the removal of the screen in 1928 was in stark contrast to their more measured response to much the same event in 1922 and 1925. The intensification of the Jewish response came from the growing confidence of the Yishuv, which had grown according to British estimates from 55,000 in 1918 to 149,554 in 1928, and had already purchased over a third of the land it would own during the mandate period.[83] To be sure, the period of 1926-28 had not been kind to the Jewish economy, but by the end of 1928 the Jewish National Home could be deemed at least a moderate success, given the fact that the Jewish community controlled the main commercial and industrial concerns in the country and operated a well-organized shadow government

---

[82] *Shaw Commission Report*, 74. The SMC also protested against Jewish actions in 1925 but this protest is not mentioned in the memorandum.

[83] The population figures were given by William Ormsby-Gore during a parliamentary debate on May 2, 1929, see HC Deb 02 May 1929 vol 227 c1714. The censuses of 1922 and 1931 showed a growth in the Jewish community from 83,790 to 174,606, with the Jewish percentage of the population rising from 11.14% to 16.90%. The information about land purchases comes from Pappe, *Buraq*, 11.

and educational system. Its success was especially noticeable when compared to the economic and political performance of the Arab community. It was therefore not much of a leap for the SMC to argue that Zionism aimed not only to conquer land and labor but also to control the holy sites of Palestine. Even if much of the Zionist protest was posturing and the Palestine Zionist Executive had absolutely no designs on the Haram al-Sharif, the provocative language and actions of certain Zionists, such as the journalists of *Doar HaYom* and the militant Revisionist Zionists of the paramilitary group Beitar, ended up confirming the worst fears of the Muslim community.[84]

XIV – British attempts to solve the crisis

By the end of the summer of 1929 neither the Arab nor the Jewish side was holding back in its defense of the sites, with both sides regularly accusing each other in print and in letters to the government of breaking the status quo at the wall. The inaction of the Palestine government would prove to be a contributing factor to this escalation in rhetoric, or more accurately it was the failure of the government to solve this crisis that allowed the two communities to escalate their struggle. Ironically, it was the government's insistence on adhering to the status quo that led to this failure.

British officials first tried to intervene in November 1928 by clarifying the Palestine government's position towards the dispute.[85] A White Paper published in

---

[84] The demand of the Va'ad Leumi came in early November 1928, which directly contradicts the Shaw Commission's portrayal of the Va'ad Leumi as a moderating influence during the dispute. See Wasserstein, *British in Palestine*, 230.

[85] See Great Britain, Colonial Office, *The Western or Wailing Wall in Jerusalem, Memorandum by the Secretary of State for the Colonies,* Cmd. 3229 (London: November 1928).

that month reiterated that the removal of the screen had been necessary and reconfirmed that the government considered the wall to be the absolute property of the Muslim community. The white paper was praised by the SMC and the wider Arab community, who expected the government to use this as the basis for its approach to the issue. At the same time however the government undercut this message of Muslim control by stating that "it would be a convenience to all the parties concerned if a protocol could be mutually agreed upon between the Moslem and Jewish authorities regulating the conduct of the services at the Wall in such a way as to satisfy normal liturgical requirements and decency in matters of public worship."[86]

Not surprisingly, this passing of the buck back to the two communities did not work and tensions continued to increase. In early 1929 the Palestine government thus decided to look to Ottoman precedent as a guide for how the site could be shared. British officials turned to the two religious communities to provide written documentation that supported their respective positions, in the hope that some compromise might be found between these documents. The SMC quickly responded to the government's request and provided documents from the Ottoman and Egyptian period, including an *irade* (sultanic decree) from 1840 and a 1910 decision from the Ottoman government, to the effect that Jews had no right to bring chairs or other objects to the wall. But the Chief Rabbinate failed to respond to the government's request. No documents existed that supported a Jewish right to bring benches or screens to the wall and so the Rabbinate and the Palestine Zionist Executive ended up

---

[86] The government's position was stated in the White Paper itself. Ibid.

reiterating their position that Jewish rights existed independently of documentary evidence.

This raised a difficult question for the Palestine government: should the government stick to its original intention and only honor documentary evidence of the status quo, which would fit with the approach towards religious matters that it had used for the first decade of its rule in Palestine, or should it be more flexible and allow for customary rights as well as formal rights? The difficulty of the situation compelled the chief secretary Harry Luke to state in a letter to the Colonial Office in November 1928 that "the more I study the whole question the more I am impelled to the conclusion that it becomes increasingly difficult among the contending claims to define the nature of the <u>status quo</u> and the extent of the area of the Wall and the Waqf property to which it may be deemed to apply."[87] Similarly, High commissioner John Chancellor wrote in June 1929 that the British couldn't do much until experts were able "to define what is meant by the phrases 'status quo', 'permitted under the Turkish regime', 'established practice' and 'allowed to take'," which were employed without much exactitude in British statements and white papers.[88] In the end British sympathies lay with the second option—the recognition that Jews enjoyed some customary rights at the wall—because that position had the best hope of satisfying their Zionist allies. This led Harry Luke and Norman Bentwich (the chief secretary

---

[87] Luke to Secretary of State for the Colonies (Amery), November 30, 1928. ISA, 3/359.

[88] High Commissioner to Secretary of State, June 14, 1929, ISA, 3/359.

and attorney-general, respectively) to work on the creation of formal rules that would

define what could and could not be brought to the site.[89]

The British decision to seek a compromise did not satisfy the mufti, who

argued in May 1929 that the government had failed to carry out the terms of its own

White Paper of November 1928. The Jewish community was also not happy with the

Palestine government for its decision in June 1929 to allow the SMC to undertake a

construction project at the northern end of the Western Wall.[90] This caused

widespread protest in the Jewish community, who saw the construction (correctly) as a

deliberately provocative action that was designed to demonstrate the Muslim

community's control over the wall. This began a period of intense and angry

editorializing in the Hebrew press and was when the supposedly passive (in the words

of the Shaw Commission) Va'ad Leumi demanded that the government expropriate

the wall and give it to the Jewish community. Jewish anger also led to the creation of

a Pro-Wailing Wall Society, which was formed by Joseph Klausner, a supporter of the

right-wing Zionist Revisionist Party of Vladimir Jabotinsky.[91]

The government's efforts to achieve an end to this tense situation were

ineffectual because they were based on the idea that a compromise could be reached

between the rival claimants, if only the truth about the status quo could be discovered.

---

[89] This would eventually lead to the high commissioner promulgating a set of rules in September 1929 (i.e. in the wake of the riots of 1929) that allowed Jews to bring certain objects to the wall—books, mats, lamps, and scrolls--but not benches or screens. See ISA, 3/359.

[90] This construction had originally begun in May 1929 but had been halted by the government and the case referred to the Law Officers in London. In the middle of May 1929 the government received a response from London that confirmed that the SMC was well within its rights to build at the site since it enjoyed complete ownership of the Haram al-Sharif. This decision was forwarded to the SMC on June 11th and construction recommenced on July 20th.

[91] Wasserstein, *British in Palestine*, 230

But as the reactions of Harry Luke and Herbert Samuel on the previous page show, the status quo was not a concrete law that could be picked up and applied but was simply an interpretation of the past by British officials. In deciding the rights of Christian sects at the Church of the Holy Sepulchre reference to the status quo was useful because these sects generally had a similar reading of the past. But when it came to the Western Wall, the Muslim and Jewish communities had radically different versions of that past. This is why the SMC could make the argument that Jews were violating the terms of the status quo by bringing benches to the wall, while at the same time the Zionist Organization could claim that the subsequent removal of those benches was a violation of the status quo.

This reality was finally recognized by High Commissioner Chancellor, who informed the Colonial Secretary in June 1929 that the Arab and Jewish positions were irreconcilable and suggested that the only way to bring about a resolution would be to rely purely on documentary evidence, which would have deprived Jews the right to bring screens and benches to the wall.[92] But the high commissioner's proposal was put on hold when he left for England on leave.

XIV – Violence and Recrimination

In the high commissioner's absence the situation descended into chaos. A Jewish demonstration was held in Tel Aviv on August 14, drawing 6,000 participants who shouted "The Wall is ours," "Shame on the Government," and "Shame on Keith-

---

[92] Wasserstein, *British in Palestine*, 232.

Roach."[93] That same night a prayer vigil was held in Jerusalem that drew a further

3,000 Jewish worshippers to the wall. The next day religious Jews once again

gathered at the wall but were joined by baton-wielding members of Beitar, who

marched to the wall, raised a Jewish flag, sang the Jewish national anthem, and

shouted provocative slogans. The next day a counter-demonstration was held by the

SMC after the completion of Friday morning prayers at the at the Haram al-Sharif, in

which Muslim protestors visited the wall, where they listened to sermons and raised

banners. According to police reports and testimony before the Shaw Commission this

demonstration also caused the burning of Jewish prayer books and of prayers on

scraps of paper that were placed in the wall.[94]

Over the next week a series of isolated incidents caused tensions between the

two communities to be raised to unprecedented levels. On August 17, a brawl

between Arabs and Jews caused a number of injuries and the death of one Jew. His

funeral on August 20 turned into a mass Jewish demonstration, followed by counter-

protests by the Society for the Defense of the Mosque of Aqsa and the Holy Places. In

response, the government attempted to diffuse the situation by having the mufti and

chief rabbi preach sermons of understanding to their followers and by arranging for a

secret meeting between Zionist and Arab leaders. But these efforts were basically too

little, too late, and so on Friday, August 23, 1929, violence broke out in Jerusalem,

mostly in the form of Arab attacks against Jews. Unlike the situation at Nabi Musa in

---

[93] It was Keith-Roach who had given the original order to remove the screen. This demonstration is
discussed in Wasserstein, *British in Palestine*, 232.
[94] Wasserstein, *British in Palestine*, 233.

1920, violence then quickly spread to other parts of the country, with particularly

gruesome attacks against Jews occurring at Hebron and Safad. All told, 133 Jews and

116 Arabs were killed and 339 Jews and 232 Arabs were wounded in a week of

violence that was only brought to an end after additional British troops were sent from

Egypt.

After the violence of 1929 the Palestine Zionist Executive accused the mufti of

inciting the Arab population to attack Jews. It also accused the government of neglect.

These charges came close to the claims in 1920 that the Nabi Musa riots were

pogroms. As I have already mentioned, the Shaw Commission report of May 1930,

acquitted the mufti of the charge of incitement, although one of its members, H. Snell,

broke with the commission's findings to argued that the mufti should bear

responsibility for the riots. The commission found that the mufti had put together the

Buraq campaign to defend the wall from what he perceived to be Jewish attempts to

take over the space, but denied that his intention had been to use the campaign for

violent means. Instead the rush to violence was caused by "the force of

circumstances," specifically Muslim fear and anger towards the Zionist community, a

perspective that would once again seem to reproduce the view that Muslims were

driven by their emotions and not by nationalist motivations.[95] The commission further

argued that during the disorder, the mufti had actually "exerted his influence in the

---

[95] *Shaw Commission Report*, 75.

direction of promoting peace and restoring order," although he along with other Arab

leaders had failed miserably in this task.[96]

Yehoshua Porath argues that the Shaw Commission's stand was unreasonable

owing to the mufti's positioning of himself as the defender of the Haram al-Sharif

throughout the 1920s and particularly his campaign in 1928.[97] This perspective is

shared by Bernard Wasserstein who states that "whatever his motives or intentions,

there can be little doubt that the key to what occurred in Palestine in August 1929 was

the Mufti's year-long campaign rousing the Arabs of Palestine to stand against the

alleged threat to the Muslim holy places in Jerusalem."[98] In other words it was the

mufi who had deliberately brought about the conflict. Philip Mattar offers a

perspective that hues closer to the Shaw Commission finding by arguing that while the

mufti contributed to the politicization of the Western Wall issue,

> He neither incited nor planned the August 1929 violence. He was
> constantly aware that if he, as an official of the Palestine government,
> challenged the British, they might exile him to political obscurity as
> quickly as they had granted him religious power in 1921. He was
> equally aware that the British were too strong for the Palestinians to
> challenge. Consequently, he practiced a dual policy between 1921 and
> 1936: cooperating with the British on the one hand while verbally
> opposing Zionism and seeking an Arab Palestine on the other. Such a
> policy worked well for him during the 1928-29 dispute: it confirmed to
> most British officials his compliance while it verified to most
> Palestinians his anti-Zionism. Already by late 1929, however, he was
> pressed by an emerging anti-British mood to choose between the two
> masters he was serving, the British and his own people.[99]

---

[96] *Shaw Commission Report*, 77.
[97] Porath, *Emergence*, 270.
[98] Wasserstein, *British in Palestine*, 238.
[99] Mattar, *Mufti*, 49.

Mattar's perspective is the more convincing because it is quite clear that throughout the 1920s the mufti was very careful in his opposition to Zionism and British policy. Using petitions, delegations, and nationalist speeches rather than violence, the mufti was able to retain his independent voice in Palestinian politics without giving his imperial masters cause to call for his removal. In 1929 he became more vocal in his support for Muslim rights but he remained careful, as the Shaw Commission reported, to make sure that he supported (or at least appeared to support) a political solution to the crisis.

XV - Conclusion

The 1929 riot led to a renewed sense of political purpose on the part of Arab political groups, such as the Arab Executive who also became involved in championing the Arab cause, but it was Hajj Amin al-Husayni who gained the most from the event. As the face of the Arab struggle he emerged as the most important leader in Palestinian politics, a hero for those in the Arab community who saw the riots as a *thawra* (revolt) against Zionist domination. His transformation into a major political player was undoubtedly helped by the fact that the struggle had been about a religious site that was already under the supervision of the SMC, although it was also due to his ability to link the fate of the Wall to the status of the Palestinian Arab community. As we saw at the beginning of this chapter, he was able to do so because of the groundwork that had been laid in the early part of the decade. The SMC's campaigns to the Muslim world and to the Arab community in Palestine had presented the defense of

Muslim religious sites as a national problem and established the SMC as the main champion of the Muslim position. To be sure, other groups had also tried to use the sites in their propaganda, such as the Arab Executive (see page 257), but the mufti's religious clout allowed the SMC to position themselves as the face of the Palestinian Muslim struggle to defend the Haram al-Sharif.

Hajj Amin's new prominence was immediately shown by the fact that he was soon elected leader of a new delegation to London that was sponsored by the Arab Executive. The decision to send a delegation to London can be seen as a return to the beginning of the 1920s when the Arab Executive sent delegations to London and Europe to plead the Palestinian Arab case against the Balfour policy. As such, it should be taken as a sign that Arab politicians saw the riots as opening up the possibility of diplomatic action, a far cry from the late-1920s when the Arab Executive had become almost moribund and the level of Arab nationalist activity had dropped precipitously. Hajj Amin's new prominence brought him into conflict with his rival Musa Kazim al-Husayni, the head of the Arab Executive, who eventually replaced the mufti at the head of the 1930 delegation. Despite this, Hajj Amin still went with the delegation to London, a sign that he was now willing to openly play the role of political advocate. It was this moment that the Foreign Office report from 1945, which opened this chapter, identified as the turning point in his political career, for it was then that he became a public political figure.

Hajj Amin's new found fame was also useful in raising his prestige in the Arab world. After the 1929 riots his appeals to the wider Muslim world, which built on the relationships he had forged during the early 1920s, were far more successful. For example, in the wake of the riots large sums of money were collected in Islamic countries to aid its Arab victims. And at the 1930 League of Nations' Commission of Inquiry into the rights of Jews and Muslims at the Wailing Wall, Muslims from outside Palestine appeared in solidarity with the Palestinian Arabs. Finally, Hajj Amin al-Husayni was able to convene in Jerusalem in December 1931 a world-wide Muslim Congress in defense of the Islamic Holy Places in Palestine.

This emergence of the mufti as a spokesperson for the Arab cause could not however have been predicted when the council was formed in 1922. As this chapter has shown, it was the struggle over religious space that brought Hajj Amin al-Husayni to prominence. To be sure, the mufti exploited this struggle for his own ends but the struggle would not have been possible without Zionist attempts to gain a more prominent position at the site. Nor would it have been possible if the British authorities had intervened early on and established a set policy at the Western Wall. The events of 1929 were not prefigured in the creation of the SMC and the appointment of Hajj Amin to the muftiship of Jerusalem, but came out of the struggle between two rival nationalisms.

As I mentioned in the introduction to this dissertation the Western Wall struggle of 1928- 1929 laid bare the intensity of this national conflict and caused British officials to realize their folly in believing that a compromise could be worked out between the two sides by building better regulations. High Commissioner John Chancellor's conclusion in June 1929 that the Arab and Jewish positions were irreconcilable was a far cry from Herbert Samuel's rosy predictions at the beginning of the decade that Arabs could be brought around to support British policy in Palestine if the benefits of colonial rule were better explained to them. After 1929, no serious plans for building a shared Arab-Jewish state were attempted by British officials, with the result that in 1937 plans were drawn up for the partition of the country by the Peel Commission into the Palestine Arab Revolt. If 1929 had brought the mufti to new political prominence, it placed him in the position of facing a confused and wary colonial administration that had no real plan for the future of Palestine.

Conclusion

Although 1929 represented the end of an era and marks the endpoint of my analysis of

Islam under the British, Hajj Amin al-Husayni continued to be the main political

figure of the Arab community until his dismissal by the British from the SMC in 1937.

This dismissal was occasioned by his decision to become the leader of the Arab

Higher Committee during the Palestine Arab Revolt of 1936-39. The AHC was

designed by the Arab elite to take control over the revolt, which had broken out as a

spontaneous insurgency from below. They had some success in organizing a six-

month general strike, although there is much evidence to suggest that the strike

ultimately harmed the Arab economy more than the Jewish economy. But ultimately

the AHC was unable or unwilling to control the spontaneity of the insurgency,

especially the attacks of Arab peasant guerillas on British targets. As a result, Hajj

Amin was stripped of his presidency of the SMC in September 1937 and soon

afterwards he fled the country to avoid arrest. He would never return to Palestine

again.

Why was the mufti removed from power in 1937 and not in 1929? The most

obvious reason was the fact that in 1936 Hajj Amin took up a political position that

was totally unacceptable for an employee of the government to take. By joining the

AHC, Hajj Amin effectively became a revolutionary. This was a far cry from his

position in 1929 when his angry opposition to Zionism was leavened by his continued

cooperation with the British authorities.

Hajj Amin's moderate tone towards the Palestine government before, during, and *after* the 1929 Western Wall riots made him useful to the British. From 1922 until 1936 the leader of the Muslim community largely limited his opposition to British policy to private reprimands of government officials or the dispatch of petitions. Although the mufti engaged in political activities this engagement could be accepted by the colonial officials who were happy not have been facing more effective expressions of popular anger, such as civil disobedience campaigns, which were successful in British Egypt and India, or armed revolts as occurred in Iraq, Egypt, and Syria.

As I mentioned in Chapter Four, the elevation of the mufti and the creation of the position of the President of the Supreme Muslim Council was intended as a means for creating a Muslim equivalent of the Latin and Greek Patriarchs and the Jewish Rabbis—a religious figure given control over the religious affairs of his community in return for expectation that he will keep his community loyal and quiet. The riots of 1929 certainly called into question the idea that the mufti was able or willing to control his community but the Shaw Commission's statement that the mufti had "exerted his influence in the direction of promoting peace and restoring order," is significant for it showed that the British were still willing to believe that he worked as a moderating influence in Arab politics.[100] As a consequence, British officials made only superficial changes to the Supreme Muslim Council after 1929, by instituting more government oversight of the council's finances but leaving its personnel intact.

---

[100] *Shaw Commission Report*, 77.

A very different situation was observed in 1937. At first, the mufti was praised by the high commissioner, Arthur Wauchope, for his moderation, "It is a remarkable fact that the religious cry has not been raised during the last six weeks, that the Friday sermons have been far more moderate than I could have hoped during a period when the feelings of the people are so deeply stirred and for this the mufti is mainly responsible."[101] Opinion quickly changed when he issued a statement that confirmed that the Supreme Muslim Council fully supported the Arab strike and he took up a position of leadership in the Arab Higher Committee. But ultimately it was his inability to control the insurgency that led to his downfall not his decision to join the strike. This was shown by the fact that the Hajj Amin's dismissal came not after he took up his position in the AHC but occurred four days after the assassination of L. Y. Andrews, acting district commissioner in the north, on September 26, 1937.

In other words, what ultimately caused the downfall of the mufti was that he could no longer be counted upon to keep order in the community. He had outlived his usefulness to the British authorities. With the emergence of figures such as the militant preacher 'Izz al-Din al-Qassam and the Syrian Arab nationalist fighter Fawzi al-Qawuqji, the mufti's brand of notable politics seemed out of date.

The mufti's fall from grace in 1936-37, if not his actions in 1929, can be seen as evidence of the failure of Britain's Islamic policy. This is certainly the perspective that was taken by British officials in the wake of the Arab revolt. The violent events of the revolt caused British policymakers and analysts to look back at their past

---

[101] Wauchope to Secretary of State, June 7, 1936, PRO CO 733/297/75156-2.

approach to the Supreme Muslim Council with a very critical eye. The Peel

Commission report of 1937, for example, criticized the Palestine government for

failing to undertake reforms of the council, thereby allowing the mufti to use the

council as his own personal fief. This reinterpretation of the past would help lead to

the idea that British officials had been either incompetent or naïve in their approach to

the mufti, which has become central to the conventional narrative about Britain's

Islamic policy.

But Britain's policy towards Palestinian Islam can also be seen as a success.

For almost twenty years (1917-1936) the Palestine government did not have to face an

armed revolt. This made Palestine very different from Iraq and Egypt. Hajj Amin had

a part to play in this success, for in office he turned out to be rather moderate in his

actions, if not in his rhetoric. Rashid Khalidi, Philip Mattar, and Taysir Jbara have all

argued that the mufti was a hesitant political actor, an assessment that is corroborated

in my own research that has shown the mufti to have been cautious in engaging in

political activities that would have put him at odds with his colonial masters.

What is interesting is that this was even true after the transformative moment

of 1929. The Western Wall struggle from 1928-1929 seemed to have indicated a new

way in which Arabs could challenge Zionism and British colonialism could be fought.

By reorienting Palestinian Arab nationalism around the issue of the defense of the holy

sites, Hajj Amin had moved Palestinian politics away from the stale legalistic

approach that had dominated most of the 1920s, by making the struggle appeal to the

Palestinian masses. But, in fact, it turned out to be no turning point at all—Hajj Amin

went back to being a moderate politician after the events of 1929. According to Philip

Mattar, the mufti was approached a month after the August 1929 riots by a Syrian

militant, Shabib Wahab and asked to organize bands of guerilla fighters, a request that

the mufti rejected in preference for effecting a political solution.[102] Instead the mufti

joined the 1930 Palestinian delegation to London. Although the Foreign Office viewed

this in a negative light, his decision confirmed that he was prepared to play according

to the rules of the colonial power. Indeed, as Rashid Khalidi notes,

> Until only a few years before the outbreak of the 1936-39 Arab revolt
> in Palestine, virtually the entire Palestinian leadership remained
> individually on relatively cordial terms with senior British officials.
> Their actions indicate that for well over a decade they believed that by
> simply continuing to negotiate with British officials, combined with a
> little genteel pressure, they would eventually be able to persuade
> Britain to change its policy and hand over the reins of power to the
> country's "natural" rulers, that is to say themselves…The mufti shares
> fully in this approach; indeed, he was a leading member of the 1930
> delegation that met with Lord Passfield.[103]

The events of 1929 may have led to the elevation of the mufti to a position of political

preeminence but it did not change the fact that he continued to tread a fine line as an

employee of the Palestine government. What had changed for the mufti is that after

1929 he no could no longer operate under the radar. As the face of the Arab opposition

to Jewish National Home he would be watched for any signs of a turn to politics.

This suggests that British officials were not as naïve or incompetent or just

plain weak as many scholars have suggested. As this dissertation has suggested,

---

[102] Mattar, *Mufti*, 51.
[103] Khalidi, *Iron Cage*, 79.

British officials had a good idea of what they were doing and acted in rational ways. As I argued in the first two chapters of this work, a particular logic governed the British approach to Palestine and Palestinian Islam. In Chapter One, I argued that British visits to Palestine in the late-nineteenth century had convinced Britons that Palestine was a place that needed to be saved. This led to the development of two discourses about the country that would be used to justify British intervention: the discourse of the "civilizing mission"—it was the duty of the British to bring development to a desolate and decayed country—and the discourse of the "protection of religious tradition"—it was the responsibility of Europeans to ensure that the holiness of the land and its people were protected. In Chapter Two, I presented how Ottoman Palestine was a territory that was undergoing a great deal of transformation in the late-Ottoman period but showed that this dynamism was elided in British views of the period that reduced Ottoman rule to the imposition of the status quo and the millet system.

In the second part of my study, Chapters Three and Four, I considered how the British took these ideas and applied them to their general approach to religion (Chapter Three) and their specific approach to Islam (Chapter Four). Here I argued that the discourse of the "protection of religious tradition," as represented by the concept of the "preservation of the status quo," won out over the civilizing mission due to the conservative and frugal nature of the colonial authorities and to the need for the Palestine government to reassure the world about their colonial policies. This led to the adoption of the millet system and the status quo as the basis for Britain's approach to religion in the country, leading in the end to the creation of the independent Supreme Muslim Council as the Muslim millet. These chapters indicated that British policies were developed as rational responses to the imperial agenda in place in Palestine and the conditions of British rule and were not developed out of ignorance or fear.

In the final part of the work, I considered how events eventually ended up transforming the Supreme Muslim Council into a political force in Palestine, a development that challenged and ultimately doomed to failure the British approach to institutional Islam. Here the breakdown of more secular Arab politics (as detailed in Chapter Five) allowed for the development of a space for the mufti to become more involved in politics. Especially important in the rise to prominence of the mufti was the fact that the major political contest of the 1920s took place over religious space— an area of Palestinian life that fell solidly within the jurisdiction of the Supreme Muslim Council. I have argued that the politicization of the SMC was not inevitable but was a product of the conflict between Zionism and Palestinian Arab nationalism. As such, it could not have been fully anticipated by British officials, who genuinely believed in the early 1920s that their policies would eventually lead Arabs to accept the terms of their occupation. It is here, of course, where the colonial power was naïve.

The dismissal of Hajj Amin al-Husayni did not end the Supreme Muslim Council but it did lead to its transformation. Hajj Amin's dismissal was accompanied by that of one other member of the five-person SMC and the resignation of a third. In the place of these other two councilors, the Palestine government appointed two new

members that were not attached to the al-Husayni bloc. Government officials also

decided to leave the presidency of the council vacant until the end of the mandate.

Another change that occurred was the creation a new three-member Awqaf

Committee, made up of two British officials and one Arab member, to take charge of

the waqf system. To assert its control over institutional Islam the Palestine

government dismissed a further nine shari'a court employees and twelve waqf

officials.[104] According to Uri Kupferschmidt, this new government-supervised council

"became what it originally had been destined for: an administrative body for the

management of Muslim religious affairs."[105] The SMC would continue to operate

under British oversight until the end of the mandate period.

The council would eventually be abolished in 1951 as the Jordanian

government—then in control of Haram al-Sharif and the Old City of Jerusalem—

chose to control Islam through its own state-run Islamic institutions. In the new state

of Israel, the British experience with the SMC became a major factor in the

government's decision to make sure that waqf and shari'a affairs were placed under

supervision of various agencies of the Israeli state.[106] As Alisa Peled has pointed out,

this had detrimental effects on Islamic institutions within Israel. The Israeli Ministry

of Religious Affairs, for example, "made great efforts in the 1950s to secure control of

the vast financial resources of the waqf, and not always for the sole benefit of the

---

[104] For a discussion of the council between 1937-48 see Kupferschmidt, *Supreme Muslim Council*, 255.
[105] Kupferschmidt, *Supreme Muslim Council*, 255.
[106] For a good account of Israeli policy see Alisha Rubin Peled, *Debating Islam in the Jewish State*. Albany: SUNY Press, 2001. Kupferschmidt also offers a brief account of Jordanian and Israeli policy, see Kupferschmidt, 257-261.

Muslim community."[107] The ministry was also found negligent in its safeguarding

and maintenance of Muslim holy sites. According to Peled, the disjointed Israeli

approach to Islam, which was built on keeping the Muslim authorities weak, ended up

creating an ineffectual leadership that would ultimately be challenged by the Islamic

Movement, an Islamist group that combines nationalism and Islam into a single

political agenda.[108] Ironically, the Israeli approach, which developed in opposition to

the British approach, ended up creating the very movement that the Israeli government

feared.

In other ways however the Israeli government has continued the British

approach, such as in the case of its approach to Islamic law and waqf. Such

continuities are detailed in Robert Eisenman's *Islamic Law in Palestine and Israel: a

history of the survival of the Tanzimat and Shari'a in British Palestine and the State of

Israel* (1978) and Yitzhak Reiter's *Islamic Endowments in British Palestine* (1996),

and attest to the manner in which Ottoman Islamic precedent has been transmitted to

the Israeli state through the British occupation.

The conflict between Arabs and Jews over Jerusalem was also passed on to the

Israeli period. In the conflict at the Western Wall in 1929 we can see the origins of

today's clashes and protests at the Western Wall, on the Haram al-Sharif, and

throughout and beyond the Old City of Jerusalem. And whether we are looking at a

Hajj Amin al-Husayni or an Ariel Sharon as the person stoking the embers of this

conflagration, the dissertation suggests that such conflict is better understood as being

---

[107] Peled, *Debating Islam*, 5.
[108] Peled, *Debating Islam*, 15.

caused by the conflict between two nationalist communities under a colonial or

national state that was/is happy to let those communities develop in isolation from

each other.